D0940635

HUNTING BUFFALO W

While he is probably best known as a novelist and short-story writer, Lawrence Block has produced a rich trove of nonfiction over the course of a sixty-year career. His instructional books for writers are leaders in the field, and his self-described pedestrian memoir, *Step By Step*, has found a loyal audience in the running and racewalking community.

Over the years, Block has written extensively for magazines and periodicals. *Generally Speaking* collects his philatelic columns from *Linn's Stamp News*, while his extensive observations of crime fiction, along with personal glimpses of some of its foremost practitioners, have won wide acclaim in book form as *The Crime of Our Lives*.

Hunting Buffalo With Bent Nails is what he's got left over.

The title piece, originally published in *American Heritage*, recounts the ongoing adventure Block and his wife undertook, criss-crossing the United States and parts of Canada in their quixotic and exotic quest to find every "village, hamlet, and wide place in the road named Buffalo." Other travel tales share space with a remembrance of his mother, odes to New York, a disquisition on pen names and book tours, and, well, no end of bent nails not worth straightening. Where else will you find "Raymond Chandler and the Brasher Doubloon," an assessment of that compelling writer from a numismatic standpoint? Where else can you read about Block's collection of old subway cars?

◁ ◆ ▷

"There's only one problem with opening a new non-fiction book by Lawrence Block: Your reading list explodes logarithmically . . ."
—*Otherdeb, Amazon Reviews*

More by Lawrence Block

NON-FICTION

STEP BY STEP • GENERALLY SPEAKING • THE CRIME OF OUR LIVES • HUNTING BUFFALO WITH BENT NAILS

NOVELS

A DIET OF TREACLE • AFTER THE FIRST DEATH • ARIEL • BORDERLINE • CAMPUS TRAMP • CINDERELLA SIMS • COWARD'S KISS • DEADLY HONEYMOON • FOUR LIVES AT THE CROSSROADS • GETTING OFF • THE GIRL WITH THE DEEP BLUE EYES • THE GIRL WITH THE LONG GREEN HEART • GRIFTER'S GAME • KILLING CASTRO • LUCKY AT CARDS • NOT COMIN' HOME TO YOU • RANDOM WALK • RONALD RABBIT IS A DIRTY OLD MAN • SINNER MAN • SMALL TOWN • THE SPECIALISTS • STRANGE EMBRACE • SUCH MEN ARE DANGEROUS • THE TRIUMPH OF EVIL • YOU COULD CALL IT MURDER

THE MATTHEW SCUDDER NOVELS

THE SINS OF THE FATHERS • TIME TO MURDER AND CREATE • IN THE MIDST OF DEATH • A STAB IN THE DARK • EIGHT MILLION WAYS TO DIE • WHEN THE SACRED GINMILL CLOSES • OUT ON THE CUTTING EDGE • A TICKET TO THE BONEYARD • A DANCE AT THE SLAUGHTERHOUSE • A WALK AMONG THE TOMBSTONES • THE DEVIL KNOWS YOU'RE DEAD • A LONG LINE OF DEAD MEN • EVEN THE WICKED • EVERYBODY DIES • HOPE TO DIE • ALL THE FLOWERS ARE DYING • A DROP OF THE HARD STUFF • THE NIGHT AND THE MUSIC • A TIME TO SCATTER STONES

THE BERNIE RHODENBARR MYSTERIES

BURGLARS CAN'T BE CHOOSERS • THE BURGLAR IN THE CLOSET • THE BURGLAR WHO LIKED TO QUOTE KIPLING • THE BURGLAR WHO STUDIED SPINOZA • THE BURGLAR WHO PAINTED LIKE MONDRIAN • THE BURGLAR WHO TRADED TED WILLIAMS • THE BURGLAR WHO THOUGHT HE WAS BOGART • THE BURGLAR IN THE LIBRARY • THE BURGLAR IN THE RYE • THE BURGLAR ON THE PROWL • THE BURGLAR WHO COUNTED THE SPOONS • THE BURGLAR IN SHORT ORDER

HUNTING BUFFALO WITH BENT NAILS

LAWRENCE BLOCK

For my Frequent Companion,
LYNNE,
that nicely-dressed lady in "The Whole World is Listening,"
the indispensable partner for a proper Buffalo hunt,
and for everything else . . .

◁ ◆ ▷

A LAWRENCE BLOCK PRODUCTION

Contents

FOREWORD

HUNTING BUFFALO WITH BENT NAILS? REALLY?

I started writing for publication sometime in the early 1950s. Someone—I think it was Hallmark—aired a TV production of *Macbeth,* and I sent the *Buffalo Evening News* a letter to the editor, protesting the over-the-top violence. "First they kill the king," I wrote, and went on to summarize the story's bloodier aspects. "Let's all get together," I exhorted readers, "and clean up television!"

I signed it "Allor Bryck," an anagram for Larry Block. Damned if they didn't print the thing, and damned again if some readers didn't rush, pen in hand, to the Bard's defense. And at some point Steve Allen read Allor Bryck's letter on the *Tonight* show, though whether or not he took it seriously I couldn't tell you. (Neither, come to think of it, could he. Not now.)

Never mind. Alas, I've been writing ever since.

While most of my writing has been fiction of one sort of another, I've produced a fairly extensive body of nonfiction. (And isn't that a curious word, defining a category of writing by stating what it is not? If it's factual, if it's not a pack of lies, if it hasn't been made up out of the whole tattered cloth, if it's not the product of some ninny's imagination, then we call it . . . nonfiction.)

Some of this work, I blush to admit, is nonfiction in name only. Back in the 1960s and early 1970s, I wrote quite a few books as John Warren Wells; they dealt with human sexual behavior, presented largely in case history form. While often informed by fact, they were largely invented.

I've also written quite a bit of instructional material for writers, enough to fill seven books. Another book, *Step By Step,* is a memoir of my career as one of the world's slowest racewalkers. A hobby led to a column for a philatelic publication, and the columns wound up collected in a book, *Generally Speaking.*

A few years ago, I realized I'd somehow contrived to write quite a bit about crime fiction and its practitioners, and I gathered up various pieces thereof and made of them a book called *The Crime of Our Lives.*

What we have here is what was left over, and I'll hew to the example of whoever came up with the word *nonfiction* and define what follows by what it is not. It's not fiction, for starters, and it's also not about writing, or human sexual behavior, or racewalking, or stamp collecting, or crime fiction.

So what have we got?

Some travel pieces, for starters. Early in our courtship, my wife and I decided to make up a list of places to which we hoped someday to travel. We didn't get very far in our list making, because it soon became evident that we were just writing down every country we could think of. It seemed we wanted to go everywhere.

And, over the past thirty-plus years, we've traipsed around a good deal of the world. This passionate traveling has always been an end in itself, undertaken for its own sake, and while I sometimes thought I might write about where we went and what we saw, I never bothered to make notes or take pictures. Why dilute an experience by jotting down words for it? Why diminish great scenery by squinting at it through a viewfinder?

In the spring of 1991, when Lynne and I prepared to embark on our most ambitious trip, a walk from Toulouse over the Pyrenees and on via the ancient pilgrim route to Santiago de Compostela, I proposed a piece on our trek to an editor at the *New York Times* travel section. She was enthusiastic. And, while we took no photographs, I did make a few notes along the way.

And then when we got home I found myself not at all interested in writing about it. We'd spent several months and had no end of adventures, and it had been a life-changing experience and perhaps a spiritual one, and the last thing I wanted to do was turn it into a travel piece.

I did write about the pilgrimage—years later, as a section of my walking memoir, *Step By Step*.

But other travel did lead to essays and articles of one sort of another, and you'll find them here. One of them supplied the title for this volume—or the first two words of it, anyway. *Hunting Buffalo* recounts an extended quest we undertook, attempting to visit every city, town, hamlet, and wide place in the road with *Buffalo* in its name.

I certainly didn't begin the Buffalo hunt with any intention of writing about it, but there came a time several months into it when we interrupted the adventure to make a trip to New York. While I was there I borrowed a desk in the *Playboy* offices and wrote *Hunting Buffalo.* I showed it to my great friend Alice K. Turner, longtime fiction editor at *Playboy,* not because I was daft enough to think it was a possible *Playboy* article but because Alice was the most perceptive reader I've ever known, and one with a good sense of media in the bargain. Maybe she could figure out where I might send the damned thing.

She immediately suggested *American Heritage,* a market which would never have occurred to me, and I had my agent send it over to Richard Snow, and damned if he didn't snap it up. It led in time to some other pieces for the magazine, among them the overview of American mystery fiction included in *The Crime of Our Lives.*

American Heritage is essentially gone now, although it lives on as a digital publication. And Alice Turner lives on, too, in the hearts of everyone who had the good luck to know her—but we lost her in January of 2015, and the world grew a little darker. As it does.

*   *   *

About the title. I don't remember where or when I heard or read about the hardy soul who had a box labeled *Pieces of String Too Short to Save*. For years I had it in mind as an ideal title for a book of odds and ends, but I wasn't the only one, and there are at least two such volumes presently on offer at Amazon, and it wouldn't astonish me to learn there are more. I'm not sure I actually believe there was ever a box so labeled, but what difference does it make?

Here, though, is something that happened. Not *to a friend*, as is the stuff of urban legends, but to me.

I was at the time living in an old farmhouse in New Jersey, a few miles from Lambertville and the Delaware River. The house kept needing work, and one thing about moving from an apartment to a home of your own is you can no longer pick up the intercom and call the super. You have to do it yourself.

So I did things myself, insofar as I could, and in the course of so doing I accumulated tools and hardware. And of course it all wound up in a jumbled mess, and of course I decided what I needed to do was organize it.

Lots of luck. My life has always been a jumbled mess, and from time to time I decide I need to organize it, and . . . oh, never mind.

Part of the jumble consisted of baby food jars, which I'd washed out and stashed because I figured they'd be handy for putting things in. So I began working my way through the ocean of nails and screws and washers and bolts and nuts and bits and pieces and doohickeys and whatchamacallits, putting each article in what seemed to be an appropriate jar. I had all this stuff, see, and if it were organized I could find what I needed instead of having to go out and buy it all over again.

What I would have to buy, though, was a label-maker. Each jar would have to have its own little plastic label, and wouldn't that be a satisfying arrangement? I picked up each jar in turn, figuring out how the label could best be worded. (Thinking up words to put on labels was a more natural occupation for me than actually sorting the crap into the jars—or, God forbid, actually trying to build or repair anything.)

You see where this is going, don't you? One jar, I realized, one which was already half full of little pieces of metal, was destined to be labeled *Bent Nails Not Worth Straightening.*

Indeed. I had produced my own equivalent of Pieces of String Too Short to Save.

And that's about as far as I ever got with the whole project. The jars and their contents stayed on a shelf, undisturbed. The greater portion of hardware remained unsorted. And as for those bent nails not worth straightening, I threw them out.

At least I think I did. I mean, I must have, right? Why on earth would I save them?

Along with travel pieces, you'll find some introductions. At some point I reached, albeit barely, a level of prominence that has led some writers and publishers to think that having my name on the cover or title page of somebody else's book might give it a boost. So invitations have trickled in over the years, and more often than not I've accepted them.

At one point my friend Don Westlake taped a note over his desk: "No More Introductions!" He'd decided that they took time and energy he might better devote to the work that mattered to him. And so they do, and that I always felt was part of their charm. If I could avoid working on something that was giving me trouble, and tell myself that I was at least working, and even bank a few dollars for my troubles—well, wasn't that better than watching daytime television?

There are, well, odds and ends. An appreciation of my mother, written for a book called *Mothers and Sons.* (I showed it to its subject; she thought she was on balance rather more intersting than I'd shown her. I suspect she was right. The book came out in 2000, and she died in 2001. And the world grew a little darker then, as it keeps on doing.)

There are a batch of pieces dealing one way or another with New York City. While I've lived there for most of my life (although I was of course born at the other end of the state in Buffalo, and clearly I set about hunting Buffalo in a subconscious quest to return to my boyhood, right? No, I don't think so) I've never tired of the place, nor apparently have I run out of things to say about it.

What else? An article on my collection of old subway cars. An appreciation of my part of town, Greenwich Village. A piece or two that perhaps more properly belong in *The Crime of Our Lives:* The extended essay on Donald Westlake written for Robin Winks' reference work, *Mystery & Suspense Writers.* A numismatic take on a master of crime fiction, "Raymond Chandler and the Brasher Doubloon." A review of my own experience with private detectives, in and out of fiction.

A little of this, and a little of that.

Bent nails, then. A jar half full of them, and believe me, they're not worth straightening.

Make of them what you will.

What I've made of them is a book, sort of, so of course I've written an introduction for it. That was fairly easy; the table of contents was another matter. How exactly was I going to put a jarful of bent nails in order?

Ah, the alphabet. I've taken note before of the sheer miracle of alphabetical order. When I taught each of my daughters to sing their way through the ABCs, I never spared a moment to thank the unsung genius who put the bloody letters in order.

You know, they didn't have to be. They're not like numbers, which come in a logical and inevitable order. The letters could be jumbled in a jar, like, oh, bent nails.

But they're not. They have an order, not preordained but man-made, and because they do we are able to put in order everything that has a name spelled with letters.

So Bob's your uncle—and you'll find him on the shelf between Uncle Arnie and Uncle Chuck. And if alphabetical order is good enough for those fine gentlemen, it'll certainly do for all the bent nails in my Table of Contents. And what but alphabetical order could position Raymond Chandler snugly between my mother and the Travelers Century Club?

I'm a big fan of alphabetical order. So, I suspect, was Chandler himself, and that old writer of espionage thrillers, Edward S. Aarons. My friend Don Westlake thought it was a terrible idea, and I never asked Roger Zelazny or Barry Zeman or Sharon Zukovsky how they felt about it, but I can guess.

Never mind.

ABRIDGE THIS!

Here's a piece I wrote for the Village Voice *in December of 2004,
a month before* Audiobook Café *was scheduled to launch on
satellite radio. I don't know if any of the episodes ever aired,
or if I ever got paid for my work, but the show was essentially
dead on arrival. Let's be charitable and say the program was
ahead of its time. Too bad—it was fun while it lasted . . .*

A couple of weeks ago, I spent Monday and Tuesday at a sound studio on 9th
Avenue, taping a month's worth of hour-long radio programs. As the host
of *Audiobook Café*, set to debut in January on XM Satellite Radio, I interviewed two authors and reviewed one audiobook for each of the four shows.
I talked in-studio with Ron Chernow and SJ Rozan, and on the phone with
Joyce Carol Oates, Ann Rule, and Tony Hillerman. I recorded my reviews of
books by Ed McBain, Philip Roth, Augusten Burroughs, and Jonathan Le-
them. And I taped some of the show's connective tissue ("Thanks, Jeff." "And
now for a word from our Twisted Sisters, Rochelle O'Gorman and Barbara
Sullivan. What have you got for us today, girls?" "Over to you now, Jeff.")

I spent the following Tuesday and Wednesday at HarperAudio's sound
studio, recording the abridged audiobook of my own forthcoming novel.
This was the 17th audiobook I've narrated, so I know the drill. It went well;
we wrapped it up early Wednesday afternoon and I headed home with a
feeling of accomplishment.

Back in the day, and a long-ago day it was, the notion of writing something and getting paid for it was absolutely exhilarating to me. It barely

mattered what I wrote, just so long as those were my words on the page and there was a pot of gold at the end of the rainbow. (And it didn't actually have to be a pot of gold. A pot of silver was fine, or copper if you were fresh out of silver. Back then, come to think of it, a pot of pot would have done, too.)

Well, my first story was published in 1958, my first book a year or so later, and there have been a lot of words on a lot of pages since then. I still like to write and get paid for it, but along the way I've discovered something even more thrilling—not writing . . . and getting paid for it.

Thus, this second career with the spoken word. It's been propelled by the same two motivators, ego and avarice, that got all those words onto all those pages, and it does make a nice change of pace from writing, and uses some different muscles.

And the muscles, I should tell you, get stronger through exercise. The first audiobook I narrated was *Burglars Can't Be Choosers*, published in audio in 1995. That was a severe abridgment, the book cut down to 26,000 words, with a running time of three hours on two cassettes. (I wrote the book in 1976, and if I'd known that I'd someday have to read it out loud, I wouldn't have named one character J. Francis Flaxford, easy enough to type but, I was to discover, almost impossible to say.)

The recording session went well, J. Francis notwithstanding, and I was out of there in six or seven hours. I got home around four and lay down for a nap, and I slept for 15 hours. All I'd done was sit in a chair and read for a few hours, but the requisite level of concentration was pretty intense, and the whole thing knocked the crap out of me.

Well, some of it, anyway.

Nowadays the abridgments are longer—six hours on four cassettes, or a little over 50,000 words. The work of narration is still demanding. You have to stay in the moment; if your mind wanders, it shows in your voice. But it's not as exhausting, and I have to say I'm getting better at it.

But I won't record an abridged audiobook again. Nor will anybody else narrate a book of mine in abridged form. There's going to be a clause to that effect in the next contract I sign. No abridgments.

Because it's been an embarrassment to me that I can't recommend my own audiobook narrations, but instead find myself steering prospective readers to the unabridged versions with other narrators. The audiobook I recorded of *All the Flowers Are Dying* runs 53,000 words; the unabridged version, which Alan Sklar will narrate for BBC America, runs to 99,000 and change. Anyone who listens to my version will get the story. They'll know what happens, although a whole subplot's been excised, but they'll miss far too much of what most concerned me as a writer. The book's the 16th in my Matthew Scudder series, and what the book is about, as much as its plot, is aging and mortality, and Scudder's response thereto. All of it grist, alas, for the abridger's mill. And how could it be otherwise? What sort of book could be cut essentially in half without losing a certain something?

The thing is, nobody really likes abridgments. The listeners who don't mind them are generally unaware of how much they're missing. (And sometimes I wonder how they manage to make sense of what they're listening to. Whole subplots disappear—but they're occasionally referenced at the book's conclusion. Characters die or abscond to Luang Prabang in some excised section, and we never do find out what became of them. I suppose the medium works to the abridger's advantage here; one's often doing something else while listening to an audiobook—driving, knitting, puzzling over chess problems, struggling with Double-Crostics, whatever—so it's easy to accept apparent inconsistencies in the text. "Oh I guess I wasn't paying attention . . ." Well, somebody wasn't.)

The only argument for the very existence of abridged audiobooks is an economic one. Retail customers, publishers maintain, will be disinclined to lay out more money for an audiobook than they'd have to pay for the bound hardcover volume. If the book's priced at $25 and the audiobook's 10 or 15 dollars more than that, the potential buyer's going to be resistant.

Well, maybe. My guess is that technology will solve the problem; with audiobooks increasingly moving from cassette to CD (as well they might, since car manufacturers have long since made the switch), and with the next generation of CDs likely to hold far more in the way of running time, it shouldn't be long before all audiobooks are unabridged.

(Well, almost all. There's a real artistic argument for abridging some lengthy nonfiction. Ron Chernow's masterful biography of Alexander Hamilton has a running time of 32 hours unabridged, and contains material of interest to a scholar but not to a casual reader. There are passages one can skim and skip in the bound book, but you can't do that on audio. The publisher accordingly made the audiobook available in two versions.)

The question of abridgment aside ("Abridged audiobooks? Yikes, how 20th century!"), what strikes me most about the medium is its enormous impact. Yes, audiobooks give a devoted reader something to do while he's driving somewhere, but that only scratches the surface of the potential audience. More to the point, audiobooks bring the world of reading to men and women who have never been able to read for pleasure.

Dyslexics are the obvious example, but I know several who have overcome the disorder sufficiently to be ardent readers of the printed word. And there are evidently a great number of persons with no clinical reading disorder who simply don't absorb information well from the page.

Forty-plus years ago I did some work for Robert Harrison, the ex-publisher of *Confidential*. If you handed him a piece of paper he'd hand it back and ask you to read it to him. At the time I figured the son of a bitch was illiterate, and years later I guessed he was dyslexic. But I'm not sure he was either one. I think he just "got" it more effectively through his ears than his eyes.

I'm the reverse—which may make me an odd choice for the host of *Audiobook Café*, but probably stands me in good stead working from a script in a sound studio. I listen to the audiobooks I review—that's my job—but

I also read the bound books, because I absorb the text better that way, and that too is my job.

It takes a while to reach nonreaders with audiobooks—they're not going to wander into a bookstore, are they? But audio is finding its audience, and we're just beginning to discover its potential impact. I wouldn't be surprised, for example, if it helps resuscitate the short story. Short fiction, in great commercial decline since the end of the Second World War, lends itself perfectly to audio; you can have a complete reading experience in the course of a single commute.

Reading, it turns out, isn't something you have to do with your eyes. You can read with your ears, too. And, if you're in the mood, try some of my writing in audio form. But unabridged, if you don't mind.

Reading this fifteen years later, I'm astonished to note that I managed to leave out my own favorite story about abridgement. I was in a sound studio in the West Sixties with a very nice fellow named Steve, who was tasked with engineering a two-cassette abridgement of one of the Burglar *books. I'm not sure which book it was, but Bernie was hanging out a lot with Carolyn Kaiser; this doesn't narrow it down much, as the two have been essentially inseparable since her first appearance in* The Burglar Who Liked to Quote Kipling.

Now Steve never read the whole book. He'd received from the publisher the abridged version, and read that the night before we recorded it. And I began narrating, and we worked for a couple of productive hours, and then broke for lunch. He ordered sandwiches from a nearby restaurant, and at one point he got a quizzical look on his face, and wondered if he was missing something in the text.

"Bernie seems like a regular fellow,"he said. "And I get the sense that Carolyn's attractive, and they get along well. So how come he never puts the moves on her?"

"Oh God," I said. "Did they manage to edit out the fact that she's gay?"

His face fell. "Gay? Carolyn? Honestly?"

Yeah. Honestly. And that, I submit, is all I have to say and all you need to know on the subject of abridgement.

ALL MY BEST EYES ARE PRIVATE

This was written for and appeared in the Fall 2019 issue of Mystery Readers Journal, *the beloved creation of my friend Janet Rudolph.*

It's no secret—well, I certainly *hope* it's no secret—that I've been chronicling the fictional doings of a private detective for something like 45 years. His name is Matthew Scudder, and he's 45 years older now than when I began writing about him, because I found early on that I'd be unable to take the character seriously unless I allowed him to age in real time.

Was that a good decision? Hard to say. He was around 35 in the first book, *The Sins of the Fathers*, and he's 80 in this year's novella, *A Time to Scatter Stones*. The man's in reasonably good shape, but 80 is 80, and he's logged some hard miles on bad roads. He's no longer able to leap tall buildings in a single bound, or drink caffeine much past two in the afternoon, or alcohol at any hour.

Well, you know, I made a similar decision in my own life, and I'm by no means convinced that aging in real time is a good idea for anybody, real or imaginary. It comes at a cost.

On the other hand, Scudder's still out there, taking it as it comes, one day at a time, and I'm still sitting here with my fingers on the keyboard, making his adventures accessible to readers.

So maybe we're doing something right . . .

*　　　*　　　*

But enough about Scudder.

(More than enough, some might say—and way more than I ever thought I'd write. When he put the plug in the jug in the fifth book, *Eight Million Ways to Die*, I figured we were done with each other. He'd come to terms with the central problem of his existence, and that would seem to suggest that his *d'etre* had lost its *raison*. Well, duh, I was wrong about that, and more books followed, until it was very clear that #16, *All the Flowers Are Dying*, was the place to stop. And then I wrote #17, *A Drop of the Hard Stuff,* and wrote a couple of short stories to fill out #18, *The Night and the Music*. And that was that, it was all over, and we heard no more from or of the fellow—until *A Time to Scatter Stones* took me entirely by surprise. Go know.)

People occasionally want to know if there was a real-life model for Scudder—there wasn't—and if I'm friends with a lot of cops and private detectives and get tips from them.

Well, I've known a few cops over the years. A couple of them wrote crime fiction, like Paul Bishop, who tweets up a storm when he's not writing books like *Lie Catchers*, and the late Bill Caunitz, still an NYPD lieutenant when I met him shortly before the publication of *One Police Plaza*. One night I rode along with him while his team busted prostitutes on a local stroll in Long Island City; it was an exercise regarded as essentially pointless by all involved, but it served as good background for an episode in *Eight Million Ways to Die*.

There were other cops who weren't writers themselves but told good war stories. My friend Jimmy Galvin recounted an incident that stuck in my mind, and morphed into a plot point in a Scudder short story, "A Moment of Wrong Thinking." I paid him back (or punished him) by giving his name to the private eye who untangles a pivotal puzzle in *Small Town*.

There was Jack, a West Village neighbor of mine whose past life included a stretch as a plainclothes cop in San Francisco. (I haven't seen him in twenty years, and have long since disremembered his last name.) He'd always struck me as a kind of a boring guy, and then one night in a coffee shop on Greenwich Avenue he told me a story of how he and his partner exacted some unofficial rough justice on an otherwise untouchable bad guy. The minute I heard it I knew I would find a place for it, and it didn't take me long to do just that in *A Dance at the Slaughterhouse*.

A great resource, wouldn't you think? I certainly figured as much. I couldn't tell you how many cups of coffee and grilled cheese sandwiches I had with Jack in the months that followed, and God knows he had a lot to say, but I swear the son of a bitch never said another interesting thing. Not a single one.

The first private eye I got to know was Anthony Spiesman, whom I met at an event thrown together by Dilys Wynn, back when she owned and operated Murder Ink, the mystery bookstore on the Upper West Side. Tony was a private detective who actually came to the profession by way of the genre. He was a serious reader of crime fiction, and it was his admiration for fictional private investigators that led him to become a real one.

And the reading informed the case work. He'd frequently ask himself what Nero Wolfe would make of a situation, and act accordingly.

I lost track of Tony years ago, and I can't think of anything he told me that ever found its way into my work, but one lasting insight he gave me was the infinite variety of real-life private detectives. The stereotypes don't tell the whole story, or even a great part of it.

Tony's own ethical and moral commitment to truth and justice extended beyond his work, all the way to his reading. He was a big fan of Matthew Scudder, but he straight-out refused to read about Bernie Rhodenbarr. The man was a criminal, he told me, however affable and endearing he was supposed to be, and he was unwilling to have any part of a criminal as a hero.

I don't even want to think about what he'd make of Keller . . .

*   *   *

I'm not certain whether I ever met Skipp Porteous in the flesh. It's possible our acquaintance was limited to email. I know he turned author himself, chronicling his spiritual odyssey from fundamentalist preacher to private eye in *Jesus Doesn't Live Here Anymore* and positing a solution to the question of legendary fugitive D. B. Cooper's identity in *Into the Blast*.

Skipp, who died in 2018 after suffering from aphasia for several years, ran a successful private investigation practice in New York, and told me a few years ago that computers and the internet had changed his work almost beyond recognition. He no longer spent much time in the streets, mean or otherwise. In fact he rarely left his desk. He could find out almost everything he needed to know via the computer and the telephone.

I don't remember that he told me any war stories, though I've no doubt he had an abundance to tell. As I've said, I'm not at all certain we ever laid eyes on one another, and our email exchanges were minimal. But, while Scudder remains an adherent of the GOYAKOD method he learned when he carried a gold shield, he's become a little more tech-savvy over the years. (And GOYAKOD stands for Get Off Your Ass and Knock On Doors. But you knew that, right?)

Cici McNair's been a friend of mine for some years, and I've had a chance to see a little more of her now that she's back in New York. She's worked as a private eye for years, in various venues here and abroad, and she's very much a writer; she's thus far published three books drawn from her professional experience: *Detectives Don't Wear Seat Belts, Never Flirt with a Femme Fatale,* and, just this year, *Murder, Actually.*

Cici got in touch one time when she'd been hired by Santé Kimes, who with her son Kenneth committed at least three murders. I don't know what exactly Ms. Kimes expected Cici to do for her, but one thing she wanted was for me to write her life story, which she saw as the road to exoneration and freedom. I wasn't interested, but Cici got me into the court proceedings one day, so I got a good look at the Kimes, which was as much contact as I wanted.

And then someone at *Esquire* commissioned me and a few other writers to write short pieces inspired by the whole affair. I wrote "Without a Body," the after-death musing of Irene Silverman, the elderly Upper East Side woman whom Kenny Kimes strangled because Santé wanted to steal her house. *Esquire* paid me for it, but they didn't publish it—or, as far as I can tell, any of the stories they'd ordered. I tucked "Without a Body" into *Catch and Release,* a collection of my recent short fiction; it's the final entry, but that's because of alphabetical order, not a judgment of its worth.

I knew Jim Thompson for a couple of years before he became a private detective. (No, not the fellow who wrote *The Killer Inside Me.* Not *that* Jim Thompson. There are, you may not be surprised to know, quite a few gentlemen with that name.)

My Jim Thompson was a professor at a New York-area college. I'm not sure what he taught. Economics, I think it was. The job fell through, and he was doing a little of this and a little of that, and a private investigation firm hired him, and he liked the work and found he had an aptitude for it.

There was a stretch when trademark and copyright infringement gave PI firms a lot of work. Tons of Batman T-shirts, for example, were knock-offs, unauthorized by whoever was in charge of licensing such use, and my friend Jim was one of the corps of operatives charged with harassing street vendors and confiscating the merchandise they were not entitled to sell.

Now this may strike one as a pointless exercise, and it sort of was, but you have to make a show of defending a trademark or risk losing it, and that's what my friend was doing on the client's behalf.

While I didn't walk around with Jim and watch him and his cohorts doing their unwholesome work, his account put me right in the picture, and my imagination made itself at home. The result was a short story, "Batman's

Helpers," which takes place at a time in Matt's career when, newly sober, he's picking up day work with the Reliable agency. It turned out that one day was as much time as he was able to spend in the fight against trademark infringement.

I'm not sure how many years Jim spent as a private eye, or if he's ever given it up entirely. He's traveled widely over the decades, spending a lot of time drifting around Latin America. And I do know that he went on to achieve a measure of distinction in another sphere, when he became the leader of a New York association of bondage and discipline enthusiasts. My wife and I attended one of their open meetings; the theme was Intimate Piercings, and one perfectly lovely young member made her way around the room, inviting all to examine the various work she'd had done in that regard.

Members of the circle referred to and addressed our friend as *Master Jim.* Let's see you match that, Philip Marlowe . . .

And so it goes. When I was researching the world of hackers and phone phreaks for *A Walk Among the Tombstones,* I sat down with a guy from the phone company to find out what technology enabled people to do on both sides of the battlefront. Could a hacker do this? Could a company guy do that?

Just put anything you want, he advised me. Because if either side can't do it now, they'll be able to in six months at the outside. Whatever it is.

You want your fictional private eyes to be realistic? Write them the way you want them to be. However you imagine your guy or gal, odds are there's somebody just like that already out there.

ALONE TOO LONG

Written as an introduction for Great Tales Of Madness and The Macabre, *edited by Charles Ardai and published in 1990 by Galahad Books.*

In the fall of 1975 I was alone, and traveling. I had left New York, reduced my worldly goods to what would fit in the back of a rusted-out Ford station wagon, and was on my way to Los Angeles. It took me nine months to get there, but then I was in no particular hurry.

I spent the month of September in Rodanthe, on North Carolina's Outer Banks. I had started work on a novel, which would turn out to be *Ariel*, the story of an adopted child in Charleston, South Carolina, who may or may not have murdered her baby brother in his crib. The book was not going well, and what I was mostly concentrating on was fishing. There was a pier sticking out into the ocean and you could fish off it all day and night. I literally lived that month on what I hauled out of the ocean, occasionally varying my fare by driving over to the bay side of the island and catching eels. They came out tasting like chicken fricassee, except eelier.

And I started writing short stories. I wrote one called "Click!" about a jaded hunter who tries to hunt with a camera instead, and it turns out that he can't, and that it's human beings he hunts, not animals. I wrote another called "Funny You Should Ask" about a young hitchhiker who wonders where recycled jeans come from, since nobody ever throws them out; he learns to his chagrin that they are a byproduct of a firm involved in processing unwary young people into pet food.

And then I wrote "Sometimes They Bite," which appears in this volume.

I sent it off to my agent, as I had done with the others. After he read it he called a friend of mine. "Have you heard from Larry lately?" he wanted to know.

"I think he's in North Carolina," my friend said.

"I know where he is," my agent said. "I wondered if you'd heard from him. He's been writing these short stories."

"And?"

"And I have a feeling he's been alone too long," my agent said.

I think he was probably right. And, if there is a common denominator in the stories you will find in this collection, I suspect it is that they were all written by people who have been alone too long. They might not have been geographically remote, as I was, and they might not have been deprived of the company of others, as I also was. But I have a feeling they were too much alone in the recesses of their own minds, too much in touch with their own madness, too often face to face with their own demons. As was I.

It is this turning inward, this view of the hidden and frequently unsettling chambers of the self, that generates the ideas from which such stories spring. "Where do you get your ideas?" some readers ask—when they read anything but especially when they read stories like these. We get them as oysters get pearls, by carefully wrapping the stuff of our innards around the sharp grains of sand that cause us pain.

I am writing these lines in Virginia, where I am briefly in residence at the Virginia Center for the Creative Arts, a sort of refuge for artists and composers and writers. My wife Lynne is here as well, making art, and we are in the good company of twenty fellow artists. A few weeks ago, however, I put aside a novel and began writing short stories, and some of them look for all the world to be the work of a man who has been alone too long.

And today we wait in the path of Hurricane Hugo. The sky is light one minute and dark the next. The trees are already being whipped by high winds, and the air is warm and dense and choked with menace.

Awful and *wonderful* once meant the same thing. This weather is awful and wonderful. Storms like Hugo are dangerous beyond description, and the sane part of me hopes that this one will miss us, or strike us only a glancing blow.

Another part of me, the part that's been alone too long, yearns for the full fury of the storm.

These stories are awful and wonderful. May you enjoy weather such as this across your inner landscape as you read them.

APOCALYPSE IN A SMALL TOWN

Shortly before William Morrow published my novel, Small Town, *I was invited to submit an essay for* Metropolis Found, *a collection to be published by the New York is Book Country festival.*

I was ten and a half when I fell in love with New York. That was in December of 1948, when my father and I took the train down from Buffalo to spend a long weekend in the city of his birth. We rode the subways and the 3rd Avenue El, saw Ray Bolger in *Where's Charley?*, went to Bedloe's island to gape at the Statue of Liberty, and caught a live telecast of *Talk of the Town*, which is what Ed Sullivan was then calling his Sunday night program. (I'd never seen television until then; I was more impressed by the monitors than by what was happening onstage.) We stayed at the Hotel Commodore next to Grand Central, so I suppose we must have slept, but I don't remember that part.

As soon as I could manage it, I moved here, and right away I began setting my fiction here. Still do. Most of my books take place in New York. Bernie Rhodenbarr and Matt Scudder rarely leave the five boroughs, while Keller and Tanner, who venture far afield, always come home to Manhattan. When my wife and I moved to Florida in the mid-Eighties, I still set everything in New York. What else could I do? What the hell did I know about Florida?

People have said that the city is a virtual character in my fiction, a presence that informs the work far beyond street names and subway lines. Any number of them, New Yorkers and others, were outraged when Hollywood transplanted Matt Scudder to Los Angeles (*Eight Million Ways To Die*) and Bernie Rhodenbarr to San Francisco (*Burglar*). I know that New York energizes my work, and that I'd be no more inclined to situate my work elsewhere than I would to (God forbid) live somewhere else.

A decade or so ago, I realized I ought to write a big New York novel, a book that was somehow not merely of the city but about the city, a massive robust multiple-viewpoint book with all the New York I could cram into it. Someday, I told myself, and went on to Other Things.

Then a little later, in 1993, I came across a quotation from John Gunther, a rich paean to the city, saying how big and bustling and wonderful the place is, and ending with the line: ". . . but it becomes a Small Town when it rains."

Beautiful, I thought, and all at once I had a title for the book I seemed unlikely ever to write. *A Small Town When It Rains*? Not quite. *A Small Town In The Rain*? Still a little awkward, but it was there somewhere . . .

Come December of 2000, I realized it was time. My publishers at Morrow/ HarperCollins were ecstatic at the prospect of a big multiple-viewpoint non-series thriller, and the title had refined itself to *Small Town*. Now all I had to do was figure out something for it to be about, and then sit down and write it.

In the summer of 2001 I went to work, and by the end of August I had a little over a hundred pages done and four or five principal characters introduced and in motion. I took a couple of weeks off, and then 9/11 happened. Way down on the long list of casualties was *Small Town*. Not that I felt like writing anyway, not that I cared much what I wrote next, or if I wrote anything . . . but the book, it seemed to me, was dead in the water. It was set in a city that had ceased to exist, a pre-9/11 city.

As I said, it didn't matter much. Nine months went by, during which time I didn't even attempt to write anything. I don't remember what I did, actually. This and that, I suppose. I write a lot, but I don't write all the time, and it's very much in my nature to take time off. This was more time off than usual, but not unprecedented; I had time booked in a writers' colony in June and July of 2002, and assumed I'd write something then.

I had no idea what it might be. It seemed to me that a New York novel of any sort was impossible. It would either be about 9/11, which was a horrible idea, or it would *not* be about 9/11, which was arguably worse. I thought some piece of fluff—a Bernie Rhodenbarr book, say—might work, but was that what I wanted to do? One thing was sure. I wouldn't be working on *Small Town*.

I surprised myself, though. Because three weeks before my colony stay I printed out *Small Town*, and a week before I drove out there I actually read what I'd printed out, and I liked what I'd read. It had to be recast, certainly, and the time frame was wrong; it had to take place not before but after the bombing. And it had to be a different story, a much bigger story . . .

Writing is magic, and I say this not boastfully but in wonder. I'm not the magician, waving his wand, pulling a rabbit out of a hat. I'm not sure what I am. The wand, maybe. Or the rabbit, or even the hat. Who cares? It's all magic.

And, magically, I sat down at my desk the day I got to Ragdale, and five weeks later *Small Town* was written. It didn't feel as though I were channeling the book, or taking down celestial dictation. It felt like work, but work I couldn't keep from doing. Some years back the Red Sox had a spirited lefthander of whom it was said that he pitched like a man with his hair on fire. Well, I wrote like a man with his hair on fire, and what came out was *Small Town*. It wound up much longer and darker and richer than the book I'd had originally in mind, with a very different story line. My agent read it and did backflips. My publishers, here and abroad, were over the moon. As

I write these lines, the book's publication is a week away, and the only really important verdict—the readers'—is yet to come. By the time you read this, it'll be in.

But, whether or not *Small Town* turns out to be what New Yorkers want to read, it is very definitely the book this New Yorker needed to write. It is, I came to realize, a post-apocalyptic novel set in New York in the summer of 2002. We've had our apocalypse, and we're New Yorkers, and we're moving on.

BACK IN THE DAY WITH DVR

When he died early in 2002, Dave Van Ronk left unfinished a
memoir of his beginnings in folk music. He'd been writing it
with Elijah Wald, who completed the book for publication as
The Mayor of MacDougal Street. *I was invited to provide an*
introduction.

Early in August of 1956 I boarded a train in Buffalo and got off seven or
eight hours later at Grand Central Terminal. I found the clock under which
I was supposed to meet Paul Grillo, and remarkably, he was there. I'd recently completed my freshman year at Antioch College, in Yellow Springs,
Ohio, where Paul had been one of my hall advisers. (In this capacity he and
his roommate had mentored me and the other fifteen or twenty residents of
my freshman dormitory.) Now, during a three-month work period, Paul and
I were going to room together, along with a third fellow, Fred Anliot.

Paul had already found a place for us to live, and furnished me with the
address—147 West 14th Street. He pointed me toward the subway and sent
me on my way. I took the shuttle to Times Square, the IRT to 14th Street.
I got a key from the landlady—Mrs. Moderno, if memory serves—and
climbed three flights of stairs to a very large room with bright yellow walls.

We lived there for two or three weeks. Then we decided the place was
too expensive—it was $24 a week, split three ways—and someone, probably
Paul, found us a cheaper place at 108 West 12th Street. The rent there was
$12 a week, but that didn't make it a bargain, and we were just about bright

enough to realize we couldn't live like that. Within two weeks we were out
of there and installed in a one-bedroom apartment on the first floor at 54
Barrow Street, where the rent was $90 a month. It must be a co-op by now,
and it's probably worth half a million dollars. Back then it was a terrific place
to live, and I was there until the end of October, when it was time to go back
to school.

So I was in the Village for only three months that year, and that's awfully
difficult to believe. Because I met so many people and did so many things.
I was working five days a week from nine to five in the mailroom at Pines
Publications, on East 40th Street. I spent nights and weekends hanging out,
and where I mostly hung out was Macdougal Street.

That very first night in New York, I had two addresses to check out, and
managed to get to both of them. One was a jazz club called Café Bohemia, at
15 Barrow Street, where I nursed a drink at the bar and listened to Al Cohn
and Zoot Sims. The other was the Caricature, a coffeehouse on Macdougal
Street, where a fellow I'd met a year earlier at Camp Lakeland—we were
both counselors there that summer—was a regular player in Liz's nightly
bridge game.

I could have met Dave Van Ronk there that first night—at Liz's, not at
the Bohemia—because, as he mentions, it was a regular place of his. But I
met him instead at one of the Sunday sessions in Washington Square Park,
which is where I quickly learned to spend my Sunday afternoons. The circle
was always overflowing with people playing instruments and singing folk
songs, and there was something very special about the energy there. This
was, you should understand, *before* the folk music renaissance, and before
the curious synthesis of drugs and politics made college kids a breed apart.
The great majority of collegians were still gray-flannel members of the Silent
Generation, ready to sign on for a corporate job with a good pension plan.
Those of us who didn't fit that mold, those of us who'd always sort of figured
there was something wrong with us, sat around the fountain in Washington
Square singing "Michael Row the Boat Ashore" and feeling very proud of
ourselves for being there.

The only thing wrong with Sunday afternoons was that they ended at six o'clock and some of us figured that there ought to be a way to keep the party going. For a while, 54 Barrow Street was our after-hours. Our apartment—living room, bedroom, kitchen—filled up with people with guitars and banjos and voices, and the party went on for four or five hours. I'm not sure how long we hosted it. We passed 54 Barrow to other Antiochians when we had to go back to Ohio, and they may have kept the party going for a few years, but eventually it moved to larger quarters on Spring Street.

By then I was a lifer. I'd visited New York twice with my parents—my father had grown up in Manhattan and the Bronx—and I'd always assumed somehow that I'd wind up living there, but it was during those three months that I became a New Yorker and, more to the point, a Villager. I've lived in other places—Wisconsin, Florida—and in other parts of New York City, but Greenwich Village has always drawn me home, and has indeed been my residence for most of the past thirty years. I started out, you'll recall, on 14th Street a few doors from 7th Avenue. Since then I've lived on 12th Street, on Barrow Street, on Bleecker and Greenwich and Jane, on Charles, on Horatio, on West 13th. Now, for about a dozen years, I've been on West 12th a few doors from 8th Avenue.

"Why should I go anywhere?" Dave said of the Village. "I'm already here."

Whenever you got here, it was better ten years earlier.

That's what people say now, complaining about gentrification. It's what they said twenty years ago, complaining about tourists. It's what they said forty years ago, complaining about hippie kids.

I suspect they've always said it. I suspect they said it to Edna St. Vincent Millay and Floyd Dell.

It seems to me—because I was around then, because I remember it fondly, because it was gone, alas like my youth, too soon—that Greenwich Village was a very special place during my first years in it. And the people who just moved here yesterday will probably think the same themselves, when their youth is as remote and as inaccurately recalled as is mine.

Once, back in the early Sixties, I decided to leave New York. I told Dave I was going to return to Buffalo. He was incredulous and asked why, a question I was somehow unable to answer. "Well," I managed, "that's my hometown. That's where I'm from."

He thought about it, then looked off into the middle distance. "I know a woman," he said, "who was born in Buchenwald."

Dave Van Ronk and I became friends during my first three-month stint in New York. The friendship lasted for forty-five years.

I couldn't begin to guess how many times I heard him sing. I caught him at no end of venues in New York, but I also managed to catch up with him in Los Angeles and Chicago and Albuquerque and New Hope, Pennsylvania, and somewhere in Westchester County. There was never a time when I didn't want to listen to that voice.

One night he and I and Lee Hoffman sat drinking in her apartment—she was then married to Larry Shaw—and co-wrote a batch of songs that wound up in *The Bosses' Songbook*. ("Songs to Stifle the Flames of Discontent" was the subtitle, and nobody got author credit for any of the songs; a note in the introduction explained that most of the authors were on enough lists already.) Another song of mine, "Georgie and the IRT," wound up on his second album. Some years later, I provided the liner notes for another album, *Songs for Aging Children*.

When Dave died, I spent a couple of weeks playing his records. The music lasts. The song's there, and so's the singer, present in every note.

What fades, what's hard to recapture, is the off-stage presence. The nights—and there weren't enough of them, just handfuls scattered over the years—spent sitting around and talking. Dave was self-taught, and never did a better teacher meet a more receptive pupil; he knew more about more subjects than anyone I've ever met.

I wish to God he hadn't left us so soon. And I wish this wonderful book he's given us could be a little longer. But then I wished that of every set I ever heard him sing. And Dave had a long-standing policy of never doing more than a single encore. You should always leave them wanting more, he said. And he always did.

I was pleased and honored when Elijah Wald asked me to write an introduction to *The Mayor of Macdougal Street.* The task has turned out to be far more difficult than I'd expected, and I can't say I'm happy with the result.

Dave doesn't really need someone to open for him. I've taken up enough of your time. I'll get off the stage now, knowing at least that I'm leaving you in very good hands.

THE BALLAD OF THE POUND

FOUR STERLING STANZAS BY HORACE BULL

The following bit of doggerel graced the pages of the Whitman Numismatic Journal *in November, 1964. Six years and three months later, the UK's currency had been decimalized, which is not the same thing as decimated, but still . . .*

You say we're somewhat backward, you may even call us fools,
But there's madness to our method when Britannia waives the rules;
Though our wealth may be uncommon, when we creep into our tents
                    In solemn stealth
                    We tally our wealth
In pounds and shillings and pence.

Canadians count in dollars, a most distressing thing;
Australians go to decimals a year from now in spring;
The present is imperfect and the future's more than tense,
                    But we'll buy and sell
                    And do quite well
In pounds and shillings and pence.

When the shoe is on the other foot it's rather apt to pinch,
For your lot measures distances in yard and foot and inch;
And so we'll ride on the road's left side (though you may think us dense)
                    And we'll reckon each sum
                    Till Kingdom Come
In pounds and shillings and pence.

There'll always be an England just as long as there's a pound,
For the dollar shall not occupy an inch of English ground;
In English eyes a dollar does not make a lot of sense
                    And we shall count
                    A fair amount
In pounds and shilling and crowns and guineas
In quids and florins and bobs and tanners
In pounds and shillings and pounds and shillings
And pounds and shilling and pence!

THE BUMPY ROAD TO INSPIRATION

An essay for the March 9, 1997 travel section of the New York Times.

In 1982 I published *Eight Million Ways to Die*, the fifth in a series of novels about a hard-drinking ex-cop named Matthew Scudder. In its course he surprised me by coming to terms with his alcoholism, which was good for him but looked to be bad for me; the book was very well received, but I couldn't see how I'd be able to write more about the guy. I did manage a sort of prequel (*When the Sacred Ginmill Closes*), but my several attempts at continuing the series stalled out after fifty or a hundred pages. And that, alas, seemed to be that.

Then in the spring of 1988 I was on a night train from Luxor to Cairo. That sounds romantic, and I suppose it might have been, but the reality was grim. There were close to fifty in our party, all tombed and templed half to death after ten days in Egypt, and every last one of us intestinally challenged in the worst way. The train's restroom supplies were exhausted twenty minutes out of Luxor, and so was everyone's sense of adventure.

Lynne and I had a squalid little roomette to ourselves, with a sort of cushioned ledge for each of us to sleep on. The floor was awash with the water we had planned to drink during the night, our water bottle having fallen and smashed open when the train left Luxor station rather abruptly. The trackbed was in terrible shape, the train much given to sudden stops and starts, and, when I finally found something to read, they turned off the lights for the night.

I dozed off eventually and slept for two or three hours. I woke up in time to watch dawn brighten the sky. That was the Nile outside our window, that great historic waterway, that cradle of civilization—and I couldn't bear the sight of it. Nor could I go back to sleep, or find anything diverting to do now that I was awake.

So I lay there, and by the time we arrived in Cairo knew what Matthew Scudder was going to do next. Some plot elements I'd ruminated on and gotten nowhere with years previously had suddenly knit themselves together. I felt confident the book would work, and by September I was ready to sit down and write it, and Scudder was off and running.

Four years and four more novels later, we spent a month in China's Sinkiang province, shlepping across the Takla Makan desert on the southern Silk Road, only the second or third party of westerners to take that godforsaken route since the days of Sven Hedin and Sir Aurel Stein.

We had known going in that the trip, like a fair amount of adventure travel, might very well be more enjoyable in retrospect than while it was going on. Even so, the event vastly exceeded expectations. It was hideous. We set out on August 1, and by the middle of the week we were telling one another, "Remember, September 1 is the first day of the rest of your life."

After two weeks of long rides and low rations, we left our wretched Jeeps and mounted Bactrian camels, striking out across the sand in search of a lost city. (Sven Hedin had found it a century or so ago, and had had the good sense to lose it again. We might have left well enough alone, but no . . .)

My camel was a mean-spirited beast, and my saddle was a wooden board that was supposed to be cushioned with padding, but wasn't. Riding on it was rather like being ridden out of town on a rail, but without the tar and feathers and attendant ceremony. Our group leader might have set things right, but the fellow was loopy with malaria. For a while we were actually afraid he might die, and then we were afraid he wouldn't.

I sat on my camel. And I found myself remembering an article I'd read at least twenty-five and probably thirty years earlier about a Last Man's Club of thirty-one men, the survivor of which would round up thirty young men and start another chapter. I had not had a conscious thought of the subject in decades, but now out there in the desert it rang like a bell, and I knew what my next novel was going to be about. I turned the notion over and over in my mind for at least as long as I stayed on that camel, and some months later I wrote the book, *A Long Line of Dead Men*.

I don't think any of this is coincidental.

As you will have gathered, I travel quite a bit—as much as I possibly can, really. I do so because it is my passion, and not in the hope that it will pay off in any practical fashion. Writers beyond number have trotted the globe in search of plots, of exotic settings, of whatever comes under the heading of inspiration. Not I. I go all over the world, on land and sea and camel, and then I come home and write yet another book set in New York City.

Even so, the travel seems to be an important part of the process. Nor does it have to be the next thing to unendurable in order for it to stimulate the flow of creative ideas. Even a pleasant and carefree trip can prove productive.

I am writing these lines in a wonderfully comfortable room in the Amari Airport Hotel, in Bangkok. A week ago I was sitting in a deck chair on a boat cruising the Irriwaddy. The river was lower now in the dry season than it would be when the monsoon came, but it was still a mighty river, the most important waterway of Burma (or Myanmar, as you prefer). There is a book I plan to begin writing three months from now; for a couple of years I've known what it's going to be about, but that's all I've known, and the plot elements have been a long time coming.

They came in a rush on the Irriwaddy. More bits and pieces joined them in the week that followed. I found myself doing the most useful kind of thinking about the book, not the thinking you will yourself to do but the sort that comes along unbidden, sometimes in a trickle, sometimes in a flood.

I don't know how it all works, or why. I'm sure the time I spend far from New York brings the city into sharper relief when I turn to it again in fiction, that I see more clearly for having temporarily turned my eyes elsewhere. But that seems inadequate explanations for the curious process by which travel serves to stimulate my creative imagination. I don't understand that part, and maybe I don't have to.

I can tell you this much. Like every writer I've ever known, I run into a fair number of people every year who ask the single most annoying question any of us ever hears—i.e., "Where do you get your ideas?"

Why do people insist on asking this question? And who could possibly come up with an answer?

Well, I could. "Oh, I get them everywhere," I can say airily. "On a train in Egypt. On a camel in Chinese Turkestan. Sailing on the Irriwaddy River in Burma, or bouncing along on a ruined road from Bamako to Mopti in Mali. Cruising in the Galapagos, or river-rafting in Peru, or walking clear across Spain to Santiago de Compostela. Ideas? I'll tell you, I get them all over the world."

You may be wondering which novel got its inspiration during that boat ride on the Irriwaddy. You wouldn't be alone. I think it would have to have been Tanner on Ice, *a return to a series character whom I'd last heard from in 1970. That seems obvious, given that the novel is set chiefly in Burma. Interestingly (well, to me, anyway) I was thinking about the book while I was in Burma, but it wasn't until months later, and thousands of miles from Rangoon and Mandalay, that I decided where the story would take place.*

I got plot components on the Irriwaddy. A few months later, back in New York, I got the idea of having Tanner's adventure take place in Burma. And it was a few more months after that, holed up in the Listowel Arms in County Kerry, that I started writing.

CHEERS FOR THE
MUCH-MALIGNED MOTEL

On March 17, 1990, the No-Fixed-Address portion of the Buffalo hunt ended with our return to New York, and the city was so glad to see us they threw a parade. And on June 3 the New York Times *ran this piece:*

Two and a half years ago my wife and I decided to try living without a fixed address. We closed our house in Florida, packed all our hopes and dreams and socks and underwear into the trunk of our Buick Century, and set off in search of America.

Most friends, on hearing our plans, assumed we'd be traveling in some sort of RV. Once they got it straight that we weren't planning to spend our nights in the Buick, their assumptions lurched off in another direction altogether. "You'll be able to stay in inns and B-and-B's," they told us. And they explained that enterprising young couples all over America had taken to restoring ancient hostelries and faithfully renovating old mansions, all with the aim of providing travelers like ourselves with a blessed respite from that blight on the landscape, that bane of the nomadic existence, that ubiquitous eyesore, the motel.

We jotted down the names and addresses they provided, paged through the guidebooks they handed us. We read about rooms furnished with canopy

beds and period chairs and armoires, about hearty breakfasts featuring bis-
cuits and muffins made from scratch and omelets made from double-yolk
organic eggs laid by happy free-range chickens. We read about hosts eager
to share everything with us—their intimate knowledge of the Delaware Valley, their recipe for chicken divan, their homemade chokecherry wine, their
views on the reunification of Ireland. We read until our eyes ached, and then
we packed those guidebooks in the spare tire well and spent the next two
years in motels.

Because the last thing we wanted, after a few hundred miles of bad road
(or a few hours on the back of a mule, or walking a trail, or in a museum), was
to spend a night up to our ears in quaint. I didn't want to worry, before dropping into a chair, that I might turn a museum piece into kindling. I didn't
want a bathroom down the hall, its plumbing fixtures as faithful to the period as the creaking canopy bed. I didn't want a talkative host and hostess and
a slew of chattering guests, their company a civilized alternative to television.

On the contrary, I wanted television. I wanted a large-screen color
set with cable reception and, for preference, a Mets game on it. I wanted
air-conditioning and hot water and a bare minimum of human contact. I
wanted to be able to skip breakfast and get an early start, or sleep through
breakfast and get a late start, without feeling that I was Missing Something
Important. (The people who tell you that breakfast is the most important
meal of the day are the very same people who try to make you feel guilty for
watching television.)

I don't want to disparage innkeeping—or inngoing either, for that matter. Bed-and-breakfasts and full-service inns provide wonderful vacations;
we've enjoyed them in the past and will doubtless enjoy them in the future.
But when you travel day in and day out, when the place you sleep is not an
end in itself but a way station along the roadside, you want something else.

Fortunately, it's a cinch to find. Motels litter the American landscape.
They line the interstates, of course, but they are also strewn along blue high-
ways all over the country. They are so easy to come by that we tend to take

them for granted. We snipe at them for their sterility, their uniformity, their anonymity, as if these were faults.

Twenty years ago a musician friend of mine told me about a musician friend of his who had finally settled down after many years on the road. He was living in Los Angeles, making good money as a studio musician, working steady, living an ordered life for a change. He had built a house, and he'd made sure that it contained ample guest quarters so that he could accommodate musician friends when they hit town.

And, so that he could make them entirely comfortable, he had hired a decorator whose job it was to duplicate the standard Holiday Inn unit as closely as possible. According to my friend, the room was a huge success, down to the lamp bolted to the dresser top and the bullfighter portraits on the wall. Once you entered that room and closed the door, you were in a Holiday Inn.

When I heard that story I thought the fellow was some sort of sadist. A little time on the road made me realize that he was in fact the perfect host. How better to make a friend feel at home than to put him in the very room he occupies 300 days a year?

Motel-hopping is simplest and surest if you find one or two chains that you like and book each night's accommodation that morning, or even the night before. Your room will be waiting for you on your arrival, and it will be as you have specified—smoking or nonsmoking, double or king, ground floor or second floor. Although there is always some variation within a motel chain, and although some individual motels will be newer and better maintained than others, you will be getting an essentially standard product at a prearranged price. You'll have few surprises, and fewer disasters.

We hardly ever did this.

For one thing, we rarely knew in the morning where and when we would want to stop that night. On the infrequent occasions when we wanted to make good time on an interstate, we wanted to be able to keep the wheels turning until we were tired. Most of the time, though, we poked around with no clear destination and in no great rush to get there. Even if we knew for certain what roads we'd be traversing that day, they were rarely the sort to attract the motel chains. They didn't draw enough tourist traffic.

So we stayed, more often than not, in independent motels that we selected essentially at random. We had some surprises, and the occasional disaster.

One room in Fort Scott, Kansas, for example, was full of flies. We checked in, we brought our bags in from the car, we got the teakettle going, and we noticed that the place was swarming with houseflies. Not just one or two. More like one or two dozen.

I went to the office to complain about the infestation. Someone must have left a window open, I said. The clerk seemed dubious but had another room available and gave me the key. I checked the room and there were no flies buzzing around, and I was mollified.

Of course there were no flies buzzing around. The little darlings were sleeping. But, by the time we had transferred our bags and shucked our clothes and got the kettle boiling, they were wide awake and ready to play, and at least as numerous as the ones in the first room.

When we turned out the lights they went back to sleep. And so, eventually, did we.

Motels, it may be said, are like families. It is the happy ones that are all alike. The unhappy ones are unhappy each in its own way.

Some have beds that sag, while others err on the side of rigidity. Some television sets get only one channel, and that poorly. Some rooms smell like the aftermath of an all-night poker game, others like a cat box. Some have thin walls, so that you hear the people whispering next door. Some have thin ceilings, so that you hear every step taken by the family overhead.

The potential for disaster can be minimized by inspecting the room before check-in, an option that is always available and that I rarely exercise.

Here are a few things we learned during two years on the road:

- Take along an electric teakettle, and whatever you like in the way of tea or cocoa or instant coffee. China cups or mugs are a pleasure, and easy enough to replace if they break. Some motels provide a doohickey attached to the wall that will supposedly heat a cup of water. It will generally take 20 minutes to do so, however.

- Unless stairs are a problem for you, or you have a lot of heavy luggage, ask for a room on the top floor of a two-story motel. You'll have more privacy and hear less road noise. And, if the acoustics of the motel are such that it is the lot of the person downstairs to be annoyed by the footsteps of the person overhead, you will be the annoyer rather than the annoyee.

- Breakfast in your room saves money and gets you on the road faster. We kept a box of cereal and a couple of bowls in the bag with the tea things, and picked up a pint of milk and a couple of oranges the night before. If breakfast to you means eggs and toast, you'll have to go out for it.

- Some motels have great soap, substantial cakes that will last a week or two. Take them with you when you leave. Then, when your next stop provides tiny chips of insoluble soap, you can use your own and feel luxurious. A similar range prevails in the realm of towels, but walking off with the good ones strikes us as over the top, not to say larcenous. You could always carry your own with you, but we never did.

- Trust your intuition. One time, early in our travels, I had us nearly checked into a motel outside of Marion, Alabama, when I got spooked and pushed the registration card back across the desk. I went back to the car and started explaining sheepishly to Lynne. "Thank God," she said. "Let's get out of here. There's something creepy about this place." Now I'm sure we could have spent the night there and lived to tell the tale, but I wouldn't be fool enough to test the hypothesis. And, now that I think of it, that clerk did look a lot like Anthony Perkins . . .

Some motels have memorable idiosyncrasies, others unanticipated delights. One in Statesboro, Georgia, insisted that you show your driver's license upon check-in; no guests were accepted who lived within 50 miles, lest the owner be an unwitting partner to adultery. (You didn't have to show a marriage license, so out-of-state adultery was evidently acceptable.) A motel in Batavia, New York, calling itself the Friendly Motel, had a whole dresser drawer full of notes from previous occupants. ("This sure is a friendly motel, and we sure did enjoy our stay here . . .") Another in Texas had a petting zoo on the front lawn. One in Mora, Oregon, had the most comfortable bed we ever slept in, anywhere.

The thing is, you're not buying the place. You're just renting it, just spending a single night in it. If it's terrific, it's a pleasure. If it's terrible, it's only terrible for eight hours. Then it's a memory.

And you can get hooked on it.

This past fall I found myself on a busman's holiday, a 20-city promotional book tour, and I did it by car. While I went on motel-hopping, Lynne suddenly found herself alone in our huge old beachfront house in Florida. After a week she started to go nuts. Little sounds spooked her, long silences unnerved her. ("It's quiet out there." "Yeah . . . too quiet.") And. when a pair of stray cats had a fight beneath the living-room floor, that about did it. She threw some clothes in a bag and decided to visit a friend in Key West.

It was evening already when she set out, and Key West was six or seven hours away. A couple of hours down the road she realized she couldn't drive the whole stretch in one shot. At Homestead she saw a familiar word in neon and pulled off the road and checked into a motel. She hung the "Do

Not Disturb" sign on the doorknob, plugged in the teakettle, sat on the bed and put her feet up.

"And I relaxed," she told me. "I was in a room 12 feet by 20 instead of a four-bedroom house. There was a phone on the nightstand next to me, but it wasn't going to ring because nobody knew where I was. I could make tea, I could watch TV, and, in the morning I could take a shower and get dressed and leave forever. I felt *safe.*"

COLLECTING OLD SUBWAY CARS

In 2006, Plume published The Subway Chronicles: Scenes From Life in New York, *edited by Jacqueline Cangro. (I include the subtitle because the main title is shared by at least three other unrelated volumes.) I wrote the following reminiscence for the book, and the words flowed as if I'd been waiting for forty-plus years to write it all down; Lord knows I'd had enough practice inflicting the story on friends in conversation.*

In 1964 I was living in Tonawanda, a suburb of Buffalo, New York. People who live in suburbs have cars, and I had a 1963 Rambler, and didn't like it much. So one day I drove it to a Volkswagen dealer and made arrangements to trade it in on a new VW convertible. As decisions go, it wasn't a bad one; it was better than the original decision to buy the Rambler, and infinitely superior to the earlier decision to move back to Buffalo from New York.

The salesman and I worked out a deal. I mostly just sat there, not really knowing what the hell I was doing, and this proved to be a good negotiating strategy, as it turned out. Then I filled out the paperwork and signed a lot of things, and arranged to come back in a day or two and give them the Rambler and drive home in the VW.

At which time the salesman kept giving me these strange looks, and I kept waiting for him to say something. And at length he did.

"Tell me," he said. "Where do you keep them?"

"Keep them?"

"The old subway cars," he said. "Where in heaven's name do you keep them?"

If I'd been a computer, I'd have picked that moment to crash. Instead I just stood there, nonplussed, until the penny dropped and I found myself plussed again. And remembered the questionnaire I'd filled out a year or two earlier.

It was in 1961, you see, that my first novel was published—or, more specifically, the first novel published under my own name. It was called *Mona,* and its impact on the world of American letters recalled Don Marquis's observation that publishing a volume of verse was like dropping a rose petal into the Grand Canyon and waiting for the echo. The closest *Mona* got to an echo was the questionnaire that Gale Research, publishers of various reference works including *Contemporary Authors,* sent to anyone who managed to break into print.

It was a fairly straightforward document, and I'd filled it out in a fairly straightforward manner. But then I came to a question about interests and hobbies, and for some reason I turned playful. "Have an extensive collection of old subway cars," I wrote. And, further down the page, I was invited to list topics on which I would welcome correspondence with readers and other authors. "Would like to hear from other collectors of old subway cars," I wrote, "esp. any with wooden cars from the old Myrtle Avenue elevated line."

And then I signed and sealed the thing and mailed it off to Chicago. I didn't really expect them to print it. I mean, really—a collection of old subway cars? And if they did, what could it matter? Who would ever read it?

Well, I'll tell you who read it. That VW salesman read it. I'd told him I was a writer, and so identified myself in the purchase agreement, and he'd decided to check up on me. And he'd found *Contemporary Authors* in the Kenmore Public Library (which, I have to say, was more than I'd ever done, never having thought to look for the listing). And he'd read about my collection, and wanted to know more about it.

I've no idea what I told him, but it must have been okay, because I got to drive home in the Volkswagen. (It was the model with the top that you raised and lowered manually. Great little car.)

The car's long gone, but the memory lingers. At the time what astonished me was that the fellow had looked me up, but over time I've decided that what's truly remarkable is that he's the only person in over forty years to make mention of my putative collection. I've no idea how many copies of *Contemporary Authors* occupy library shelves, or how many persons, salesmen and others, may have consulted them. Nor could I begin to guess how many other reference works might have cribbed data from that article. But what I do know is that not a single person has ever raised the subject of old subway cars with me.

It's a damn shame, too. I mean, there has to be somebody out there with a wooden car from the old Myrtle Avenue El. Wouldn't you think?

I love the subway. Always have.

I grew up in Buffalo, and came to New York for the first time when I was ten and a half years old. My father, a native New Yorker, brought me for a weekend of male bonding years before someone dreamed up a term for it. We rode the Empire State Limited to Grand Central, stayed next door at the Commodore Hotel, and for three or four days he showed me the city. We went up to the top of the Empire State Building, we took a ferry to the Statue of Liberty, we saw a Broadway show (*Where's Charlie?* with Ray Bolger) and a live telecast (*The Talk of the Town*, the Ed Sullivan show, which was remarkable to me less for the fact that it was live than that it was television; I'd not yet seen TV back home, and found the monitor more interesting than the show on stage). We went all over by subway, and my most vivid memory is of a Sunday morning ride on the 3rd Avenue El, all the way down to the Bowery. I recall seeing a fellow run out of a saloon down there, let out a blood-curdling shriek, then turn around and run back in again.

It seems to me that I knew then that I'd eventually live in New York.

I moved here for the first time in the summer of 1956; I'd just completed my freshman year as an Antioch College student, and the school had (and continues to have) a co-op plan whereby students spend half the year in jobs in their field. My job was as a mail room flunkey at Pines Publications, on East 40th Street, and I commuted by subway from an apartment on Barrow Street. I would board the 7th Avenue IRT local at Sheridan Square—they call it the 1 train now—and switch to the express at 14th Street, and get off at Times Square and walk a couple of blocks.

Curiously, that's always been my train. I've lived in various parts of the city—mostly in Manhattan, but for awhile in Greenpoint, Brooklyn—and I've had occasion to ride most of the city's subway lines, but I've always thought of the West Side IRT as my line. Early on, I wrote a song about it, a parody of an old Carter Family classic about a heroic engineer who died at the wheel of a train sabotaged by strikers—one of the rare pieces of folk music written to glorify a scab. Here's the song, which my friend Dave Van Ronk recorded on an early album:

Along came the IRT, a-cannonballin' through
From 242nd Street to Flatbush Avenue
At 5:15 one Friday eve she pulled into Times Square
The people filled the platform, and Georgie, he was there.

The people filled the platform, they milled and massed around
And Georgie looked upon that train, and it was Brooklyn bound
He vowed at once that train to board, the weekend not to roam
For Georgie was a shipping clerk, and Brooklyn was his home.

The people poured into that train, ten thousand head or more
George used his elbows and his knees until he reached the door
But when he reached those portals, he could not take the gaff
The conductor shut the door on him and cut poor George in half.

The train pulled out of Times Square, the swiftest on the line
It carried poor Georgie's head along and left his body behind
Poor George he died a hero's death, his martyrdom's plain to see
And the very last words that Georgie said were "Screw the IRT."

So when you ride that IRT and you approach Times Square
Incline your head a slight degree and say a silent prayer
For his body lies between the ties amidst the dust and dew
And his head it rides the IRT to Flatbush Avenue.

They don't write songs like that anymore, and it's not hard to see why. Oddly, it had a close brush with success. The Kingston Trio, a very successful pop-folk act at the time, was considering covering it, but recorded their MTA song ("He will ride forever 'neath the streets of Boston; he's the man who never returned") instead. And they decided one subway song was enough.

The West Side IRT, then, was my subway line. And there's something special about one's own subway line.

This became evident in the early nineties, before the crime rate plummeted in New York. The city was then perceived as a dangerous place to be (although even then the perception was probably out of proportion to the reality) and someone sponsored a survey to find out not how safe or unsafe the subway system was, but how safe or unsafe it was thought to be by the hapless souls who rode it.

Most of them, it turned out, gave the system bad marks, allowing that the trains and tunnels were perilous. But the great majority of those surveyed noted an exception—one line in particular, they maintained, was much safer than the rest of the network.

And which line was that? In all the city, which line was the safe one?

Why, it was whatever line the passenger in question rode on a regular basis. D train riders felt safe on the D, but kept their guard up on the N. West Side IRTers were nervous when they had to ride the East Side IRT. And so on. Familiarity, it seems, breeds not so much contempt as contentment. We will, if circumstances compel us, take the train less traveled by—but we won't be happy about it.

I've always been puzzled by people who don't take the subway.

Oh, I can understand that out-of-towners might find it daunting. I remember the first time I had to find my way through the system. It was my first summer in New York, and I'd arrived by train from Buffalo and met my roommate-to-be at Grand Central. He told me he'd found us temporary lodgings on West 14th Street, and said I should take the shuttle to Times Square and the IRT downtown. 14th was an express stop, he said, so I should take the express, but the local would also get me there. Just so I took the IRT, he said, and made sure I was headed downtown.

I hoisted my suitcase and found my way. The Times Square station was swarming with more people than the average American sees in the course of an average day, or even a week, all of them hurrying this way and that with that incomprehensible purposefulness rarely seen outside of an anthill. I didn't pay much attention to them, and they paid no attention to me, and I did what I was supposed to do and emerged at 14th Street and 7th Avenue with a sense of having accomplished something.

A lot of tourists, I've noted, tackle the subway with the same spirit of adventure, and emerge with the same sense of accomplishment. Others take cabs, and I can understand that, although it seems to me they're missing something. But what I find harder to grasp is those New Yorkers who would sooner plunge naked into a sewer than descend into the subway tunnels.

"I haven't taken the subway in over twenty years," a novelist friend informed me. "Thank God and my agent I don't have to."

Success, I guess, means to him that he gets to cram his large body into a small taxi and listen to one side of a cell phone conversation in Urdu while waiting helplessly for the light to change, and change again, and change a third time. The hell, I say, with that.

If it's late and you're exhausted, and if you're trying to get from 89th and York to 23rd and 10th, well, yes, there's something to be said for flagging a cab. But in the ordinary course of things the subway is faster and more comfortable. (It's less comfortable at rush hour, but makes up for it in speed. You're a little more miserable, but for considerably less time.)

The only times I've been late for appointments in the past several years have been when I was pressed for time, and reflexively took a taxi in the hope of getting there faster. And, of course, I'd have gotten there sooner by subway. One almost always does.

My characters know this. Most of my books are set in New York, and most of my characters get around the same way I do, dropping a token in the slot (in the earlier books) or swiping a Metrocard.

In *A Walk Among the Tombstones,* a dope dealer in Bay Ridge wants to hire Matthew Scudder to find the men who abducted and dismembered his wife. They don't hit it off, and the man dismisses him and gives him $200 for his time and expenses. Scudder won't take it:

> "Take the money. For Christ's sake, the cab had to be twenty-five each way."
>
> "I took the subway."
>
> He stared at me. "You came out here on the subway? Didn't my brother tell you to take a cab? What do you want to save nickels and dimes for, especially when I'm paying for it?"
>
> "Put your money away," I said. "I took the subway because it's simpler and faster. How I get from one place to another is my business, Mr. Khoury, and I run my business the way I want. You don't tell me how to get around town and I won't tell

you how to sell crack to schoolchildren, how does that strike you?"

They worked things out, I'm happy to report; otherwise there'd have been no book. And Scudder has continued taking the subway.

In *A Long Line of Dead Men,* he's investigating a string of deaths over a period of several years among the members of a particular club. One is that of a man who jumped, fell, or was pushed in front of an oncoming subway train, and Scudder talks to the transit cop who was the investigating officer, who at the scene's conclusion talks of his own take on the subway:

> *"What I do, I take the subway all the time. I'll be honest with you, I love the subway, I think it's a wonderful and exciting urban rail system. But I am very careful down there. I see a guy who don't look right, I don't let myself be between him and the edge. I got to walk past somebody and it's gonna put me close to the edge of the platform, I wait until I can step past him on the other side. I want to take a chance, I'll go in a deli, by a lottery ticket. I'll go by OTB, put two bucks on a horse. I love it down in the tunnels, but I don't take chances down there."* He shook his head. *"Not me. I seen too much."*

While I find it hard to understand why any New Yorker would avoid the subway, I'm really puzzled when the person's a writer. One of the many reasons New York is such a splendid city for writers is that one is constantly in contact with one's fellow citizens. In most of the rest of the country, people spend all their in-between time in cars. They listen to their radios or natter away on their cell phones—or, alas, both—and they're effectively insulated from everything going on around them.

If a Los Angeleno's SUV is a culturally sterile environment, a New York subway is a veritable Petri dish, swarming with life. Sometimes it's too much, sometimes the peddlers and the mooch artists and the nodding junkies and the militant non-bathers are more than one can bear, and all one wants to do is hide behind a newspaper and tune it all out. But it's life, it's the city, and in a very real sense it's why most of us live here—not for the theater, not for free concerts in the park, but for the urgent pulse of the metropolis.

Overheard in New York is a favorite website of mine—and, indeed, of almost everybody I know. It consists of the snippets of conversation submitted by the readers who have in fact overheard them, on the street or in the elevator or, often, in the subway. You don't overhear a lot of interesting things when you're driving around in your car. *Overheard in Los Angeles?* No, I don't think so.

People ask writers where we get our ideas. It's an annoying question; we get them, mysteriously, from our imaginations, and only someone lacking an imagination would presume to ask the question. But our imaginations, certainly, are stocked by our experience and observation, and we don't enrich them by isolating ourselves.

Writers who don't take the subway? They must be out of their minds.

When I first moved here, I sort of assumed New York's subway was the only one in the world. I didn't think about it much, but whenever another subway was brought to my attention, I was somehow surprised. I'd read no end of French novels with scenes set in the Paris Metro before it dawned on me that the damn thing was a subway.

My wife and I have traveled quite extensively during the past twenty years, and it's been our pleasure to ride the local subway whenever we get the chance. We've taken the Metro in Paris and the Underground in London, naturally, but we've also sampled the subway in Madrid and Barcelona and Stockholm and Rome, in Prague and Budapest, in Minsk and Kiev and Moscow and Tashkent, in Taipei and Singapore . . . and, I'm sure, in other foreign capitals I've temporarily forgotten.

All of these cities have surface-level public transportation as well, but we hardly ever take the bus. When we do, we more often than not get lost. A bus, I've found, cannot be trusted. You think you know where it's going, and then the damn thing takes a turn you didn't expect, and you don't know where the hell you are. You're above ground, you can *see* where you're going, but you're still lost. Underground, where all you can see are the tunnel walls, it's not all that hard to get on the right train and take it to the right destination.

I've noted a few things about various subway systems. I can tell you that the platforms in Paris smell of Gauloise cigarettes, that the tracks in earthquake-prone Tashkent rest upon rubber cushioning, that one line of the Budapest subway is only a few feet below street level, that you risk arrest if you eat or drink anything in the Taipei subway, and that transferring from one line to another in either Madrid or Barcelona involves a longer walk than seems possible. But this is about New York's subway, so all I'll tell you is this: almost every other system, in this country or abroad, is more modern, more efficient, and more comfortable than ours.

There are, I should point out, some solid exculpatory reasons for this, and chief among them is that we were there first. Our infrastructure is older, and there are no end of things we'd do differently if we'd had the experience of others to build upon.

Remember, too, that New York's subterranean urban transit system began life as three independent subway lines, the IRT, IND, and BMT, each of them authorized by the city but operated by private firms in the wistful hope of profit. That's why, until relatively recently, you couldn't transfer from the E train (IND) to the Lexington line (IRT). The trains crossed one another at 53rd Street, but you had to get out of one, walk a block, and spend another token to board the other; it took decades after the whole business had become a single system before the requisite tunnels were excavated and the two lines fully integrated.

So Paris has maps with little red lightbulbs that show you the best route from one station to another, and London's Underground has genuinely comfortable cushioned seats, and Singapore's trains are—big surprise—as antiseptically clean as Singapore's streets. So what? This is New York. All things considered, we're doing pretty well.

We'd be doing better, I have to say, if they'd built the 2nd Avenue subway. They started, sometime in the late sixties, and dug up a huge stretch of that thoroughfare, and managed to kill a batch of local retailers and restauranteurs in the process. Then they ran out of money, and left things as they were, and sometime in the Seventies they gave up and put things back the way they were. (They didn't actually fill in the tunnels they dug, and all that's needed is an appropriation of a few billion dollars and they can start in again where they left off. But don't hold your breath.)

During my first years in New York, I was acquainted with a fellow who was planning a series of stories about a subterranean subculture, a world of runaway children who'd taken up permanent residence in the subway system, rarely if ever emerging on the surface. You didn't have to, he pointed out. You could live on hot dogs and peanuts and Mars bars and Cokes, which was what most kids lived on anyway. You could buy clothes when what you were wearing got too ratty, and, if you wanted to look respectable, you could even get your hair cut and your shoes shined. (There's still at least one barber I know of, in the Columbus Circle station, and shops to shine and repair your shoes all over midtown.)

And, as Edmund Love reminded us in *Subways Are For Sleeping,* you could get forty winks and more quite comfortably.

I don't think the stories ever got written. Everybody, as I recall, had something wonderful he or she was going to write, and that's often as far as it went. (I myself decided my first novel would be a stirring tale of Ireland's fight for freedom, set in the 1920s. But first, I realized, I really needed to know the whole history of Ireland, and in order to put it in context I'd have to have a thorough grounding in English history. So I went out and bought Oman's six-volume work on Britain before the Norman Conquest. I never got more than a chapter or so into it, and never did write a word of my Irish novel, but I managed to amass an impressive library of English and Irish history. When I wrote my first novel, it turned out to be a story of a young Midwestern woman in Greenwich Village coming to grips with her sexuality, or trying to.)

Life, of course, imitates art, even when the art never makes it past the state of conception. A decade or more ago, when homelessness flowered in New York (and, I suppose, elsewhere, but it was always more visible here), our subway system became home to no end of people. The 14th Street pedestrian passageway, running between 6th and 7th avenues, turned into an underground equivalent of the Hooverville shantytowns of the Great Depression. One soon learned not to walk there; it wasn't dangerous, although it may have felt that way, but it was unhygienic in the extreme, and the stench was overpowering.

That's changed now, and the homeless have largely disappeared from the subways, although people still sleep on the trains. (Some of them are homeless, and some are heroin addicts on the nod, but others are just drunk, and a few are merely tired. Years ago a good friend of mine, a writer whose name you'd recognize, was tired—well, yes, he'd had a few drinks—and he dozed off on the L train on his way home to Canarsie. When he woke up he discovered that someone had stolen his shoes. These things happen.)

It was in 1948 that I first rode the subway, and both it and I are a good deal older now, and have had irregular maintenance over the years. I still ride the subway, and am in fact the proud possessor of a Senior Metrocard, one of the few tangible benefits of having ascended into Old Farthood.

The card—with my name and picture on it—works just like any other Metrocard, but it gets me onto the subway (or, more rarely, the bus) for half price. And that's terrific, a true perk of age, but it's the least of it.

I never have to refill it. It's linked to my credit card, and it refills automatically. And—get this—every month I receive a statement in the mail, with every occasion I've used the card noted, and the time and place specified. I could, if I cared, use the thing to find out where I'd been, something I'm less and less likely to recall on my own with the advancing years.

I loved the card from the moment I got it, and was heartbroken when I lost it. I figured I'd have to go through a ton of red tape to replace it, and I might even get a scolding before I got a new card. Then I called the designated number, had a five-minute conversation, and a few days later received a replacement card in the mail. I didn't even need to have a new picture taken; they had the old one on file.

Of course! They were dealing with the senescent, a batch of doddering oldsters who needed the card not least of all to remember our own names. Naturally they'd be prepared to deal with lost cards.

The second time I lost my card, I knew just what to do. And I didn't get a scolding that time, either.

I wish people wouldn't hold the doors. I wish the public address systems in the stations weren't inaudible. I wish they'd get back to work on the 2nd Avenue subway. I wish they'd replace those cars they bought from Japan, the ones with the sculpted seats, artfully designed to accommodate a population with smaller behinds. I wish each train had a designated car for passengers who stink to high heaven, so they could all ride together and leave the rest of us alone.

And what I really wish is that I'd hear from other collectors of old subway cars. Hey, if you've got any of those wooden cars from the Myrtle Avenue El, get in touch, you hear? Maybe we can do some swapping . . .

DONALD E. WESTLAKE

Maureen Corrigan and the late Robin W. Winks compiled and edited an extensive two-volume reference work, Mystery and Suspense Writers: The Literature of Crime, Detection, and Espionage, *published by Scribner's in 1998. I was assigned the entry for my good friend, Don Westlake. I've since published* The Crime of Our Lives, *with a good deal included about the man and his work, and only through oversight failed to include this piece. It's a little late to try splicing it into* TCOOL, *and yet I hate to see it forever unavailable. (The books live on in libraries, to be sure, but can be hard to find; aftermarket ex-library copies seem to consist almost entirely of Volume 1, and this piece, through the miracle of alphabetical order, is in the second volume. The first volume, I'm sufficiently egocentric to note, does include Charles Ardai's very flattering essay about, um, me.)*

Donald E. Westlake was born in New York City on July 12, 1933. His parents were natives of Albany, New York, and the family moved there when he was six years old. He was educated in Catholic schools in Albany, and attended Champlain College, in Plattsburg, New York, and, after two years in the Air Force, Harpur College (now the State University of New York at Binghamton).

By the time he'd enrolled at Harpur, Westlake had written an unpublished novel about the Air Force, as well as a slew of short stories, some of which he had managed to sell. He had chosen his career much earlier.

"I knew I was a writer when I was eleven," he has written. "It took the rest of the world about ten years to begin to agree . . . Neophyte writers are always told, 'Write what you know,' but the fact is, kids don't know *anything*. A beginning writer doesn't write what he knows, he writes what he read in books or saw in the movies. And that's the way it was with me. I wrote gangster stories, I wrote stories about cowboys, I wrote poems about gold prospecting, I wrote the first chapters of all kinds of novels. The short stories I mailed off to magazines, and they mailed them back, in the self-addressed stamped envelopes I had provided."

One year short of graduation, Westlake moved from Albany to New York City. There, like no end of young men who would spend their lives in writing or publishing, he became a fee reader for Scott Meredith, the literary agent. He read "sixty short stories or eight novels or some mix thereof every week," writing letters over Meredith's signature "about how *this* story doesn't quite make it but shows really amazing talent and do try us again with another story and another check."

The work was both an education and an apprenticeship for an emerging writer. Reading slush submissions taught one what did and didn't work on the page, while one's presence in the office led to frequent assignments for anyone who proved himself a decent utility infielder. Westlake wrote confession stories and magazine articles on assignment, and was able to give up his job altogether for steady freelance work writing 50,000-word soft core paperback sex novels.

These aside, his first real novel was published in 1960. "The stories that were getting published were more and more frequently mystery stories," he has said, "and I think it's a natural tendency to go where you're liked, so the next time I tried to write a novel it was a mystery novel. That's when I began to describe myself as a writer disguised as a mystery writer, a remark I continued for ten or fifteen years, until the face grew to match the mask."

Westlake moved to Canarsie, in Brooklyn, then to New Jersey, and has continued to live in and around New York to this day. Since 1979 he has been married to the writer Abby Adams, his two earlier marriages having ended in divorce. In addition to some fifty novels, almost all of them at least peripherally in the field of mystery and suspense, he has written reportage, essays, book reviews, and a children's book. In addition, he has written successfully for the screen, and was nominated for an Academy Award for his adaptation of Jim Thompson's *The Grifters*. In 1992 he was named a Grand Master by the Mystery Writers of America.

Well, a computer could have written the foregoing, and would very likely have had an easier time of it than I. Objective journalism has never been either my strong suit or my predilection. How, indeed, am I to be objective about Don Westlake? He has been my friend for almost forty years.

I made his acquaintance in print before I met him in the flesh. In early 1959 I was in Yellow Springs, Ohio, proving that Thomas Wolfe's observation about going home applied as well to returning to college. I had worked the previous year for Scott Meredith, and was writing sex novels for Midwood Books when I should have been writing papers on Henry Fielding and Tobias Smollett, and I read other Midwood titles when I found them, in a spirit of professional curiosity. One led to a note to Henry Morrison, my (and Don's) agent at Scott Meredith at the time.

"This one's pretty good," I observed. "Who wrote it?"

Come summer I met the author. We introduced ourselves at the Scott Meredith office, where we'd both come to pick up checks or drop off manuscripts, or both. I went back with him to his apartment on West 46th between 9th and 10th Avenues (not a bad neighborhood now, but it certainly was then). I met his wife and their infant son, and we had dinner and talked for hours.

I've been his friend ever since, and I've been his enthusiastic reader as well. There was a period in the late sixties when we didn't speak, and even then I went on reading his books. (I was occasionally mean-spirited enough during that brief span to hope I wouldn't like his latest work, but, dammit, I always did.)

Moreover, there have been startling parallels in our careers. We both worked for, and were subsequently represented (and misrepresented) by the same agent. We sold stories to the same magazines and sex novels to the same purveyors of schlock. We both wound up mystery writers without having consciously chosen the field early on. We both wrote voluminously under pen names, and were intermittently neurotic about keeping our true identity a secret. And each of us, in a world that reveres brand names, has stubbornly insisted on writing more than one sort of books. "How can you write some books that are so funny and others that are so hardboiled and serious?" I get that question all the time, and so does Don.

Sometimes people confuse us. (That sentence can be read more than one way, but it's still true.) "I remember the first book I read about Matthew Scudder," a fan told me a while ago. "It was an early one, and he was spending all his time building a wall in back of his house." It was a very early one, I agreed; Scudder's name was Mitch Tobin at the time, and he was a character in a book by Tucker Coe, a pen name of Westlake's. And more recently a woman asked me if my novelettes about that Jewish cop with a bad heart would ever be published in book form. "The book was *Levine*," I told her, "and it was published in 1984, and I used the pen name Donald E. Westlake on it."

So how can I be objective about either the man or his work, when I have been uncommonly fond of both for so many years? I won't even try. What I can and will do is discuss some of the tissues and organs in his remarkable body of work. I'm not sure this needs doing—one of the work's most re-markable qualities, after all, is its sheer accessibility—but that's what they want me to do, and what they're paying me to do. So I'll do it.

*　　　*　　　*

Westlake's first novel (not counting the pseudonymous sex novels, which we could call finger exercises if it didn't sound dirty) was *The Mercenaries*. Lee Wright, whom Westlake calls "the best editor I've ever had," bought the book, saw the author through several revisions, and published it at Random House.

The narrator of *The Mercenaries* is a mid-level corporate executive, essentially, but the corporation employing him is an organized criminal enterprise. There's a murder, and he has to solve it, using the skills he's acquired on the job and the resources (bought cops, criminal informants) available to him.

No one had done anything quite like this before, and Lee Wright was sufficiently impressed with its novelty to ballyhoo the book in a manner that helped and harmed it in the same breath. She heralded it as "the first new direction in the tough mystery since Hammett." That guaranteed the book a certain amount of attention, and also pretty much assured that a lot of people's response would fall somewhere between "Oh, yeah?" and "Sez who?"

The book doesn't live up to its billing, but it's hard to see how it could. For one thing, there had been several new directions since Hammett; for another, *The Mercenaries* wasn't that great a departure. It was (and is) a terse, tough-minded mystery with a lead character who, while by no means unsympathetic, is the sort who gets called amoral. It received a fair amount of attention, given that mysteries were ghettoized at the time, and received an MWA Edgar nomination as best first mystery of the year. (It didn't win, coming in second to a book by Jack Vance which, while arguably a first mystery, and thus technically eligible for the award, was by no means a first novel.)

With the publication of *The Mercenaries* and Random House's acceptance of his second mystery, *Killing Time*, Westlake began to feel secure as a writer. I can vividly recall sitting in his upstairs flat in Canarsie while he confided that he figured he had it made. The way things were shaping up, he said, he could pretty much count on being able to make $10,000 a year as a writer, year in and year out.

*   *   *

No one would have called *Killing Time* the first new direction since Hammett. It was, on the contrary, very much a turn *toward* Hammett. Westlake has always admired Dashiell Hammett enormously—he is considerably more restrained in his enthusiasm for the other putative founder of the hardboiled school, Raymond Chandler—and his second book is very much an homage to Hammett, with persistent echoes of *Red Harvest* and *Blood Money*. ("Homage," according to Westlake, is the French word for plagiarism.) A hard, fast, nasty book, it was a good sequel to the author's first novel and seemed to confirm him as an heir to the Black Mask tradition.

Nowadays, "sequel" is almost always taken to mean the next book in a series, but the genre was a different place back then. Publishers were not nearly so inclined to urge writers to produce a series of books about a single character. The feeling persisted that a book in a series amounted to rather less artistically than one which stood alone. A full-fledged novel, it was assumed, ought to use up its lead character by its end, either providing him with a catharsis or killing him dead, or both. Readers might prefer series, but so what? Since a mystery novel was presumed to have an audience of four to six thousand copies, what difference did it make what readers liked?

Times have changed, God knows, and a young Westlake today would find himself keeping Clay alive at the end of *The Mercenaries*, and writing a dozen books about him. They might have been interesting books, but, fortunately for Westlake's development, he was instead encouraged to write varied books and find his own way as a writer. He followed *Killing Time* with *361*, my personal favorite of his hardboiled period, and to my mind the first book in which he found a voice that was uniquely his. *361*—the title is the numerical heading for "killing" in *Roget's Thesaurus*, and the epigraph is that entry, with its host of synonyms for slaughter—concerns the two sons of a gangster and their efforts to help him regain power after his release from prison. But it is also about the narrator's search for his father—someone somewhere said all American crime fiction is about the search for one's father—and it is a book that derives unmistakably from the author's own personal mythology.

(The interested reader might refer to Westlake's fascinating and immensely readable essay in the *Contemporary Authors* autobiography series.)

Westlake's early hardboiled period, if you will, concluded with *Killy*, about a labor union troubleshooter, and *Pity Him Afterwards*, a suspenseful tour de force about a psychopathic killer at a summer theater. (Westlake hammered out *Pity Him Afterwards* in four or five days to overcome a siege of writer's block; it's probably a better book than he realizes.)

During this time, Westlake wrote what we were then wont to call a "serious" novel. (We used the word to indicate a mainstream novel with literary aspirations; it would, in fact, be hard to explain why *361*, say, was anything other than serious.) Westlake called the book *Memory*, and describes it thusly:

"At the beginning of the novel, an actor on tour is hit on the head and hospitalized. His brain is damaged, so that his longterm memory goes; his memory loss is accelerated; last month is lost to him. By the time he comes out of the hospital, the touring company is long gone and so is his past, though he has enough memory to function in normal ways, and has fitful glimpses of a brighter and more interesting yesteryear. The book is about the functions and uses and glories of memory, and about the slow despair of the hero."

I read *Memory* in manuscript, which as it turned out was the only way anyone would ever read it. I sat up all night with it, certain I was reading a great novel, unquestionably worthy of being mentioned in the same breath with the best existential fiction.

It was never published.

Virtually all the editors who saw it turned *Memory* down in terms more glowing than they would have dared apply to the books they accepted. They all loved it, they all praised it, and they all said they couldn't figure out how to sell it. They compared it to Dostoevsky, to Kafka, to Twain, to Thomas Wolfe, and said they were confident someone else would figure out how to publish it successfully.

I remember this when I hear people whining about how hard it is now, how the fabled midlist book no longer has a chance. I read *Memory* almost thirty-five years ago, in publishing's kinder, gentler era. The book was important, and of the highest quality, and, incidentally, an edge-of-the-chair read . . . and nobody could summon up the gumption to get it into print. Things may be not so hot now, but don't try to tell me that was a Golden Age back then. I don't think so.

Years later, Westlake read *Memory* after an agent told him it would probably now be publishable, only to decide against trying to market it. His feeling was that the book was too much a creature of its time.

I wonder if his perception was accurate. Oddly enough, I'm not sure the author is the best person to make that sort of decision. I know that I find it impossible to read my own early work, and I tend to judge it far more harshly than I judge the early work of my friends. The sentences seem choppy, the transitions awkward, the scene-shifting clumsy and cumbersome. More to the point, I don't welcome the look I get at the callow youth who wrote those sentences.

But this doesn't keep me from allowing publishers to reprint those early books.

Would I be similarly sanguine about publishing an early book that had never seen print before? I have such a book, it was unpublishable then, and I'd prefer it stay unpublished now. But that's different, it seems to me. *Memory* wasn't unpublishable, no one ever called it unpublishable. It was simply unpublished.

I wonder, too, if it's really as good as I thought it was. I may have been easily impressed. Hard to say.

Another thing to wonder about—and we can wonder all we want, because we'll never know the answer—is what Westlake would have gone on to write if *Memory* hadn't been consigned to the dustbin of literature.

Throughout his career, Westlake has written the books he's wanted to write. While his intent has always been commercial, he has been led more by artistic considerations than commercial ones. If, *Memory's* failure notwithstanding, he'd been overtaken by an idea for another novel of the same sort, I don't doubt for a moment that he'd have written it.

But, as he's said, it's a natural tendency to go where you're liked. And the subconscious, the part of the self from which literary ideas flow, is no less inclined to steer clear of doors that have been slammed in its face, and to close a few doors of its own. If *Memory* had been a success, who can doubt for a moment that he'd have had ideas for other serious literary fiction? But it wasn't, and he didn't.

Let me interrupt myself to advise you that, after DEW's death on the last day of 2008, I mentioned Memory *in a memorial piece I wrote. This led Don's widow, Abigail Adams Westlake, to search his files and discover a ragged manuscript of that novel; it was published in short order by Charles Ardai at Hard Case Crime, and is readily available—and, I must say, every bit as powerful as I remembered it.*

"Use the accident" is a catchphrase in the visual arts. What it generally means is that one ought to be guided, even inspired, when something other than one intended emerges on the canvas. Whether it's a slip of the brush or a bubbling up of the unconscious, don't obliterate it precipitously. Maybe there's a way to make use of it.

The accident that Westlake has used, more than once, is humor.

His sixth novel for Random House was designed to be one more variation on a hardboiled theme, an innocent on the run, but it started coming out funny. Westlake was worried, and called his agent, who reminded him that there had been no funny mysteries since the death of Craig Rice, and told him to stop what he was doing and do something else.

The advice struck him as eminently sound, but he was fortunately unable to take it. The book demanded to be written, and he decided to give in and get it out of his system and go back to being serious. "The fact is," he recalls, "it had never occurred to me that I could write funny. [In childhood] I wasn't the funniest kid around, I was the funniest kid's best friend. So what this book was trying to do I had no idea, but I followed it, and it kept on being funny."

The book was published as *The Fugitive Pigeon*, and it confounded everybody by doubling the author's sales domestically and doing very well abroad. And it is, as we've seen, natural indeed to go where you're liked; accordingly, in the years that followed Westlake produced one comic novel after another, all of them the sort of work we have come to call Westlakean. Before *The Fugitive Pigeon* there was no such thing as a comic mystery novel; within a few years such a category did in fact exist, and Westlake essentially owned it.

In one book after another, Westlake pitted his hero, an imperiled innocent, against an all-powerful but inept system. The world reflected in books like *The Busy Body, The Spy in the Ointment, God Save the Mark,* and *Somebody Owes Me Money* is a far different place from the setting for Westlake's earlier work. It's filled with criminals, and they perpetrate felonies and occasionally kill one another, but good always triumphs, and nothing too terrible ever happens to anyone we care about.

The most casual reading of his work makes it quite clear that neither the serious nor the comic novels can claim exclusive title to the "real" Donald E. Westlake. Both provide accurate reflections of their author. I would contend that he (like everyone else) has a light side and a dark side, and that he (unlike the great majority of writers) is equally capable of writing from either of these sides.

And, of course, there is dark in light, and light in darkness. His hardest, toughest work is not without the leavening of humor, nor is his lightest, airiest confection entirely devoid of substance.

With *The Fugitive Pigeon*, Westlake would seem to have gone over entirely to his light side, and to have remained there but for such anomalous later works as *Kahawa* (1982), *Sacred Monster* (1989), *Humans* (1992), and

The Ax (1997). In point of fact, he never ceased to produce darker work as well, but did so under pen names.

Mitch Tobin, the guilt-ridden depressive ex-cop who is the hero of five novels written under the name Tucker Coe, provides an ideal window onto Westlake's darker side. The source of his anguish is this: while he was cheating on his own wife in the bed of the wife of a criminal he had previously arrested, his partner is shot dead by another crook—and Tobin's not there to back him up. This is enough to turn Tobin severely dysfunctional, and to make him a pariah in the NYPD. (And this does strain credibility a bit. While I'm willing to believe Tobin might agonize over his role in his partner's death, he'd never get such an extreme reaction from his fellow cops. But never mind.)

Tobin mends things with his wife, sort of, though a little couples therapy might not be amiss. And he devotes the greater portion of his energies to building, slowly and meticulously, a concrete wall around the perimeter of his back yard, walling himself in, walling the world out.

It's a wonderful metaphor, and Tobin's character, quite perfectly realized, fits it superbly. He is drawn reluctantly away from his wall, and back into the world, by the cases he has to take in order to make ends meet. As a de facto private eye, Tobin works in areas of the demimonde a cop would regard from a distance, and with contempt—homosexuals in *A Jade in Aries*, hippie kids in *Don't Lie to Me*. An outcast himself, Tobin is sympathetic to the people he meets in spite of his prejudices.

Over five books, Tobin gradually began to heal, even as his wall neared completion. What helped him as a human being made him no longer compelling as a dark hero, and Westlake stopped writing about him.

*   *   *

"When the shit hit the fan, Parker threw himself in front of it."

No, none of the Richard Stark novels opens that way, though I live in hope. Westlake began writing about Parker in 1960, and produced sixteen books about him (and four about his colleague, Grofield) in the space of fifteen years.

I remember reading the first chapter of what would be the first Parker book, *The Hunter*. In it, Parker, walking across the George Washington Bridge into New York, is offered a lift by a motorist and tells the guy to go to hell. I read the chapter through and asked Don if he knew where the book was going. He said he didn't.

He found out as he wrote it. Parker, a professional thief, has escaped from custody and is looking to get even with the people who betrayed him, and to recover money that is rightfully (or, since he stole it in the first place, wrongfully) his. The book was never intended as the first volume of a series, and in fact Parker was back in police custody at the book's end; he was set free when an editor at Pocket Books said he'd publish *The Hunter* if Parker were to escape, and reappear in three books a year. Westlake agreed at once; he'd only had Parker recaptured because he thought he had to, that villains had to die or get caught at the end.

Parker's concern—to get back the money he's owed—drives the first three books. (This is a recurrent theme in Westlake's fiction; for a lighter treatment, see *Somebody Owes Me Money*.) The books that follow are caper novels. Book after book, Parker plans a job, assembles a crew, pulls it off, and then something goes wrong, and he has to mend his fences and salvage what he can. There is even a standard formal structure for the books. They are in four parts, like a symphony, all but three of them narrated from Parker's point of view. The second or third section—it varies—has each of its chapters told from the point of view of one of the other characters.

The minor characters—some turn up in more than one book, some are heard from but once, and some, of course, are killed off in these harsh and violent books—are brilliantly realized and economically sketched. The bits of color—Parker buys a stolen truck, Parker arranges financing for a job—are clever and vivid and engaging. But it is Parker himself, a coldly logical but not inhumane sociopath, who is eternally fascinating.

It is impossible to guess what will or will not be read years hence. (And does it really matter? Why should we value posterity's ill-informed judgment more highly than our own?) That said, it's my opinion that the Parker novels will prove to be Westlake's most enduring work. I base this not on their merit, which I think is considerable, but on the special hold they have on readers. People don't just read the Parker books. They reread them, over and over and over. And if any quality makes a book last over time, I think that may be it: not that the book cries out to be read, but that it insists upon being read again and again.

In 1974 Westlake wrote the sixteenth Parker novel, *Butcher's Moon*. It was longer than the others, and in it he brought back surviving co-conspirators of Parker's from throughout the series, all assembled to help Parker rescue Handy McKay, his closest thing to a friend. If the series had to end, that was a good book to end it on, and it looked as though Westlake had done just that. He made several attempts to write further about Parker, and it didn't work. "I don't know why Richard Stark retired," he has written. "I tried several times to put him back to work, but he was tired and leaden. His imagination was gone, the simplicity of his prose was gone, the coldness of his view was gone. It never worked. On the other hand, I've learned from embarrassing experience never to make absolute statements about the future."

Indeed. Parker returns in 1997's *Comeback*, and it's as if he'd never been gone. He hasn't lost a step.

Several years before Richard Stark's extended temporary retirement, Westlake ran into problems trying to write about Parker. The story idea he was developing had Parker called upon to steal the same thing over and over, and there was something inherently antic in the premise; when he wrote it, it kept coming out funny.

If this had happened in Parker's initial appearance in 1960, Westlake would have either abandoned the book as a bad idea or simply allowed it to be funny, as he would do a few years later in *The Fugitive Pigeon*. But he'd already written enough books about Parker to have established beyond doubt that Parker was not a funny guy.

So, handed a lemon, he made lemonade. He recast the book and created John Dortmunder, a sort of anti-Parker, not a bumbler but a supremely unlucky fellow, who inhabits a kinder, gentler criminal universe and whose jobs go horribly wrong in unfailingly amusing ways. Dortmunder was never intended as a series character, he was just something to do with that lemon, but then neither had Parker been so intended, and a couple of years after *The Hot Rock* was published, Westlake saw a bank temporarily housed in a mobile home, and thought of a way to steal it. Thus *Bank Shot*, and, since then, a whole string of books about Dortmunder and Kelp and Murch and the gang. Though they're all good, some of the books are better than others. I'd say *Drowned Hopes* is the strongest book to date, though *Jimmy the Kid* can claim to be the most interesting; in it, Dortmunder's men steal the plan for their caper from a (fictitious) book by Richard Stark.

I haven't said anything much about Westlake as a screenwriter, and I don't think I will—not that there's nothing to say, but that I'm not at all the person to say it. I haven't seen that much of what he's done, and film and television writing lie well outside my area of interest, let alone expertise. I can say that I thought his work on *The Grifters* was superb, and would have made Jim Thompson himself happy, if anything could have that unlikely effect.

In recent years Westlake has made a substantial portion of his income from screenwriting, and what I find remarkable is not what he has or hasn't done for Hollywood, but that he has managed to touch pitch without being defiled. Hollywood ruins most of the writers who get anywhere near it. Most of them stop writing prose fiction after a few years out there, and those who make the effort generally find out they've lost the knack.

Perhaps Westlake's secret lies in the fact that he has kept his distance from the place while getting wholly (and happily) involved in the work. He doesn't go out to California, except for the occasional meeting. He stays in New York, or in his house upstate, and works on screenplays the same way he works on novels, batting them out on his manual typewriter.

He continues, after so many years, to be as productive and as wonderfully unpredictable as ever. In the past two years he has produced *Smoke*, a savage indictment of the tobacco industry in the guise of a rollicking invisible-man comedy; *The Ax*, a taut, hard-edged novel about a victim of corporate downsizing who assures himself a job by killing off all the better-qualified prospects; and *Comeback*, Parker's long-awaited return. He has always written rapidly and well, and he has never written better or faster than he's writing now. After all those years, and all those books.

EAST SIDE, WEST SIDE:

Tales of New York Sporting Life, 1910-1960
by Lawrence S. Ritter
Introduction by Lawrence Block

The invitation to write a foreword for East Side, West Side *was
an easy one to accept. The book, to be published in May of 1998
by Total Sports Publishing, was a wonderful nostalgic look at
a half century of the New York sporting scene, written by the
man whose* The Glory of Their Times *is a brilliant and enduring
account of the game of baseball as recalled by the vanishing
array of men who played it in its early years.*

*I don't know if some editor recommended me, or if Larry
Ritter was already familiar with my work, but after one look
at his book and the dates it spanned I thought immediately of
my own father, born in New York in the last weeks of 1908 and
gone by the end of 1960.*

*New York, my father, and the world of sports. Combine and
stir, and here's what I came up with:*

In December, 1948, my father and I rode the Empire State Limited from
Buffalo, where we lived, to New York, where he'd been born and raised. We

stayed at the Commodore Hotel, right next to Grand Central Station, and for three or four days my dad showed me New York.

It seems to me we did just about everything there was to do. We rode the subway, of course, and the 5th Avenue double-decker bus. There was still an el on 3rd Avenue, and Sunday morning we rode it clear down to the Bowery. Right on cue, a derelict dashed out of one of the hellhole saloons down there, screamed at the top of his lungs, then turned around and ran back in again.

There had been els on 6th and 9th Avenues as well, my father told me, but they'd been torn down, and one of them—I forget which—had been sold for scrap to the Japanese, who made bombs out of it and dropped them on Pearl Harbor. He shook his head at this, at American shortsightedness or Japanese perfidy, or both.

We took a ferry to the Statue of Liberty, on what was still called Bedloe's Island, and we rode up to the top of the Empire State building. We saw *Where's Charlie?* on Broadway, with Ray Bolger, and we attended the live telecast of *The Toast of the Town*, which was what they were calling the Ed Sullivan show. I'd never seen TV, and the whole concept was new to me. I spent my time ignoring the action on stage and staring in fascination at the studio monitor.

I'm tempted to say that, by the time we boarded our train back to Buffalo, I already knew I'd wind up living in New York. The die may indeed have been cast, but I'm sure I wasn't aware of it. All I knew about the future was that I was going to be a veterinarian, and it turned out I was wrong about that.

I can't recall everything my dad and I did that weekend, but I know we didn't get to a sporting event. We'd have been limited at that time of year to hockey or basketball, and my father had no interest in either one. (Nor do I, to this day.) There must have been a boxing card during our visit—there were fights all the time, all over town—but I don't know that we'd have been able to fit it in.

My dad liked boxing and I've been a lifelong fan myself. We used to listen to fights on the radio, and watched on Wednesday and Friday nights once we had a television set. We only went to the fights once, and that was a few months before or after our trip to New York.

We went to Buffalo's Memorial Auditorium to see Willie Pep fighting what I have since learned to call a tomato can, an easy target who must have needed a transfusion by the time the fight was over. Pep was the dirtiest fighter in the world, my dad told me, with grudging admiration. "According to Pep," he said, "'You can take a round away for a low blow, but you can't take the whole fight away.'"

Whenever Willie Pep's name comes up, I remember that I saw him fight.

By the time I was fifteen I knew somebody else would have to spend his life giving rabies shots. I was going to be a writer, and of course I would go to New York to do it. A couple of years later I was writing professionally, and in the spring of 1960 I got married and took an apartment on West 69th Street, between Broadway and Columbus.

One Monday night that summer my then-wife and I walked down Columbus Avenue and ate an early dinner at Vorst's, a neighborhood institution, a sort of Luchow's without the oompah band and the tourists. Then we walked a block or two to St. Nicholas Arena, where we sat ringside for five bucks apiece and watched six or eight bouts. Miles Davis was there, looking hip and sinister, and the word at ringside was that he had an interest in an up-and-comer named Vince Shomo, who headed the prelim card that night and won handily.

The feature bout pitted two heavyweights, Ronnie Cohen of New Rochelle and Irish Eddie Jordan. Cohen threw sweeping roundhouse punches that were not without effect, and one of them put Irish Eddie Jordan on the canvas. He got up and they took turns hitting each other, until Cohen went down and stayed down. The fight made up in drama what it lacked in science. I never heard a word about either fighter after that, and it was probably just as well.

My dad was a Yankee fan all his life. We watched the Bisons many times over the years at Buffalo's Offerman Stadium, and we watched Cornell football at Schoellkopf Field, but we only once got to a Yankee game. That would have been in the late Fifties, when I was living in New York, working days at a literary agency, writing short stories and articles at night and selling them for twenty-five or fifty or seventy-five dollars. He came into town on business, and we caught a ball game and had dinner at Keen's Chop House, on West 36th Street.

Keen's is still there, and so is Yankee Stadium, although the latter's days may be numbered. Vorst's is gone, and St. Nick's is gone, and my dad is gone, too; an aortic aneurysm took him out in December of 1960, twelve years after our trip to New York and one day before his 52nd birthday.

I don't know why this turned out to be a remembrance of my father. For some reason I kept thinking of him on every page of Larry Ritter's wonderful book. As a boy, he lived all over New York. His mother died when he was a little kid, and he wound up moving around a lot and attending thirteen different grammar schools. (When his father remarried, his stepmother cleaned house and threw out all my dad's Yankee scorecards. He never did forgive her for that.)

Along with memories of my dad, *East Side, West Side* brought back other moments. I must have dropped in eight or ten times at Tony Canzoneri's midtown bar. (I always ordered the same thing there, Bushmill's with a beer chaser, and the bartender always explained they didn't have beer on tap and furnished instead what he called a nipper beer, a bottle containing four ounces or so. We went through this ritual every time I walked into the place.)

I remember the Neutral Corner, too, and I saw Jack Dempsey countless times, greeting diners at his restaurant. I only went there once because I considered the place too pricey; now, looking at the menu, I can't believe how little everything cost.

In *The Langoliers*, Stephen King pictures the future as a tribe of rapacious monsters who race through time devouring the past. New York, to be sure, is a town that eats its own past for breakfast, licks its chops, and goes on about its business. We throw buildings up, we knock them down, we build new ones. You got a problem with that?

It's always tempting to idealize the past, and it's impossible for anyone with the slightest aesthetic sensibility not to lament the loss of the old Penn Station, or Stanford White's Madison Square Garden. And yes, you can't make an omelet without throwing out the baby with the bathwater. Old New York used to be the most exciting city in the world, and it still is. And it's capacity for reinventing itself is one of the reasons why.

There's no reason, though, why we can't now and then drop in on the town that used to be It's a nice place to visit, whether or not you'd care to live there. And it's easy enough to get to.

Just turn the page . . .

East Side, West Side *not only gave me a chance to write about my dad. It also brought me a few years of friendship with Larry Ritter, a fine gentleman whose Wikipedia entry is worth a look.*

We had a few lunches together, and I wish there'd been time for more.

He died in 2004, after a succession of strokes, and two years after this observation, quoted in his New York Times *obituary, on modern baseball: "I don't like the players, I don't like the umpires, I don't like the owners. But I love the game."*

He's been gone fifteen years now, and I don't have occasion to think of him that often, but I enjoy the memories when they come along.

And the books live on.

FOLLOW THE SERENDIPITY ROAD

Around the time 1987 was giving way to 1988, Lynne and I closed our house in Florida and set off for a couple of years of life without a fixed address. That, of course, was the beginning of the Great Buffalo Hunt, which had as an additional objective our determining where we might want to live next. Fort Myers Beach hadn't really worked for us, and while we thought it not unlikely that we'd wind up back in New York, why not see what other possibilities presented themselves?

We'd been on the road for two years when I wrote this piece for the Sophisticated Traveler section of the New York Times. *They ran it on March 4, 1990; not quite two weeks later, on St. Patrick's Day, we returned to New York, and have been there ever since.*

Which is not to say we've quit knocking around, as the dated list of Buffalos at the end of this book's title story will illustrate. (We even managed an encore visit to the Corn Palace, and found it no less remarkable the second time around.) And the motif of serendipity upon which I expounded here has characterized our travels ever since.

On a Sunday some months ago, my wife, Lynne, and I were driving west on U.S. 14 from Brookings, South Dakota. We had spent the night there, after a visit to the South Dakota Art Museum, with its exceptional collection of paintings by the South Dakota artist Harvey Dunn. At De Smet we stopped for a tank of gas, and I studied the map.

"If we turn south here," I said, "we can go to Mitchell. It's out of our way, but I think it's worth it. We can go to the Corn Palace."

"Oh, goody," said Lynne, who has always been a creature of ready enthusiasm. "What's a Corn Palace?"

"You'll see," I said.

De Smet is not without its own attractions, most of them linked to Laura Ingalls Wilder's Little House books for children. Some of them, including *Little House on the Prairie,* are set in De Smet; a couple of Ms. Wilder's homes have been restored and there are other sites and buildings mentioned in the series. I'd toured them in 1976 with my daughters, who were heavy-duty *Little House* fans. Lynne is not, so we pushed on to Mitchell.

A town of 14,000, Mitchell is on Interstate 90, about 60 miles west of Sioux Falls and almost directly south of Aberdeen. The Corn Palace is right in its center, and there were ample signs pointing us in that direction. We were soon driving along the main street, and there it was—a huge square structure capped with a dome and festooned with towers and turrets and minarets in a riot of Byzantine splendor one does not expect to encounter a stone's throw from the Little House on the Prairie. Its architecture alone would make the Corn Palace stand out, but its embellishment makes the building one of the wonders of the world. It is covered, inside and out, with elaborate and utterly glorious murals composed entirely of ears of corn, kernels of corn and colored grasses.

The Corn Palace was first constructed in 1892. It has been rebuilt twice since then, but in a sense it is rebuilt annually. As you might expect, birds and the elements take a heavy toll, and every year the murals are replaced for the Corn Palace Festival, which is held during September. The festival runs for eight or nine days, and name bands entertain; John Philip Sousa and his band played there in 1904; Mel Tillis and Crystal Gayle performed in 1989.

The sight of the Corn Palace hurled Lynne into instant rapture, which came as no surprise to this reporter. Here is a woman whose heart chakra opens up every time Christo wraps an island in pink plastic, and whose own work as an artist centers on the production of Port-A-Shrines, tiny reverential dioramas of devotional subjects housed in tortuously decorated sardine tins. How could she fail to be moved to joy by something as loopy as the Corn Palace? There was only one problem. We couldn't find a place to park. "It's a big weekend," I observed. "Lots of tourists on the road."

"There wasn't much traffic on the interstate," Lynne pointed out.

"Of course not," I said. "They're all here in Mitchell."

By the time we found a spot and tucked the car into it, a subtle pattern had begun to emerge. People seemed to be heading on foot toward the Corn Palace, most of them in family groups and all of them very nicely dressed. The girls and women seemed to be wearing white, and most of the dresses looked homemade. Not your typical tourist regalia, I had to admit.

We followed the crowd, entered the Corn Palace and discovered we had just crashed a high school graduation. We stood along one wall while the band struck up "Pomp and Circumstance" and a fine-looking group of seniors marched into the room. We watched in awe as the school chorus took the stage and sang something inspirational. Then, when someone started to make a speech, I grabbed Lynne and hurried her out of there.

My own daughters graduated from any number of schools and I never went to witness their passage. Why should I watch total strangers graduate in Mitchell, South Dakota? (And yet isn't that the whole point of travel, to do at a distance what one never gets around to doing at home? I always return from trips resolving to visit New York's museums, but I hardly ever follow through. I've never been to the Cloisters, for heaven's sake, or the Museum of the American Indian. Stick one of them in Logansport, Indiana, and the other in Roseburg, Oregon, and I wouldn't dream of missing them.) A visit to the Corn Palace could not have been disappointing at any time; that we had the luck to catch it on graduation day was a happy bonus. But perhaps the best thing about our visit to Mitchell was its wonderfully serendipitous nature. Our happiest moments as tourists always seem to come when we stumble upon one thing while in pursuit of something else.

Such moments have come to us often in recent years. Ever since February of 1988, Lynne and I have been entirely nomadic, driving back and forth across the country, living in motels and artists' colonies and friends' guest rooms, leading a life that lends itself remarkably well to serendipity. The focus of our trip, insofar as it has one, is at least as wacky as wrapping islands in pink plastic. We have been on an extended serial pilgrimage to towns named Buffalo, and at this writing have managed to visit 54 of them. Before our stay in Brookings, we hit Buffalo Trading Post and Buffalo Ridge, both in South Dakota's Minnehaha County. Our next destination was Buffalo Springs, just outside of Bowman, North Dakota. The trip to Mitchell delayed our arrival in Buffalo Springs, but so what?

When you're not going anywhere special, and you don't care when you get there, you begin to realize the infinite richness of tourist attractions in this country. Travelers who speed along the interstates, or (God forbid) fly over everything, do not know what they are missing.

For a start, there are museums absolutely everywhere. Towns you've never heard of, towns that are the merest dots on the map, towns that don't even have a speed limit, are apt to have a museum. Some, like the Woolaroc Museum outside of Bartlesville, Oklahoma, or the Buffalo Bill Historical Center in Cody, Wyoming, are worth a special trip and an extended stay. Others are a delight when you just happen on them.

We have fond memories, for example, of the John Dillinger Historical Wax Museum in Nashville, Indiana, and the Dalton Defenders' Museum in Coffeyville, Kansas, near the site of the bank the Dalton Brothers were trying to rob when they were gunned down. (The Dalton Museum also has mementoes of Wendell Willkie and Walter "The Big Train" Johnson, who pitched for the Washington Senators. Who knew?)

In Harlowton, Montana, we stopped for lunch en route to (where else?) Buffalo, and happened on a little museum that contained, among other strange and exotic items, a collection of over a hundred small wooden goblets carved by a local eccentric, each from a different kind of wood. They looked for all the world like wooden goblets carved from different kinds of wood. Another citizen had collected the 50 different cans issued by the 7-Up people a few years back, each honoring a different state. He had donated this treasure to the museum, and there it was, displayed so that anyone could marvel at it. You'll never see anything like it at the Metropolitan.

The same museum also had a couple of Charles M. Russell's letters. Russell, the famous cowboy artist, must have been the best pen pal anyone ever had. He wrote delightful letters, made it a virtual point of honor never to spell a word the same way twice, and illustrated his correspondence with sketches and colored drawings. It was an unexpected pleasure to run into his letters in Harlowton. You should understand that Harlowton is a town of fewer than 1,200 souls, and the seat of a county with a population of 2,300. That it should have any museum at all was surprising, and this one was a treat.

But museums are only part of the treasure awaiting the serendipitous tourist. Consider the clay factory. We found it in Huntington, Indiana, a small city 30 miles or so southwest of Fort Wayne. We were going to pass through Huntington en route to Buffalo, Indiana, so I looked it up in the Mobil Travel Guide and discovered that a local clay factory offered a free industrial tour. We managed to locate the factory—I don't imagine it would be terribly difficult to locate anything in Huntington—and a woman met us at the door with a smile.

"I'll bet you're here for the tour," she said. "We get people every now and then."

The factory opened originally because there was a fine supply of clay in the area around Huntington. Now the factory's there because it's there. It buys the ingredients necessary for the modeling clay it produces from various sources; they are combined in the proper proportions at the factory, and the resulting clay is dyed one of several colors and packaged so that small children can mold it into unrecognizable animal shapes that their parents can unwittingly grind into the carpet.

An obliging young woman walked us through every step of the clay-making process. We watched as a workman combined clay granules and oil in a hopper and then churned the resulting mess, and we watched as the clay went through machines that extruded it and lopped it off and gathered it and packaged it. We didn't take notes, so I can't tell you too much about the operation, but then how much do you really need to know? What actually interested us more than what we learned about the manufacture of clay was the perspective we got on life at the clay factory. There were perhaps two dozen men and women employed there, and they seemed to have a pleasant existence.

"We could get jobs here," Lynne said. "We could live nearby and walk to work."

"Carry lunch boxes," I suggested.

"Or even come home for lunch, if we lived close enough. And at night we could talk about what we did on the job."

"'Made a fair amount of blue today,' I might say. 'Not so much yellow, but a fair amount of blue.'"

"I'm sure there are stresses," Lynne said. "Some days a machine must get fouled up and everybody has to pitch in and straighten things out or—"

"Or things get gummed up."

"Right. It can't all be smooth sailing. But they certainly seemed happy, didn't they?"

"They did. It was nice of them to give us this clay, wasn't it? What do you want to do with it?"

"You can make unrecognizable animal shapes," she said, "and I'll grind them into the rug."

The rest of the world, of course, knows Huntington as the home of Vice President J. Danforth Quayle. To us, though, it will always be first and foremost the site of the clay factory, where we long to be employed whenever the world is too much with us.

I'd like to go on more industrial tours. We went through Michter's Distillery, not far from Buffalo Springs, Pennsylvania. And we tried to tour the Sun-Maid Raisin factory in Kingsburg, California, but we wound up in court instead.

Kingsburg is an interesting town, 18 miles south of Fresno. It was settled by Swedes, and there's a lot of Swedish heraldry and folk designs on the buildings in the historic downtown area. We stopped for a quick look around before we went on to the Sun-Maid plant, and we passed one storefront that seemed to be the focus of a lot of activity. It turned out to be a courtroom, and court was in session, so we went in.

We sat there for hours, as one migrant farm worker after another pleaded guilty to operating a motor vehicle without license or insurance. It doesn't sound all that fascinating now, but we couldn't leave. And there were a couple of interesting cases, including one involving a long-haul trucker who had stolen his employer's truck and run off to Las Vegas with it.

Afterward, we chatted with the judge. "I wondered what you were doing here," he said. "Well, you're welcome to come to my courtroom any time you're in the area."

By the time we got to the raisin factory, we'd missed our last chance to tour the place that day. But we decided that was okay. If part of serendipity is finding things you're not looking for, the other part is not finding some things you *are* looking for. Fair enough.

*　　　　*　　　　*

The first rule of this sort of travel is that there are no rules. But Lynne and I have established a few guiding principles that serve us well, and you might find them of some value.

1. Less is more. The less publicized and advertised an attraction, the more likely it is to prove a happy surprise. If something is hyped by signs along the interstate and flyers in the motel lobby, it will probably be disappointing.

2. Everything run by the National Park Service is worthwhile, and a good deal. The major national parks and monuments are obvious destinations, not serendipitous surprises along the way. But the Park Service operates no end of lesser national memorials and national historic places. I'd be sorry to have missed Bent's Old Fort in Colorado or Sunset Crater in Arizona or Fort Scott in Kansas or the Theodore Roosevelt Inaugural National Historic Site in Buffalo, New York. Buy a Golden Eagle Pass for $25 on your first visit to a Park Service operation, or any Federal recreation area that charges an entrance fee, and all their other locations are open to you for the rest of the year. (If you're over 62 and a United States citizen, the equivalent Golden Age Passport is yours free.)

3. Develop a close relationship with maps and guidebooks. I spend a great deal of time with both, probably because I'm often more involved with where I'm going than where I happen to be at the moment. The Mobil Travel Guides serve us particularly well; I can look up nearby towns and find just the sort of attractions that don't call for a special trip, but that are well worth our time when we're in the neighborhood.

4. It helps if you're easily amused. If you approach this sort of travel with the attitude of a wine snob, looking for imperfections and inadequacies in everything you taste, you will probably not have a great time. If you dwell on the fact that the museum in Harlowton

can't compare to the Metropolitan Museum of Art, you'd have done better to stay at home.

If you travel in this fashion long enough, there comes a point at which you realize certain truths. That every place is the right place to be. That you are never on the wrong road, because every road leads where you're going. And that these truths apply whether or not you're traveling.

Meanwhile, happy trails. And I hope you don't run into too long a line at the clay factory.

I honestly don't expect anything I've written to outlast me by more than a few seasons. One tells oneself one is writing for the ages, and this form of self-delusion may be useful if one is to get anything written at all, but one ought to face facts. Everything one writes might as well be written on water. One's words, however well- or ill-chosen, will go away and leave no trace— and meanwhile one is trapped in a sentence in which one refers to oneself forever as one, and I trust you can appreciate how unutterably tiresome that can be.

But if I'm remembered for anything, it will probably be this evidently imperishable sentence: "Our happiest moments as tourists always seem to come when we stumble upon one thing while in pursuit of something else."

I guess the words struck enough of a chord with enough people to make it turn up in no end of compendia of quotations. People who compile these quote banks evidently use the quote banks of others as a chief source, and thus momentum builds momentum, and—

Never mind. If this will come closer than anything else to providing me with a few months of immortality, well, okay. For now I'm happy to appreciate the irony of such a result coming— yes, serendipitously—while I was looking for something else.

GANGSTERS, SWINDLERS, KILLERS AND THIEVES

In 2003, Oxford University Press proposed that I edit a volume to be compiled from their multi-volume reference work, American National Biography. *I was to select the entries for fifty villains, write an introduction for each entry, and furnish as well an overall introduction for the volume. It wound up being more work than I'd expected, but it was interesting, and when the book was published in 2004 I was happy with it. OUP supplied the title, and it has a nice ring to it, doesn't it? It reminded me of something, and it took me a while to realize what it was; the penny dropped one morning, when the song I couldn't get out of my head was Cher's "Gypsies, Tramps and Thieves."*

The book's still in print, and at the present rate of sale it should earn out its advance sometime in 2067. Here, to whet your appetite, or perhaps to deaden it altogether, is my introduction:

Villains. There's something inherently fascinating about them. Sometimes they're bad-bad, the people you love to hate. Sometimes they're good-bad, and you love them and hate yourself for it. Either way they draw your attention and stick in your mind, and more often than not the heroes who oppose them pale in comparison.

The late Jean Kerr recounted the story of her son's disappointment at landing the role of Adam in the Sunday school play. He'd wanted to play the snake. But Adam was the hero, Kerr told him, and the boy agreed that this was so. But, he countered, the snake had all the lines. And *The Snake Has All the Lines* became the title of Kerr's next book.

*   *   *

> Back in his room, Keller tried the book again but couldn't keep his mind on what he was reading. He turned on the TV and worked his way through the channels, using the remote control bolted to the nightstand. Westerns, he decided, were like cops and cabs, never around when you wanted them. It seemed to him that he never made a trip around the cable circuit without running into John Wayne or Randolph Scott or Joel McCrea or a rerun of Gunsmoke or Rawhide or one of those spaghetti westerns with Eastwood or Lee Van Cleef. Or the great villains—Jack Elam, Strother Martin, the young Lee Marvin in The Man Who Shot Liberty Valance.
>
> It probably said something about you, Keller thought, when your favorite actor was Jack Elam.

The passage above appears in *Hit Man*, my own novel about a curiously sympathetic hired killer, and if it does indeed say something about you if your favorite actor is Jack Elam, it very likely says even more if you persist in writing fiction about characters an impartial observer would have to characterize as antisocial. Keller, born in a short story, has gone on to appear in two novels, with a third on the horizon. Bernie Rhodenbarr, a professional burglar who runs a secondhand bookstore as a hobby, stars in a series of mysteries that runs to ten volumes. Martin Ehrengraf, who defends criminal cases on a contingency basis, has committed crimes ranging from fraud and forgery to homicide on his clients' behalf in a dozen short stories.

Even in my books about Matthew Scudder, ex-cop and sober alcoholic turned private detective, it seems as though the snake gets all the lines. Scudder's best friend is Mick Ballou, a hoodlum gang leader with gallons of blood on his hands, and his assistant and surrogate son is a young black kid with street smarts and little reverence for the law. Scudder himself is not the traditional private eye with a code; if he ever had one, he's long since lost the codebook, and is a moral relativist who makes it all up as he goes along.

"I think you're doing something very subversive," a woman told me at a signing in northern California. "I was reading *Hit List,* and I really like Keller, although I don't think I should. And at one point I looked up from the book and said to myself, 'Well, so he kills people. What's so bad about that?'"

Perhaps it was my predilection for chronicling the adventures of fictional bad guys that got me the gratifying job of compiling this collection of very real villains, drawn from a couple hundred years of American history—and, specifically, from the pages of Oxford University Press's incomparable *American National Biography.* Here, for your enjoyment and edification, are the life stories of half a hundred thieves, murderers, gangsters, assassins, outlaws, and all-around menaces to civilized society. Each, individually, has an absorbing story to tell; collectively, they add up to an antisocial whole that's greater than the sum of its parts, enlarging our sense of just what it means to be a villain, and what another's villainy means to us.

Some of them make us ache physically with the need to see them punished. Ted Bundy, the clean-cut handsome boy-next-door who killed attractive young women for sport, is perhaps the quintessential serial killer of the twentieth century, and makes the perfect poster boy for capital punishment—or, if one recoils at the notion of government-sponsored homicide,

at the very least for life imprisonment without parole. Ed Gein, whose ex-
periments in taxidermy led to Robert Bloch's and Alfred Hitchcock's *Psycho,*
inspires horror more than loathing; we want to see him put away, far away,
where we won't have to look at him, or at ourselves.

You'll meet assassins here, three very different men who took the lives of
three American presidents. John Wilkes Booth, Lincoln's assassin, saw himself as the last-ditch defender of a lost Confederate cause; Charles Guiteau
believed himself to be divinely inspired to shoot James Garfield; Leon Czol-
gosz's half-digested anarchist sympathies led him to assassinate William
McKinley. All three died for what they did, and it was a forgone conclusion
that they would; the enormity of their acts, the prominence of their victims,
pretty much guaranteed their deaths.

You'll encounter quite a few gangsters in this book, including Owney Mad-
den and Al Capone, Bugsy Siegel and Meyer Lansky, Lucky Luciano and
Dutch Schultz. "We only kill each other," Siegel told his Hollywood friends,
although of course that wasn't always true. One of the guiding principles
of the Lepke Buchalter's original Murder Incorporated gang was that con-
victions became unlikely if witnesses disappeared, and no end of witnesses
were consequently murdered. The deaths of presumably innocent bystanders
were another by-product of the violent side of organized crime, and contemporary drug dealers coined the term *mushrooms* for the passersby caught in
drug war crossfire—because they just pop up out of nowhere.

Still, we can overlook the occasional innocent victim as we give ourselves over to the myth of the gangster, as it unfolds in fiction like *The God-
father* and *The Sopranos* or in real life. Criminal enterprise, we tell ourselves,
is a time-honored way for immigrants to gain a foothold in their new home.
They claw their way up, using methods more direct and arguably more honest than those used in climbing the corporate ladder. They may have to kill

someone, they may get killed in return, but their sons and daughters will go to college.

If our urban mythology embraces the gangster, the outlaw with the six-gun plays a similar role in our view of the frontier. Here we'll encounter William Clarke Quantrill and a few of the outlaws—Jesse James, Cole Younger—who made their bones in his Civil War guerrilla band. Quantrill's Raiders were vicious murderers or heroic soldiers, depending in part upon your Union or Confederate sympathies, and the ones who turned to crime after the war's end remained heroes to a portion of the population. They and others who robbed banks and trains benefited from a populist sentiment that saw financial institutions and railroads as parasitic exploiters; those who preyed on the predators were quickly cast as latter-day Robin Hoods, although evidence that many of them actually went so far as to give to the poor is hard to come by.

While not every outlaw was so treated in his lifetime, legend continues to burnish images, often with no discernible justification. Tiburcio Vasquez, a Mexican bandit hanged in California, has achieved what may be the most extraordinary posthumous rehabilitation; they've named a medical facility after him in Alameda County.

Vasquez, for all we know, may have been a nice guy, but no one who knew him said the same for John Wesley Hardin. Time and pop music have been kind to him; Bob Dylan, who saw fit to tack on a G and call him John Wesley Harding, portrays him in song as a fair-minded, courageous, socially-conscious fellow, a true stand-up guy. That just goes to show what an extra consonant will do for a man, because the real John Wesley Hardin, as you'll see, was an ill-tempered homicidal sociopathic racist with no redeeming qualities whatsoever.

The Robin Hood myth, the image of the outlaw as an individual fighting a lone battle against a corrupt and corrupting system, survived the loss of the frontier. The bank robbers of the years between the two world wars achieved that sort of mythic status long before the film *Bonnie and Clyde* made the life look glamorous. John Dillinger, Pretty Boy Floyd, and of course Clyde Barrow and Bonnie Parker, raced their fast cars along country roads and blazed away with their tommyguns, much as Butch Cassidy and the Daltons rode fast horses and fired Colt revolvers. The motorized outlaws of the Dust Bowl and Depression years were in it for the money, of course, but that's not to say that they were unaware of the mythic aspects of their role even as they enacted them. In Dillinger's jail break and Bonnie Parker's poems, we can almost see performers playing consciously to an audience.

One of the things we seem to have trouble believing about those we elevate to mythic status is that they're dead. If we regard them as immortals, how can mortality have its way with them?

It's not only criminals who get this treatment, as the rash of Elvis sightings demonstrates. No one has turned up claiming to be Elvis—unless you want to count all those Vegas lounge acts—but for awhile there was a fresh Anastasia popping up every decade or so, and before that poor lady there were all the Lost Dauphins of France.

Of our criminals, quite a few have demonstrated a comparable reluctance to stay dead. In one case, that of John Dillinger, a substantial body of evidence exists to suggest that lawmen did indeed shoot another man altogether in front of the Biograph Theater, though what subsequently became of the real John Dillinger is a good question. Butch Cassidy's death is also hard to substantiate; he may have been killed in South America, but he may as well have returned to the US and lived out his life in quiet obscurity.

In other instances, the outlaw's posthumous life represents the triumph of myth over hard fact. The death of Jesse James is probably the best example. Before the body was cold, a broadside ballad had been widely circulated, so that the whole country knew that Robert Ford, the "dirty little coward who shot Mr. Howard," had laid poor Jesse in his grave. The craven betrayal became part of the legend of Jesse James—how he was hanging or straightening a picture on the wall, how Ford shot him in the back, and so on.

With his end so well documented and so widely acknowledged, you'd think Jesse wouldn't have had much trouble staying in his grave. You wouldn't suppose there'd be much opportunity for men claiming to be the living Jesse, nor would you expect the public to pay much attention to such claims. But claims were made and attention was paid, even to the old codger who turned up 103 years after Jesse's birth.

Introductions are a curious literary form. A book like this seems to call for one, yet the whole enterprise strikes me as essentially pointless. While I suppose some people will read these lines, I can't avoid feeling they'll do so largely out of politeness.

Explaining his literary style, novelist Elmore Leonard said he just tries to leave out the parts that people will skip. Introductions, I'm afraid, are frequently skipped, and with good reason. And yet I soldier on.

And, thinking of Elmore Leonard, I find myself struck by the fact that he has written with great success over the years in two genres of popular fiction, the crime novel and the western. (So, coincidentally, has Loren Estleman, and I feel duty-bound to point out that both of these gentlemen live in Detroit. Make of that what you will.)

Few readers of crime fiction read westerns. Few fans of westerns read crime novels. But if you read examples of Leonard's or Estleman's work in both genres, you realize how little difference there is between the two. You meet the same sort of characters, on both sides of the law. The milieu varies, from sagebrush and open range to mean streets. Men ride horses and rustle cattle in one book; in another they hotwire SUVs and deal drugs.

By the same token, the villains you'll meet here, for all their differences, haven't changed that much over the centuries. There are some you may wish you could know, and others you'll be very grateful never to have encoun-tered. Some will inspire grudging admiration, others contempt, still others fear and revulsion. All in all, though, I think you'll be glad to have made their acquaintance. I know I am.

GETTING BUSTED

Periodically the Mystery Writers of America raise funds for the organization by publishing an anthology. The contents are always short stories, works of fiction contributed by MWA members.

Except in 1978, when Brian Garfield took a turn as editor and invited members to write about actual crimes to which they had a personal connection. At Brian's suggestion, I wrote an incident that had taken place a full twenty years before I was to write about it.

Brian's anthology, published by Times Books, was entitled I, Witness. *That title, with and without the comma, has been used several times since then by other writers, as an Amazon search will quickly reveal.*

It was the summer of '58. I had just turned twenty and was tentatively approaching the age of reason. After a year in the employ of a marginally disreputable literary agent, a year during which I spent my time encouraging the continued literary efforts of earnest souls who couldn't write their names in the dirt with stick, I had decided to visit Mexico.

My companion was Steve, my best friend and erstwhile college roommate; I'd be returning with him to college after the summer. We bought traveler's checks, had ourselves inoculated against a full complement of diseases, stocked up on Kaopectate and penicillin pills, and got on a plane for Houston.

We hitched from Houston to Laredo, and as I recall it took us thirteen rides and almost as many hours to cover the distance. We got a room in a grungy hotel in Laredo and walked across the border to Nuevo Laredo, the little cesspool conveniently located on the other side of the Rio Grande. Word had it that Nuevo Laredo was a great place to buy marijuana, which we hadn't had all that much experience with, and to get laid, which was another area in which we felt we could use some refinement.

Getting laid in Nuevo Laredo was about as tricky as getting warm in Hell but scoring marijuana proved more difficult. Here's how we managed it. We crossed the bridge, made our way to the public square, and were immediately approached by a dude with a sombrero and a horse-drawn cab who wanted to take us to his favorite whorehouse. "*Actualmente,*" I said, "*deseamos comprar alguna marijuana.*"

After I translated this into English for the cat he frowned and shook his head. "No, no, señor," he said. "Marijuana illegal in Mexico."

We walked another four paces and another hack driver hit on us. This time I skipped the old Español and pitched him directly in English. "No, no, señor," he said. "Marijuana illegal in Mexico."

Steve and I looked at each other and shrugged. I said, "This isn't going to be all that easy."

We continued circling around the plaza. We walked no more than a hundred yards when a chap with a mustache and what he must have thought were snappy clothes sidled up to us and winked. "Hello, there," he said. "I understand you boys would like to buy a little marijuana."

No kidding.

We bought three or four bombers from our new friend, who announced that his name was Ernesto. We took them back to our stateside hotel and smoked them. I think they cost fifty cents apiece or thereabouts.

The next day we crossed the border again and ran into another Ernesto who knew a really sensational whorehouse that he'd be delighted to show us. We repaired there. The next morning I caught Steve checking out the want ads, looking for job opportunities in beautiful Laredo. "I think I'm in love," he said.

I got our tourist cards processed and dragged him onto a bus for Mexico City. "Someday I'll thank you for this," he said. "But not just yet."

The girl's name was Letitia.

On the bus we both had stiff necks from sleeping under a fan. We sat next to a girl named Dorcas who was on her way to a Quaker encampment near Cuernavaca. Dorcas was no Letitia and neither of us fell in love with her.

Mexico City was terrific. A tout zeroed in on us at the bus station and told us he had just the hotel for us. I think his name was Ernesto, too, but I don't expect you to believe me.

Someone had hipped us to a friend who was studying at Mexico City College on the GI Bill, and through him we met a lot of beat types and learned to drink Dos Equis beer and smoke Delicado cigarettes and hang out at the whorehouse at No. 9 Medellin.

I think we were in Mexico City for about a week. We drank a lot and managed to fit in a little sightseeing in the off hours. We hooked up with another Stateside friend named Phil and dragged him around to the house on Medellin. Later that night he ate up all our penicillin pills, but to no avail. He came down with some form of galloping clap that baffled a team of Park Avenue urologists for a year and a half. He also drank all our Kaopectate and that didn't do him a lot of good either.

But Steve and I led charmed lives. Loved and ate whatever looked good and didn't catch so much as a cold.

Then we went to Guadalajara and the roof fell in.

It seemed a good idea at the time. Mexico City was expensive compared to the rest of the country. Besides, we had it on good authority that it wasn't the "real" Mexico. Guadalajara, however, would be a step toward the real

Mexico, and we could take a further step from there by crossing to Puerto Vallarta on the Pacific coast.

We took a bus to Guadalajara, got a hotel room, and went out to visit a man I knew through correspondence from my days at the literary agency. He was a prize guppy, conned into "collaborating" with my employer, which merely meant that he sent in an outline which was criticized by me, then did a first draft, then revised it as I told him, and ultimately was assured that his manuscript was in perfect shape and was being marketed. What happened was they cached his hopeless script in a filing cabinet and left it there throughout eternity.

So we went to see him and he turned out to be a paraplegic in a wheelchair, and that visit did not turn out to be one of the happier times of my life.

We didn't stay there long. Steve spent the afternoon watching a John Wayne movie with Spanish subtitles. He said it was better, all things considered, than watching a foreign movie with English subtitles. I spent the afternoon reading *The Brothers Karamazov* until Steve came back from the theater; and I stopped reading and we went out and had dinner.

The restaurant we chose was on the opposite side of the plaza from our hotel, a few blocks away down a side street. We walked through the plaza on our way to dinner and, naturally enough, intended to walk through it again on our way back to the hotel.

But in the meantime somebody started a riot.

At this time Mexico was getting ready to have an election, which is evidently something they do every now and then as a matter of form. I don't know why they bother. The PRI party always wins these elections. At the time the head of the party, and thus the President of Mexico, was one Adolfo Lopez Mateos. I have no trouble remembering his name even unto this date because I saw it everywhere I went in Mexico. All the barns and rock outcroppings and sundry surfaces that say *Chew Mail Pouch* in America said *Adolfo Lopez*

Mateos in Mexico. There were other political parties and no doubt they were running candidates in opposition to Adolfo, but I don't know much about them.

I do know one thing. One of these parties, a right-wing group of some sort, was known as the PAN party. That acronym spells the Spanish word for bread, and I'm sure it stood for something, but whatever it stood for the PAN party was having a south-of-the-border version of a rally-cum-fundraiser, which is to say they were holding a riot.

The plaza was circled by public buildings, and the PAN enthusiasts were heaving bricks and rocks through the windows of these buildings and shouting slogans and shrieking and generally contributing to the furtherance of the democratic process.

The police were meeting this challenge calmly and professionally by lobbing tear-gas shells all over the place and firing rifles over the heads of the crowd. (At least that's the presumption. We didn't see anybody get shot. But then it wasn't possible to see very much because of the tear gas.)

A little perspective. This was 1958. Eisenhower was in the White House. There was no such thing as SDS. There was such a thing as Vietnam but stamp collectors were the only people who had heard of it. The only urban guerrillas were housed in cages at the Bronx Zoo. Tear gas was something the cops used on television. Cops, for that matter, were something on television.

We were very excited about the whole thing. It would be terrific to tell our friends about. We felt sorry for poor Phil back in Mexico City, sitting on the toilet and missing out on all this.

Of course the tear gas was extremely unpleasant, and it really worked in practice the way it was described in books; and enough, sooner or later, was enough. By the time one enormous cop pointed a finger in our direction and told us to get the hell away from there, we were only too anxious to comply.

But that wasn't the easiest thing in the world to do. Whenever we started in one direction, somebody dropped tear gas in front of us and a mob of people began running toward us and we had to go with the flow or get trampled. And in no time at all we lost whatever sense of direction we had possessed and didn't know which way was the hotel, or even which way led away from the core of riot activity.

At that point the cop who'd yelled at us before came not exactly to our rescue. He got us off to one side, asked us who we were and what we were doing, and demanded our identification. We explained that we were students, that we were trying to get back to our hotel, that our tourist cards were at the hotel. Meanwhile we showed him such things as drivers' licenses.

Thereupon he bundled us into the back of a police cruiser, drove us to a building a mile or two from the action, and, before we really knew what was going on, led us to a cell and slammed the door on us.

Things apparently were beginning to get a little hairy. After all, who hadn't heard stories of people vanishing into Mexican jails and languishing there for the rest of their lives?

I yelled in Spanish for someone to come around who spoke English.

Nothing happened.

We called out the same request a few times in English, with similar non-results, and then we decided to shut up lest we aggravate somebody.

It was still something of a lark. I suspect it was our stupefying innocence that made it seem frivolous. We were decent middleclass kids from good homes and we lived in what we were sure was a well-ordered universe. In an hour or certainly by morning the men in charge would realize that they had made a mistake. We would be returned to our hotel and released—perhaps with a warning, more likely with an apology. Naturally, in the heat of the moment, arresting us might have seemed like a good idea: after all, we were foreigners; we were dressed a bit scruffily; we had beards, albeit tentative ones. And we had ignored a direct order to leave the area. We'd tried to obey the order, but perhaps El Jefe had been unaware of that. Assuredly, señores, there was a certain amount of justification for jugging us, if only for our own protection. Assuredly.

*　　*　　*

The jail itself was not the sort of stuff nightmares are made on. I don't recall that it was terribly clean, and the sanitary facilities were limited and generally foul, but I don't recall an all-pervading stench or anything that would constitute the last word in squalor. In retrospect I think we were probably in a tin can of a jail where they put people who'd gotten drunk or fallen behind in alimony payments or something about that dangerous to the community.

It was the only jail we had and we made the most of it, pacing back and forth like Rubashov in *Darkness at Noon*, then searching our persons for incriminating documents. I found two pieces of identification in the name of Leonard Blake. One was a Social Security card and the other wasn't. I can't recall why I'd ever thought to provide myself with them in the first place. "If they find these," I said, "they'll think I'm some sort of agent."

Steve checked his own wallet and turned up his NAACP membership card. "If they find this," he said, "they'll think I'm a Communist."

We giggled at both notions—agent, Communist, sure. But why be careless when it's so much more dramatic to be careful?

We ate these incriminating documents forthwith. Just as well, too, because it was all we got to eat that night. De Maupassant, I have been given to understand, ate some human flesh once so he'd be able to describe it. Unhappily I can't remember what the cardboard tasted like. Probably it tasted like the *plat du jour* in a fast-food joint.

Of course no one ever checked our wallets. Not to look for false ID, anyway. But I don't want to get ahead of my story.

There were a dozen cells like ours circling a large empty room. I seem to remember that they let us out sometime during the night to exercise in the large open area. Most of the other cells were unoccupied. Of our few fellow prisoners, none seemed conversant with English. For the most part they appeared to be drunks sleeping it off.

I suppose we slept a little.

In the morning it seemed there was a problem. Someone had checked our hotel and we did not seem to be registered under the names we'd been booked with. Oddly, we had forgotten this altogether, and it had come about for a curious reason. The beat-generation type we'd palled around with in Mexico City had tried to borrow money from us, and had muttered something about dropping in on us in Guadalajara, and we saw him as a possible source of future annoyance. To duck him—and, I don't doubt, out of a desire to dramatize ourselves—we had used last names different from our own in signing the hotel register. We were only going to be in Guadalajara a couple of days, we reasoned.

We explained this to the cops. Our friend from the night before was present, and it might be a good time to describe him. He seems to have been eight feet tall and built like King Kong, but I'm sure memory has distorted reality. I know that he was very large, very gruff, and that he spoke perfect English. He told us something about having served in the American Army during the war but he did not say he'd been educated at UCLA.

He wasn't delighted with our explanation of the false names. In fact he took pains to make this look like a serious offense, and at the time I thought it really disturbed him. Then he and his partner, who looked like an accountant, accompanied us back to our hotel room where we were to be searched and questioned.

And that was when the feces and the fan really collided.

The first thing the search disclosed was my diary of the trip. This was a very sketchy account of things, as I've never been temperamentally inclined to keep a detailed diary, but it did disclose that we'd visited a whorehouse now and again. This threw the cop into a frenzy. Here we rotten Yanquis had come south to ruin the sacred virgins of Mexico. He really seemed livid about this.

Next he got hold of our tourist cards. There's a blank there for religion, presumably so they'll know what sort of last rites to give you if the dysentery does you in. I'd put Jewish and Steve had put None. The cop read all this out loud and didn't know whether to defecate or go blind. "To be Jewish is bad enough," he announced, "but to have no religion is even worse." Steve and I couldn't even bear to look at each other. Clearly we'd both flunked that test.

But the worst revelation was yet to come. A systematic search of our belongings yielded up the literature we'd brought along, my copy of *The Brothers Karamazov* and Steve's edition of *Ten Days That Shook the World*. "My God," the cop roared, "you're Communists! Agitators from Moscow! Reading Russian books! Coming here to stir up the poor peasants of my country!"

Let me tell you something. It sounds a lot funnier in print, and in retrospect, than it ever felt at the time. Because this son of a bitch was one hell of an actor, and even though it was fairly obvious that he was acting, it was also eminently possible that he'd get carried away with the role. By this time he had his gun out of his holster and was waving it around the room. He was really into the part he was playing, condemning us as Jew pervert Communist bastards, and we weren't too innocent to know how easy it would be for him to report us as killed trying to escape, or something of the sort, and . . .

I don't think he actually hit us with the gun. He swung at us a few times but I don't think he connected. And I don't remember what if anything we said in our defense but I'm fairly sure it's nothing we'd be terribly proud to remember.

After what was probably only a few minutes of this deliberate rage he calmed down and his partner, who looked embarrassed, explained that he thought he might be able to reason with the monster. Of course there were problems, there were expenses. He'd have to see just how much cash we could scrape together and if it would be enough.

They knew how much money we had because they'd searched us. We had six hundred dollars' worth of traveler's checks between us. You know about traveler's checks. They're better than cash because you don't have to worry about losing them and they're accepted everywhere. Well, the second part of the statement is true enough. The fuzz in Guadalajara couldn't have been happier than to accept our traveler's checks. We signed them over one by one, and the good cop solemnly held us at gunpoint while the bad cop trotted off to cash them. I figured if the bank didn't turn those checks into pesos we were going home to our parents in plastic bags.

While we waited the partner felt silly pointing a gun at us and put it away. Then he got me to show him how the camera worked. They'd had to confiscate it, of course, on the chance that we might have taken subversive photos, and since it was confiscated he wanted to know how to operate it in case he felt like taking a couple of photos of his mother.

Then, he frowned and asked why that particular model didn't come with a case. I found the case under the bed along with some unexposed film. He packed it all up and couldn't have been happier.

When the big guy came back with our money he promptly made another confiscation—my pornographic diary and our three subversive Russian books. He also went through our wallets, leaving us bus fare to the border and a few odd pesos for Delicados and tacos en route.

The two of them drove us to the bus station and told us we had twenty-four hours to get out of the country. After that we'd be subject to arrest, imprisonment, and God knew what else. Summary execution, I suppose.

It occurred to us, while we waited for that bus, that there was almost certainly an American consulate in Guadalajara and that we could most likely go there and pitch a bitch. We decided that this was not a safe and sober thing to do. We had the feeling we were being observed, that some official all-seeing eye would stay on us until we boarded that bus. A single step outside the station was more risk than we were prepared to take.

We did learn something, though, while waiting for the bus. We picked up a copy of the local paper and I had enough Spanish to dope out what had happened. The PAN party had indeed rioted, and twenty-seven rioters had been duly arrested by the heroic police. Then in another article there appeared a list of twenty-five rioters who had been carted off to jail—not our jail but another one.

It seemed pretty clear that we'd been singled out for special treatment from the start. The police were busy busting up a riot, all right, but they were willing to take time off in the middle of it to jug a couple of Americans who might turn out to be a good source of cash.

We also found a picture of the enormous bastard who'd waved his gun in our faces. The caption identified him as the chief of the district police or something of the sort.

The rest is a blur in memory and I think it was pretty much of a blur at the time. Our bus was a local, taking forever to carry us eastward as far as San Luis Potosi, where we waited four grim nighttime hours for a connecting bus to the border. We sat in a grimy café sharing out the Delicados to make them last—Delicados were six cents a pack at the time, but they hadn't left us with abundant cash. Our bus finally did come, and it did take us to Laredo, and we got back across the border and did indeed stoop to kiss the ground of Texas, an act I for one had never expected to perform.

One hideous moment. The Mexican border guard gave our luggage, such as it was, only the most cursory sort of search. But he did take his time opening Steve's tobacco pouch and helping himself to a good hearty sniff of its contents. Now we'd been dumping our roaches in with the tobacco earlier, and had forgotten about this altogether in the course of our prison experiences, and I think that's as close to cardiac arrest as I care to come. But he evidently didn't smell anything more authoritative than tobacco and we were on our way.

Our parents wired money and we flew home the following day. We made an attempt through the traveler's-check company to get our money refunded, arguing that we'd signed over our checks under duress, and a fat lot of good that did us. The company chap told us, as diplomatically as possible, that he figured we lost the dough in a crap game. I can understand his position and I suppose it's one I'd take were our roles reversed, but it'll be a while before I buy traveler's checks again. Perhaps as long as it'll be before I return to Mexico.

Remembering all this, certain things occur to me. I guess the most striking is the realization of just how massive a source of guilt this entire experience was for us. In spite of the fact that we were certain we'd been marked as pigeons the minute El Jefe laid eyes on us, I've never been able to dismiss the notion that it was our fault. Couldn't we have gotten away from the riot area, at least after our warning? Shouldn't we have had the sense not to bring Dostoevsky and Reed with us? And Barry Ulanov, for God's sake? Where did I get off mentioning whorehouses in my diary? Why hadn't we thought to list ourselves as Catholics on our tourist cards?

And what power had so possessed us as to lead to our registering at that hotel under false names? That's one detail we didn't bother mentioning to our parents.

Another line of thought suggested that, given the situation, there should have been some way we could have acquitted ourselves more manfully. I don't know just what we might have done—I certainly had no illusion that I could possibly overpower that gorilla and take his gun away from him.

I had dreams about that cop for years, daydreams in which I slipped into the country with a rifle and blew his head off.

I can't say what I gained from the experience, or what it may have cost me besides a couple of hundred dollars, a camera, and a typewriter. I have, since that Mexican trip, written more cops-and-crooks stuff than anyone should have to read, let alone write, but if I've ever drawn on the experience I did so subconsciously and still don't know about it. I'm left with prejudices—that people named Ernesto are shady but reliable, for instance, and that civilization stops at the Rio Grande. I suppose one of those theories makes about as much sense as the other but I prefer to go on believing both of them just the same.

A lot of forms contain the question, *Have you ever been arrested?* For awhile I answered *Not in this country,* which invariably led to some interesting conversations, but that got to be too much of a hassle. So I just put in *No,* and so far I've gotten away with it.

And time does fly, and heals wounds. Phil's a VP at an ad agency now. Steve's a college dean, and at the very institution where we once roomed together. I find that slightly incredible, but not that much more incredible than the fact that my eldest daughter is very nearly the age I was when I took that trip.

Why, those cops may well be dead by now.

I certainly hope so. I hope they died hard, the bastards.

I did in fact make it back to Mexico, perhaps two or three times over the years, but never without an uneasy recollection of this incident.

The luckless Antiochian I mention as having joined us at the Mexico City bordello, whom I called Phil, was in fact my friend Peter Hochstein. I don't think he'd mind my mentioning this aspect of his medical history at this late date. I still stay in touch with him, as I do with Steve Schwerner, my fellow pájaro de la cárcel, *who retired after a rich career as Dean of Students and moved back to Brooklyn.*

GREENWICH VILLAGE
THROUGH THE YEARS

The New York Times *commissioned this piece for their November 20, 1988 magazine supplement:*

In *The Maltese Falcon,* there's an aside wholly unrelated to the plot in which Sam Spade recounts the story of a man named Flitcraft. One day Flitcraft was on his way to or from his office when a beam at a construction site fell as he passed, narrowly missing him. Flitcraft then disappeared without a word. By the time Spade had tracked him down he was living under another name in another city, having settled there in circumstances not unlike those he'd left, with a job and a wife similar to those he'd walked away from.

And that, Spade explains, is what he'd always liked about the case. Flitcraft had discovered he was living in the kind of world where beams were apt to fall, and so he'd adjusted himself to the fact. And then no more beams fell, and so he'd adjusted himself to that.

In Greenwich Village, the beams don't exactly fall. They slant, jutting out at oblique angles like the funny, slanty little streets there. When the beams in your own life slant, you move to the Village and feel at home. When the beams in your life straighten out again—if they ever do—you move out.

*　　　*　　　*

The funny, slanty little streets. At the very least they are metaphorical, with the area's skewed geography underscoring a skewed state of mind.

The rest of Manhattan makes such perfect sense. Numbered streets and avenues cross one another in a perfect rectilinear grid. Then you get a few blocks south of 14th Street and chaos descends. Most of the streets in the Village have names instead of numbers, but even the numbered streets find themselves caught up in bizarre behavior. West 4th Street drifts crazily northward. Briefly, 10th Street heads south before heading east; 11th and 12th Streets hesitate, then tag along in her wake.

And they all crisscross! When you find yourself for the first time at the intersection of West 4th Street and West 10th Street, you cannot but realize that you have stepped into a non-Euclidean universe. The great security of living in an ordered world where parallel lines never meet is lost forever to you now. You are indeed in a world where beams slant. (My own favorite intersection is that of Waverly Place and Waverly Place. That street, the most resolutely pious in New York, insists upon crossing itself. To contemplate such an intersection is to gaze anew at the whole nature of physical reality.) Not everyone in the bars and coffeehouses knows this, but the place did start out as a genuine village. When New York itself was a cluster of houses down around the Battery, Greenwich Village was an altogether separate community a short distance up the Hudson. A portion of the West Village was carved from a farm owned by a man named Charles Christopher Amos, and his three names were parceled out among three of the new streets.

The city eventually grew to engulf and incorporate the village, but never entirely to assimilate it. The Village has always retained a sort of spiritual autonomy. It has always been different, and it has always drawn to itself people who see themselves as different, and who as like as not glory in their differentness.

Bohemians. Intellectuals. Artists. Writers. Revolutionaries. Decadents. Hipsters. Beats. Hippies. Every imaginable sort of social or sexual or political unorthodoxy found a nurturing environment in the Village, and took root there. If Villagers can be said to have such a thing as a common denominator, it would have to be their eccentricity.

*   *   *

Some years ago I was apartment hunting. One of the places I looked at was a studio in the West Village. Milligan Place, I seem to remember, but maybe not.

It was two flights up, and tiny. Just one big room, and the room was utterly dominated by a concert grand piano. You had to hug the walls to get around the piano. There was—barely—room for a daybed along the wall behind the piano, and there was room for nothing else. It was impossible to guess how anyone could have gotten the piano into that room, and inconceivable that anyone would ever get it out.

The apartment's tenant—and the piano's owner—was a cheerfully melancholy little man who explained that he was a piano teacher. "Actually," he went on, "I only have one student. It's not my real occupation. What I really am is a psychotherapist." "It's good you've got the couch." "Well, it's my bed," he said, "but of course you're right. My clients lie on it during their sessions. And I sit at the piano."

He would have had to. There was no place else to sit in the room, and no room for a chair.

"Sometimes they talk," he said dreamily, "and sometimes I play for them. As a matter of fact, after the first few sessions that's how we usually do it. They stretch out and close their eyes, and I play for them."

"Oh," I said.

"It seems to help them," he said. "Especially Mozart."

I never put that fellow in a book, and I wonder why. He'd fit perfectly in Bernie Rhodenbarr's world; he'd be a natural neighbor for Bernie's Village pal Carolyn Kaiser, on Arbor Court. But I never thought to use him.

I used the Sikh, though.

One day maybe 8 or 10 years ago, I was walking east on Bleecker Street in the middle of a weekday afternoon. Walking west on that same thoroughfare was a gentleman who stood at least 6 inches over 6 feet tall. He was tricked out in full Sikh regalia—beard, crisply ironed military uniform, white turban. I don't suppose there was really a jewel on the turban, or a scimitar swinging on his hip, but he wouldn't have been any more impressive for such accouterments.

If the same fellow had walked down the street in Des Moines, say, or Spokane, or almost any town this side of the Punjab, he would have drown a crowd. People would have picked up their phones and called their neighbors. "You're not gonna believe what I just saw," they'd say.

This was Greenwich Village. Nobody took a second look at him!

A few months later I was writing *The Burglar Who Liked to Quote Kipling*, in which Bernie Rhodenbarr, the titular hero, runs a bookstore on 11th Street off University, when not letting himself into other people's houses. At one point the plot ground to a halt, and I remembered a precept of Raymond Chandler's: "When in doubt, have two guys come through the door with guns in their fists."

The principle's a sound one. Somewhere down the line you'll figure out who they are, where they came from, and what they're doing with the guns. In the meantime, you've added some tension to the story.

I brought in a Sikh with a turban and had him point a gun at Bernie. Worked like a charm.

Now none of this is to suggest that everyone to be found north of Houston and south of 14th Street is unusual. The Village, built on a human scale with its narrow streets and low-rise dwellings, is an exceptionally pleasant place to live; you don't have to hear a different drummer to find it congenial. But it's not what it used to be. Ask anyone. It's changed beyond recognition. The good shops are gone, the good restaurants are gone, the great saloons are gone. The best people—the real artists, the true intellectuals, the genuine bohemians—have long since vanished. The rents are too high. Only yuppies and coke dealers can afford the place now.

Now that's all true, in any number of ways, and yet it must be said that they've been saying pretty much the same thing ever since they cut streets through Charles Christopher Amos's farm. When I first came to the Village in the summer of '56, all the old Village hands were eager to tell me how the place wasn't the same anymore. A friend who grew up there says she heard the same refrain in her childhood, with old-timers lamenting the glorious days of the '20s. I suppose Edna St. Vincent Millay and the radical journalist Floyd Dell had to listen to the same crap way back when: "Hey, you guys should have been here for the draft riots. That was when this place really swung."

Oh, there have been changes. But before we consider them, let's savor a perfect autumn day in the Village of 1988.

We'll sleep late—Villagers have always tended to sleep late, or not at all—and then pick up the paper and have breakfast at the Bagel, on West 4th Street. We'll walk east afterward, and shop for books at Pageant, on East 9th, and the Strand, on Broadway, before cutting through Washington Square, where we can listen to someone play a guitar, or kibitz a chess game at the stone tables at the park's southwest corner.

We could spend half the afternoon on Macdougal, stopping for espresso at the Caffé Reggio. Then we'll window-shop at the Den of Antiquity, later crossing the street to have a drink at Minetta's. We could have dinner right there, or we could walk down a few doors to Monte's or the Derby.

There may be a play we'd like to see at the Provincetown Playhouse, or at the Cherry Lane Theater, nearby on Commerce. If we go there we'll probably want to stop for a drink afterward at the Blue Mill, or maybe drop in at Chumley's, hidden away on Bedford.

*　　　　　*　　　　　*

Just an ordinary Village day. You can do all of this today.

And, interestingly enough, you could have done it all 30 years ago. All of the establishments I have mentioned were in the Village then. All of the pleasures they offered then are still available, essentially unchanged. Of course there has been change in the neighborhood. For instance, there used to be bookstores everywhere. Not just on 4th Avenue, but all over the place. Dozens have vanished, and many of them are sorely to be missed—Martin's, Marloff's, 8th Street. But others have opened, and if there are now fewer general bookshops, there are probably more wonderfully specific ones—the Biography Bookshop on Bleecker sells nothing else, and Foul Play, up the street on Abingdon Square, specializes in mysteries.

It's true that jazz clubs have closed, and coffee houses have closed, and Italian restaurants have closed, and antique shops have closed—and others of each have opened.

All of this, I would suppose, is as it should be. The Village, after all, is not a museum, not some toy Quaint Towne in some urban Epcot Center. Its survival requires that it change, that it evolve. Stasis is death.

Structurally, it is remarkable how little change has occurred. On an island where buildings get knocked down and replaced before they have finished settling upon their foundations, the Village has managed surprising stability over the past quarter of a century. There were some losses, certainly, before the preservationists swung into gear, and every white brick building stands upon the grave of a structure that was more attractive, more livable and more in harmony with its environment. (Will our descendants one day mourn those white brick castles even as we lament the passing of the buildings that made way for them? I rather suspect they will.) A tug-of-war goes on forever between those who would landmark every taxpayer and parking lot and those who would cheerfully cantilever an office building over the Taj Mahal if somebody would sell them the air rights. And, while the battle rages, the Village survives.

*   *   *

There are a couple of buildings, one old, one new, that epitomize the Village for me—the way it has changed, the way it has remained the same.

The first, the Jefferson Market Courthouse, on 6th Avenue and West 10th Street, with its turrets and minarets, its exuberance and its beauty, has served for the past two decades as the most charming public library branch imaginable. To my mind, the extraordinary thing about this magnificent structure is that it came within a hairbreadth of ceasing to exist. It is hard to credit this now, but the old courthouse was that close to being torn down. To see it today is to glory in the survival of the entire neighborhood.

The second, around the corner on 11th, between 5th and 6th, is one house in a row of stately houses that differs from its neighbors even as it complements them: a portion of its facade is cocked at a rakish angle.

In 1970, some radical student activists set up a bomb factory in the house that then stood on this spot. After they accidentally blew the house up, and a few of themselves along with it, the lot stood vacant while people tried to figure out what to do with it. Weather Park, the kids called it.

The present house, built in 1978, is an architectural triumph. It fits among its fellows while quietly asserting itself as an original, not a reproduction. And the tilt of its facade is the skewed stance of the nonconformist, the side-goggled slant of a West Village lane. Perfect.

I have my own history in Village buildings. My first home there was a huge top-floor room in a tenement on West 14th Street, a house of questionable, if not positively ill, repute. The walls, I recall, were painted in four-inch vertical stripes of black and canary yellow. Then I lived briefly in a furnished room on West 12th; the building was demolished to make way for the huge, red brick Mark Twain, and not a moment too soon. There was a place on Barrow Street, too, on the first floor; the folk singers came back there on Sunday nights, after the police had rousted them from the park, and the party would go on until the neighbors complained.

Later, I lived in a three-room warren on Bleecker at Sullivan. And then there was the nice airy railroad flat on Greenwich Street near Bethune, where I figured to remain until it was time to toddle around the corner to the Village Nursing Home. Best-laid plans and all that—a relationship ended, and she kept the apartment, and I moved to a basement lair in a back house on Jane Street, with low ceilings and mushrooms growing out of the walls. In and out and to and fro, and I don't doubt that you could tie it all up with beams that slant and beams that fall. A couple of years ago, I moved to Florida, where beams for the most part get eaten by termites, and for the past year I have lived nowhere at all, crisscrossing the country and staying in various equivalents of the Bates Motel. I don't know just where the beams in my life repose these days; it's easier to spot them in one's neighbor's eye.

Will it be time, at the next shifting of the beams, to move back?

I don't know. How can anyone afford to move here?

Then again, when you think about it, when was it ever easy? For at least as long as I've known the Village, it has commanded a premium. When rents were reasonable, apartments were impossible to find. Now there seem to be plenty of listings, but everything costs the earth.

On balance, I think it does get harder every year for the young and the impecunious to find a place to live in Greenwich Village. And I'm certain the quality of neighborhood life has to be adversely affected by the increasing age and prosperity of its inhabitants.

Still, it's the Village. It's always been special. Somehow I don't think it's done yet.

Nor am I by any means certain that I am done with it.

And of course I wasn't. I wrote this for the Times *in 1988, when Lynne and I had left Ft. Myers and were crisscrossing the country in relentless pursuit of the wily and elusive Buffalo. Two years later we moved back to New York, and to Greenwich*

Village, first to a studio sublet on West 13th Street not much larger than the motel rooms we'd learned to love, and then a couple of blocks south and west to a condo.

Has it changed since 1988? Indeed it has, for better and for worse. Relentless gentrification has made it impossible for most people to afford to live here, and the demographics have changed and go on changing. Quirky little shops keep disappearing as their leases expire; chain drugstores and banks take their place. On the other hand, little squares and triangles that were not much more than patches of asphalt are now sweet little pocket parks, oases in the urban desert. It seems to me that in the most important ways it's still the place that charmed us all those years ago. We enjoy most of the places we visit, and tend to feel at home wherever we find ourselves, but the Village has been our true home since got here.

I might add that the Hammett's Flitcraft story, which opens the piece, seems to be everybody's favorite passage from The Maltese Falcon, *and perhaps from all of Hammett. Which speaks to the power of the written word; virtually everything else in the book turns up essentially verbatim in John Huston's film, but Flitcraft didn't make the cut. I would have to guess that a beam fell, and this time it didn't miss.*

HAM FOR BREAKFAST

When I was invited to furnish a foreword for Jewish Noir 2, *an anthology edited by Ken Wishnia, I agreed—partly, I'm sure, because it would give me an excuse to avoid working on something else, but also because one of the stories was the work of my daughter, Jill D. Block. I didn't think I'd have anything to say, so how was I going to come up with a thousand words?*

Oh really? As it turned out, I nattered on for something like 3200 words, and while a reading might suggest that I did indeed have precious little to say, I seem to have said it at length.

Go know . . .

Fifteen years ago, I got to spend the night at Terrace Hill, the Iowa Governor's Mansion in Des Moines. I was on a book tour in aid of *The Burglar on the Prowl*, and in my experience book tours don't come with a lot of perks. You are, after all, not a rock star. You are a mere writer. You don't get to insist there be no brown M&Ms in your dressing room. You don't get any M&Ms, brown or otherwise. You don't get a dressing room. What you may get, if you're lucky, is a coffee mug or a T-shirt sporting the store's logo, for which you thank all concerned profusely. (After you've done this a time or two you learn to leave the stuff in your hotel room.)

But when I embarked on that particular book tour, Tom Vilsack was governor of Iowa, and his wife Christie was a dedicated reader and a great booster of literacy, and when she learned I'd be visiting four Iowa libraries, including one in Des Moines, she extended an invitation. I turned up in time for iced tea and conversation on the porch with her and her husband, then drove off to another library event up the road in Ames. I returned to Terrace Hill and slept the dreamless sleep of the pampered, and in the morning I got dressed and went down to the kitchen, where the wife of the governor of the state prepared my breakfast. My breakfast and hers, that is to say, and it was ham and eggs, and the eggs were perfectly acceptable, but the ham was absolutely superb. I said as much, and Christie told me it came from a particular farm in southeast Iowa, and that she'd never had better.

I was blogging every night during the tour—I can't remember what made me think this was worth doing—and I blogged about that breakfast, with particular reference to that slice of ham. (Well, I think it may have been two slices.) It was, I noted, the best ham I'd eaten since I'd been a boy on Starin Avenue in Buffalo, New York. My mother always bought hams from a Buffalo butcher named Nate Gordon, and for all I know he got them from a farm in southeastern Iowa, because they were just wonderful.

My parents were Jewish, but we belonged to a Reform temple, and I grew up a couple of generations removed from the laws of Kashruth. We observed the holidays, I attended Hebrew school to prepare for my Bar Mitzvah—but we ate ham and bacon and shellfish without a second thought.

But something occurred to me as I was sharing all this in my blog. My mother never served anything with the word *pork* attached to it. No roast pork, no pulled pork, no pork chops.

I wish I'd had a chance to ask her about this. She died in 2001, two weeks and two days after the towers came down, and there have been many things I'd have liked to ask her since then, but this would certainly have made the list. Why ham and bacon but no pork chops or pork sausage or—

It had to be the word, and it could only be an unconscious choice. We were Reform Jews, we'd no more separate milk and meat or have separate dishes for Pesach than we'd grow *payess* and strap on *tefilin* or do any of that

Orthodox *mishegos*, but we were Jews, and everyone knows Jews won't eat pork, and—

So I shared this revelation in the blog, and got an immediate response from a woman who reported the same damn thing from her own childhood. Ham, sure. Bacon, why not? Fried shrimp, oysters Rockefeller—but nothing that called itself pork.

She didn't know why either.

Over the years, I've written introductions for quite a few volumes of short stories. Some of them, like this one, have been anthologies; others were single-author collections. In each instance, I can only suppose someone thought it would be to the book's advantage to have a few words of mine start things off.

For my part, I accept these commissions more often than not. I'm seduced by the prospect of getting paid for a job of writing that will require little time and less effort. Of course it always turns out to be more work than I figured, and takes more time, but never mind. If nothing else, the task at least requires me to put aside some other and more important piece of writing, something that's probably giving me trouble and that I'm yearning for an excuse to abandon.

So I'll read the stories—well, some of them, anyway—and when the deadline looms in front of me, or overhead, or wherever it is that deadlines loom, I take a deep breath and start in. And more often than not I begin by advising the reader to skip the introduction and get on to the happier business of reading the stories.

I've even done this when I've been the anthologist. I recently delivered *The Darkling Halls of Ivy,* eighteen splendid stories set (as the title might suggest) in the world of higher education, and my foreword bears the title "Something to Skip."

Now that may be false modesty, which is the only sort I have available.

Or perhaps it's irony, as so much lately seems to be. But I suspect it's nothing more or less than plain description. Introductions are indeed something to skip.

My late friend Donald E. Westlake was apt to pin up little notes to self over his desk, and one day I spotted one that said "*No More Introductions!*" The first thought that came to me was that Don, always a genial and gracious host, had for some reason decided that he'd no longer make the rounds at a social event, introducing one guest to another. From here on in, he'd evidently decided, they could jolly well handle it themselves.

That seemed uncharacteristic, not at all consistent with the affable chap I knew, and of course it turned out that this note was to remind himself to turn down requests for introductions to collections and anthologies. They were a drain of time and energy, he explained, and diverted him from the work he felt he ought to be doing.

And so they are, and so they do, and isn't that reason enough to accept such assignments? So it seems to me, and that's why I typically take them on. So that's why I'm writing these lines, but that doesn't mean you have to read them.

And what is one to say in an introduction? That the stories are excellent? Well, perhaps they are and perhaps they are not, and you don't need me to tell you one way or the other. In the present instance, you and I could both take the merit of the stories for granted, and I could go on at some length about the two words of the title, *Jewish* and *Noir*.

I already tackled the second word in my foreword to *At Home in the Dark,* my cross-genre anthology of dark stories:

> "*Early on, it became attached to a certain type of motion picture. A French critic named Nino Frank coined the term Film*

Noir in 1946, but it took a couple of decades for the phrase to get any traction. I could tell you what does and doesn't constitute classic film noir, and natter on about its visual style with roots in German Expressionist cinematography, but you can check out Wikipedia as well as I can. (That, after all, is what I did, and how I happen to know about Nino Frank.)

"Or you can read a recent novel of mine, The Girl With the Deep Blue Eyes. *The protagonist, an ex-NYPD cop turned Florida private eye, is addicted to the cinematic genre. When he's not acting out a role in his own real-life Film Noir, he's on the couch with his feet up, watching how Hollywood used to do it.*

"That's what the French word for black is doing in the English language. It's modifying the word film, and describes a specific example thereof.

"Now though, it's all over the place."

I think that's enough about *noir.* Maybe I can write a little about Jewishness.

Here's every Jewish holiday in three sentences: (1) "They tried to kill us." (2) "We survived." (3) "Let's eat!"

While the third sentence is generally the chief reason for getting together, numbers one and two would seem to define Jewishness—and make combining it with noir almost inevitable. Because ever since Haman got sore at Mordecai, no end of people have put the subjugation and extermination of Jews at the top of their wish lists.

You may be familiar with the *Shit Happens* guide to comparative religions, a classic internet shape-shifter. Here are a few examples:

Taoism: Shit happens.
Zen Buddhism: What is the sound of shit happening?
Hare Krishna: Shit shit. Happens happens.
Scientology: Shit happens on page 152 of Dianetics *by L. Ron Hubbard*
Christian Science: Shit is in your mind.

And so on. And, tellingly:

Judaism: Why does this shit always happen to us?

So it has always been. So apparently will it always be.

Perhaps the worst result of the Holocaust, a well-bred Englishman was heard to say, was that it made anti-Semitism an untenable position.

For a while, anyway.

Shall we move on to the second precept?

(2) "We survived."

And that, it seems to me, is at least as remarkable as the fact that, again and again, they've tried to kill us. There's a line spoken by George Arliss in either *Disraeli* or *The House of Rothschild*—for an upright Episcopalian, the fellow played a lot of Jews. "We seem to be eternal," he said, and so we do.

You know, I think that's more remarkable than the persecution. For over two thousand years of Diaspora, the Jewish people have continued to exist. Hated and persecuted and scapegoated everywhere, expelled from one country after another, we have gone on living and we have gone on being Jews.

What keeps us going? What explains that Jewishness has somehow survived the destruction of the Temple and the dispersion of all of its people?

Well, who's to say? You can call it God's will, if you want, though telling me something is God's will is like saying *Because I said so* to a little kid. But here's the answer I come up with:

We continue to survive because they never stop trying to kill us.

And if I'm going to make sense out of that, I'm going to have to tell you about the wolf and the caribou.

You know what a wolf is. And you very likely know what a caribou is, too—an antlered ruminative quadruped rather like a reindeer. The chief distinction is that reindeer have been domesticated, while caribou roam the Arctic in great herds.

Wolves prey on them.

And there is a saying in that part of the world. "*The caribou feeds the wolf. The wolf keeps the caribou strong.*"

It's easy to see how the caribou is essential for the wolf's survival, but it works the other way round as well. Packs of wolves thin the caribou herd, picking soft targets, bringing down the old and the sick and the weak. That's not so great if you happen to be old or sick or weak, but it's good for the herd.

The caribou, it should be noted, cheweth the cud and parteth the hoof. Not so the wolf.

When Jews first settled in China, there were no wolves.

No anti-Semites, that is to say.

The history's a little sketchy, but the gist of it seems to be that a Jewish community was established in Kaifeng, a city on the Silk Road, well over a thousand years ago. The Chinese among whom they settled didn't know that Jews were supposed to be hated as a matter of course, and instead accepted them—with the result that intermarriage and assimilation resulted over the centuries in the essential disappearance of Kaifeng Jewry.

I could go on. I could suggest that without a Holocaust there would be no state of Israel. Yes, Theodore Herzl and Zionism. Yes, the Balfour Declaration. Yes, a small continuing Jewish presence in Palestine for generations beyond number. Yes, yes, and yes . . . but do you seriously think Israeli statehood would have come about without Auschwitz?

As I said, I could go on—but why? I'd much rather change the subject. I don't have a firm enough grip on the hem of History's garment to dazzle you with my erudition, so let me shift gears altogether and amuse you with wordplay.

Playing on words has precious little to do with noirness—*noirishkeit*? Never mind. Nor can we claim it as the particular property of the Jews. But it's certainly more fun than thinking about the Holocaust, and one thing that has struck me over the years is how much it's a matter of pure luck.

A late friend of mine, the science fiction writer Randall P. Garrett, was a high church Anglican who took the whole business seriously, though not without humor. He met regularly with his spiritual adviser, an Episcopalian canon, and their long conversations were occasionally marked by jokes which Randy told, and told well. Some of these were, if not precisely off-color, a few degrees removed from lily white, and Randy thought to ask the man if it was inappropriate to tell such jokes in that particular setting.

"Oh, not at all," the clergyman replied. "They're fine jokes. Besides, I can always use them as fodder for one of my sermons."

"It's a wise canon," said Randy, "that knows its own fodder."

Now the brilliance of such a piece of spontaneity is not something I need to point out to you. One can do no more than ponder it, and nod in admiration. But one thing that strikes me is Randy's great good fortune in having the opportunity.

His spiritual adviser could as easily have been a bishop or an archdeacon. Or a dean, a provost, or a prebendary. If he's anything other than a canon, there's nowhere to go with it. "It's a wise prebendary that knows its own fodder?" No, I don't think so.

And, of course, the canon has to say *fodder*. If he calls those off-white jokes anything else . . .

Well, you get the idea. The canon gave my friend a gift, floating one belt-high right over the middle of the plate, and Randy did the rest.

I received a similar gift some years ago on a visit to Ashland, Oregon, where my friend Hal Dresner had just about finished overseeing the building of a house. It might have been described as a chateau, and was the sort of thing God might have done if he'd had the money.

It was topped by a newly-completed tile roof, to which Hal pointed. "Can you believe," he said, "that there's thirty-two thousand pounds of ceramic tile on that roof?"

I said, "Sixteen tons, and what do you get?"

Now that's not up there with Randy's canon fodder inspiration, but it shares the element of fortuity. If the number Hal mentions is anything other than thirty-two, I don't get to quote the Merle Travis song. Look at our exchange if he'd rounded it off:

Hal: "Can you believe that there's thirty thousand pounds of tile on that roof?"

Me: "No kidding? Sure is a lot of tile."

Wonderful.

And here's another example, and it's bound up in Jewishness, as you'll see, and whether or not it touches on noir is up to you to decide.

It was in July of 1964, and I had just accepted an editorial position in Racine, Wisconsin, at Whitman Publishing, a division of Western Printing and Lithography. I was at the time an avid coin collector, and after I'd sold a couple of articles to the *Whitman Numismatic Journal*, I was invited to come edit the thing. It was the first job I'd had since leaving college for the life of a freelance writer, and it would be the last, but it served me well for the twenty months I spent there.

I went to Racine and settled into the job, while my then-wife stayed in Buffalo long enough to see to the packing and moving. Before she was to join me, a colleague invited me over for dinner. He was Neil Shafer, and he sat at the desk next to mine in Whitman's numismatic division. Neil was—and still is—an expert in the field of Philippine coinage and paper currency. He was also no longer the only Jew in the employ of Western Printing, and seemed grateful for my presence.

So I went to the Shafer home for dinner. He had married fairly recently, and his wife, Edith, was enthusiastically keeping a kosher home. It's perhaps worth noting that she had not grown up in one herself. I believe her parents were Reform Jews in Milwaukee, who found her new commitment to the dietary laws puzzling; as for Neil, while he certainly identified as Jewish, he was not at all observant.

I don't remember what we had for dinner. I'd guess lamb, but it may have been beef. (It goes without saying that it was not baked ham from a farm in southeast Iowa.)

I don't recall what the three of us talked about, either. But I do remember that we had coffee after the meal, and that Neil asked about the cake that reposed in the kitchen. Edith reminded him that the cake had been made with milk and butter, and they'd had meat during the meal, so that she couldn't serve him a piece of that cake until a specific amount of time had passed. (An hour? Two hours? Hey, I'm the last person to ask. I grew up on cheeseburgers, you'll remember. And Nate Gordon's ham.)

Neil did not welcome this news, and made his views known. And Edith stated her position, backed by the authority of rabbis all the way back to Hillel. And the conversation, peppered with no end of darlings and sweeties and honeys, did nothing to change anyone's view of the matter.

And during a pause for breath, I uttered these words: "Neil, there's something you have to realize. You can't have your cake and Edith too."

I know. And it didn't hurt a bit that Neil was irredeemably addicted to wordplay, and quite the master of it.

But consider the fortuity, will you? Had her name been anything other than Edith. Had the designated dessert been pastry or pudding or, really, anything but what it was.

"Neil, you can't have your Banana Cream Pie and Florence too."

Yeah. Right.

No, I won't apologize. Why should I? Didn't I tell you to skip the introduction?

Now it's time for the stories. *Jewish Noir 2*, a rich collection of wonderful tales wonderfully told. They're what we're here for, and they're here for you. All you have to do is turn the page.

So what are you waiting for?

HOW TO BE A WRITER WITHOUT WRITING ANYTHING

A few years ago I was commissioned to write a monthly column for Unitas, *a high-end Taiwanese literary magazine. (I am, I should say, quite the hot ticket in Taiwan, where my publishers, Faces, treat me like a rockstar.) I kept the column for two years, and most of the time I delivered a reworked version of an instructional essay on writing or, now and then, a short story.*

But once in a while I wrote something brand new for Unitas, *and here are three linked columns that ran in separate issues of the magazine. Parts One and Two later found a home at* Mystery Scene.

PART ONE: GETTING GHOSTED

When I first set my sights on writing as a profession, one clear vision energized and sustained me: wouldn't it be wonderful if I could come up with ideas and spin words into stories? And then they would grow into books with my name on them—and I would get paid for my efforts. Wouldn't it be wonderful?

And that's what happened. My imagination flowered, my words flowed, and my books and stories were published. It didn't happen overnight—though neither did it take forever. And my success, in both critical and monetary terms, was both gradual and modest.

But the books did begin to appear, on an ever-lengthening shelf. And they did have my name on them. As did the checks I received—because I was indeed getting paid for my work.

And yes, it was wonderful. Years passed, and the process continued. I wrote, and I got paid for it, and it was wonderful.

And, gradually, the vision changed.

What would truly be wonderful, it seemed to me, would be if that shelf of books with my name on them continued to grow, and if checks with my name on them continued to find their way to me.

And if this miraculously happened without my having to come up with ideas and spin them into stories. Yes, by golly, it was marvelous to get paid for writing. But wouldn't it be even better to get paid without having to write anything?

Quite the metamorphosis. Early on, the writing was everything. Oh, getting paid was important, not merely because it validated the work but because it enabled further work. So it was important—but not nearly so important as dreaming up those stories and writing them down.

So what changed? I've known for some time that Ego and Avarice are the two coursers who haul my chariot through the streets of Literature. That was true when my dream was to write and get paid for it, and it remained true when I was more taken with the idea of *not* writing . . . and getting paid for it.

If the same forces drove me, why had the dream changed course?

Well, you know, there was a certain amount of Been There Done That involved. There is a remarkable sense of accomplishment that attends the completion of one's first novel. For all the weaknesses it may possess, for all the uncertain nature of its reception, there it is—a book, spun from one's own inner self, the product of one's own thoughts and imagination, something that existed now and had not existed before.

When it's actually published, when the fruit of one's hard work has actual physical form in the shape of a bound book, that sense of accomplishment is magnified enormously—and not only in one's own mind. "Oh, you're a writer? Have you had anything published?" How satisfying to be able to say yes, and to point to that book. Its reviews may be mixed, and thin on the ground. It may never earn out its advance, let alone bring in royalties. But it's a book, and it's all yours, and you got paid for it—and that's a thrill.

And your second book is a thrill, too. You've proved you can do the impossible not once but twice. Perhaps you get better reviews the second time around. More attention, stronger sales. Perhaps not. Either way it's exhilarating.

But it's not quite the same, is it? You never get a second chance to make a first impression—or to write a first novel.

And when your new book is your twentieth? Your fiftieth? Your hundredth?

Oh, there's still a sense of accomplishment. *I did it again,* you tell yourself, and if you're voicing congratulations, you're also expressing relief. You've got the book finished, and your publisher will have it in hand before the contractual deadline—or at least not too long after it. You'll get paid—and not a moment too soon or a dollar too much, as your expenses have always managed to stay a step or two ahead of your income.

I did it again, you reiterate, and wonder to what extent this newest book is in fact a new book at all. Have you been repeating yourself, writing the same book over and over? It didn't feel that way while you were writing it, because the books certainly haven't become easier to write, as you'd think they would if you were just doing the same thing over and over again.

If anything, it seems to be getting more difficult to do what you've always done. It's harder to figure out what happens next, and sometimes you find yourself marking time in order to delay that decision. And it's harder to get the words down, harder to stay at your desk long enough to stay on schedule.

Oh, never mind. You did it again, didn't you? Another book with your name on it, another check with your name on it, another deadline met, another obligation crossed off the list.

That part still feels good. But wouldn't it be nice if you could feel this way without having to go through all that horrible business of *writing* something?

What was it the Duke of Gloucester said to historian Edward Gibbon? "Another damned thick book! Always scribble, scribble, scribble! Eh, Mr. Gibbon?"

Increasingly, writers have found themselves looking for a way to cut out the scribble-scribble-scribble, and the more successful the writer, the more inclined he is to leave that scribbling to others. Just as eager young entrepreneurs start up businesses in the hope that they'll be able to sell their entire operation to some larger corporation, so do writers work to establish themselves sufficiently as brand names that they can enlist co-writers to do the actual writing.

Perhaps the Brand Name Writer contributes an outline, which the co-writer turns into an actual novel. Perhaps the two discuss the story together and work out its details. Perhaps, when the co-writer delivers the manuscript, the BNW gives it an edit and polish.

Or perhaps the Brand Name Writer just signs off on his co-writer's work without even bothering to read it.

However the process works, it's evident it has advantages for both parties. The Brand Name Writer satisfies Ego and Avarice without having to write anything. His collaborator, who may have been having trouble getting published, or decently compensated for what he did manage to publish, now has a guaranteed income. And the readers for the most part don't seem to notice any difference between the original writer's work and the new product.

And how do I feel about the whole business?

A while ago I'd have been quick to deplore it, with no end of negative judgment on both parties to this sort of transaction. But by now I know several writers on both ends of such partnerships, and can understand their reasons for playing the game. Then too, age puts a brake on the rush to judgment. Who am I to cast aspersions, let alone stones?

At the same time, it's very clear to me that this is something I personally would not want to touch with a barge pole. My heart sinks when I contemplate putting my name on work that's not my own, even as my gorge rises at the thought of other hands mucking about in the imagined lives of my characters.

But don't be too quick to stake out a claim for me to the moral high ground. After all, what could be easier than turning down that which has never been on offer? I haven't had the kind of Brand Name Writer success that leads publishers to dream of co-writer franchises. While readers are kind enough to clamor for more books about Matthew Scudder and Bernie Rhodenbarr, and while any number of publishers would be willing, even eager, to publish the next book in either series, the prospect doesn't make them drool.

But suppose Liam Neeson's portrayal of Matthew Scudder in *A Walk Among the Tombstones* had been not merely a critical success, but had delivered big-time at the box office, selling enough tickets to get the studio to greenlight a sequel.

As it was, the film gave a big boost to Matthew Scudder in book form. But if one film had led to another, book sales would have done more than edge up. They'd have soared, and publishers would have done more than salivate. They'd have come calling, coaxing me to write another book about Matthew Scudder.

But, you know, it seems to me I've said all I have to say about the man. Maybe I could rise to the occasion, maybe the carrot and the stick would nudge Ego and Avarice into overdrive—but maybe not. All those books on the groaning shelf, all those pages ripped off the calendar . . . I'll tell you, I'm not sure I could still do it.

"Suppose we found you a co-writer, LB. Someone to do the heavy lifting, someone to get your vision onto the actual page . . ."

I'd like to think I'd turn them down. But, really, how can I possibly know for sure?

And, of course, sometime in the inevitable future it will no longer be my choice to make. As the title of the fourteenth Scudder novel reminds us, *Everybody Dies*—and, while I like to think that perhaps an exception will be made for me, I'm not counting on it.

Death, however, while it certainly slows a person down, doesn't absolutely ensure that he'll have to stop writing. Consider V. C. Andrews, who has contrived to write 78 novels since her death in 1986. (A few were at least in the planning stages when Ms. Andrews died; their completion and all the subsequent novels are the work of one Andrew Neiderman—unless he's farmed the books out to other hands in recent years, and who am I to say one way or the other?)

Robert Ludlum hasn't slowed down much since his death, and the official explanation is that he planned a batch of series for other to write under his name. Well, maybe. And Max Allan Collins has been finding no apparent end of notes and fragments and partial manuscripts by the late Mickey Spillane, which he's seen through to completion. Well, why not?

The Nero Wolfe mysteries were the absolute favorites of at least one woman, who despaired at the thought of having no new books to read after the death of Rex Stout. Her son, Robert Goldsborough, wrote a new Nero Wolfe solely for her amusement, and enough people liked it to call it to the attention of Stout's publisher, who engaged Goldsborough to continue the series. One argument advanced at the time, to get Stout's heirs to sign off on the project, was that only by bringing out new books from time to time could the originals continue to hold a sizable audience.

I'm not sure this is true, but neither can I say it's not. And it's a powerful argument isn't it? "If we don't let this fellow write more books about Grampa's characters, then Grampa's name and all his work will be forgotten, and how can we allow that to happen?"

Robert B. Parker left us a couple of years ago, and various hands have carried on various of his series, with Ace Atkins writing the Spenser books while Reed Farrel Coleman chronicles Jesse Stone. I was in the room one time when Reed was answering questions about his experience. He very much enjoyed writing the Jesse Stone books, he said, but the character he really wanted to write was Matthew Scudder.

I checked my pulse, shook my head. "Not yet," I said.

While I have a pulse, it's my hope that any books bearing my byline will in fact be exclusively my own work. After I'm gone, this sort of decision will no longer be mine to make, and I don't find myself inclined to make advance arrangements one way or the other. I'd rather have my characters follow me into the oblivion that awaits us all, but if other hands give them further life, well, I rather doubt I'll ever know one way or the other. And if the Universe should surprise me with an afterlife, I trust it'll hold more things to interest me than what's going on with some musty old books on a planet called Earth.

Some thoughts, then, on being a writer without writing. But there's another way, as I've discovered, and it involves something a little more hands-on than getting other people to write your books. One continues to be a maker of books by becoming a compiler of anthologies . . .

PART TWO: THE ANTHOLOGY GAME

When I first set my sights on writing as a profession, one clear vision energized and sustained me: wouldn't it be wonderful if I could come up with ideas and spin words into stories? And then they would grow into books with my name on them—and I would get paid for my efforts. Wouldn't it be wonderful?

Last month I talked about the dilemma of the veteran writer. (Well, this veteran writer, anyway.) Having started out with the dream of writing and getting paid for it, one ultimately dreams of *not* writing—and getting paid for it. And we had a look at the increasing practice of enlisting ghost writers or co-writers or collaborators of one sort or another, either during or after one's lifetime.

There is, happily, another way to create books and generate income without selling one's fictional children down the river. One enlists not a single co-writer but an entire table of contents thereof. Each of them contributes a story, and you take the bows as an anthologist, and Bob's your uncle.

It took me a while to get around to it. I published my own first story in 1958, and it was forty years later when I was invited to edit an anthology—and even then I didn't really edit it. I fronted it.

I was a member of the International Association of Crime Writers—still am, in fact—and someone proposed that the IACW raise some money through an anthology. Marty Greenberg offered to put the thing together, and I was asked to serve as its nominal editor.

Martin H. Greenberg was the founder of TeknoBooks, a company based in Green Bay, Wisconsin, devoted to the packaging of anthologies. He was the quintessential Mr. Anthology, generating ideas for innumerable anthologies, selling publishers on these ideas, selecting an editor for each volume, commissioning original stories and picking reprints, securing rights and permissions, and placing the result on the publisher's desk, ready for the printer.

And he did all this without needing to see his own name in print. Now and then he took a credit as editor, but more often he was happy to remain in the background. Over the years, he picked no end of short stories of mine for one anthology or another, and while I can't say either of us bought a Lear Jet with the proceeds, the transactions were always fair and amiable. Somewhere down the line I dedicated a book of my own "To Marty Greenberg and the Green Bay Packagers," probably because I was so proud of the fortuitous phrase—which I was very likely the seventy-third person to think of. Oh well.

That first anthology, published by Cumberland House as *Death Cruise*, appeared in 1999, and consisted entirely of crime stories set on the high seas. Two stories (by Agatha Christie and Richard Deming) were reprints; the rest were originals, written by IACW members for the anthology. I didn't contribute a story, but I did bat out an introduction, in which I told of my own very limited experience on cruises, and of the good fellowship I'd experienced in the IACW, and assured the reader that this collection of stories was an estimable one. I didn't single out any stories for special mention, and how could I? I don't believe I actually read any of them.

I'm sure I must have been paid something for my role in *Death Cruise*, but I never thought of the book as part of my body of work, since the only actual work I did for it was to write the introduction. Cumberland House produced a truly handsome volume with a striking cover, so the book was certainly nothing to be ashamed of, and I guess it brought in a few dollars for IACW while serving to introduce some of our European members to an American audience.

But the seed was planted, I guess. By the time *Death Cruise* was in print, Marty had suggested I come up with an idea for an anthology, and I pitched one to be called *Master's Choice*. "Each writer picks a favorite story," I explained, "and writes a page or so explaining why it's his choice."

Marty liked the idea, but wanted clarification. "A favorite story of his own? Or a favorite story by another writer?"

Now that was a question I hadn't thought to ask myself, but I didn't have to think long and hard for the answer. "Both," I said.

This time I had actual work to do. I came up with a list of writers, sent each an invitational email, nagged them gently as the deadlines approached, and sent everything to Marty so he could draw up contracts and clear rights. Berkley published the book—and, a year or so later is sequel, *Master's Choice 2.*

And Cumberland House published *Opening Shots* and *Opening Shots 2.* The premise here was simple enough, with each contributor introducing his or her own first published story. The hardest part for me was finding a way to justify including a story of my own in each volume. I'd quite properly put "You Can't Lose" in the first volume, and in the second I found room for "A Bad Night for Burglars," which missed being my first published story by something like 18 years. "After all," I wrote in my introduction, "who's editing this book?"

Other books followed. Marty came up with a series and sold Cumberland House on it: Seven anthologies, each featuring one of the seven deadly sins, each anchored by an original long story of mine and filled out with reprinted stories by other hands. Marty would round up the other stories, and his people would wrestle with permissions and contracts. All I would have to do was write the stories.

Novellas, as it turned out. I started with *Speaking of Lust,* and came up with a distinctly old-fashioned 20,000-word tale in which four aging archetypes—a soldier, a priest, a doctor, and a policeman—sit at a card table and tell stories from their experience. It was great fun to read and turned out rather well, and I brought the quartet back for *Speaking of Greed*—and that was as far as the series ever got. I *tried* to write my story for *Speaking of Wrath,* but I could never get anywhere with it.

Now and then someone asks what happened to my four garrulous card players, and all I can do is quote "The Gambler," the Kenny Rogers song. "You gotta know when to fold them," I explain.

Meanwhile, Johnny Temple of Akashic had been in touch. His Urban Noir series has been around so long and runs to so many books that it's easy to assume it's been around forever, but the fact of the matter is that it started with a book called *Brooklyn Noir*. That single volume was successful enough to launch a series, and I was invited to edit a Manhattan volume. I invited fourteen other writers to the party, and they all wrote original stories for the book. I added one of my own, "If You Can't Stand the Heat," and wrote an introduction to the volume.

It did well enough to spawn a sequel, *Manhattan Noir 2: The Classics*, consisting of reprints. I've always been uncommonly proud of the selection I managed to come up with—Edith Wharton, Stephen Crane, O. Henry, Damon Runyon, Langston Hughes, Irwin Shaw, and poems (!) by Edgar Allan Poe, Horace Gregory, and Geoffrey Bartholomew.

And then the whole business pretty much stopped. (Not the Akashic series, it's thriving, and should continue to add volumes as long as there's a geopolitical entity worthy of a turn in the noir spotlight. I've been persuaded to write stories for *Bronx Noir, Indian Country Noir,* and *Buffalo Noir*—and received benefits far beyond the pittance I was paid for the stories themselves. In "If You Can't Stand the Heat" I'd written about a charmingly homicidal young woman, and for the Bronx volume I dispatched her to Riverdale. By the time she'd scalped a hapless chap in an Indian casino in Michigan, I realized I was writing a novel in installments—and the eventual result was *Getting Off*, a very violent and intensely erotic novel published by Hard Case Crime. And my story for *Buffalo Noir*, "The Ehrengraf Settlement," helped round out a collection that was decades in the making, published by Subterranean Press as *Defender of the Innocent: The Casebook of Martin Ehrengraf*.)

But I seemed to be done with the anthology business. Oh, I put together a non-fiction collection—*Gangsters, Swindlers, Killers and Thieves*—for Oxford University Press, for which I selected the entries of assorted nogoodniks from OUP's *Dictionary of American Biography* and furnished introductions and connective tissue. And I introduced and stuck my name on *Blood on Their Hands,* a Mystery Writers of America anthology, to which I felt about as connected as I had to *Death Cruise.*

But publishers stopped being greatly interested in anthologies, and Marty Greenberg was no longer around to stir the pot; this extraordinary gentleman, who according to Wikipedia edited 1298 anthologies and commissioned over 8200 original stories, contended with glioblastoma before succumbing in 2011.

Well, some time went by, as it generally does. And I had coffee with Peter Carlaftes, who with Kat Georges runs Three Room Press, a tiny publishing operation right here in my own Greenwich Village neighborhood. Peter and Kay had put together several New York-based anthologies, reprinting a story of mine in each, and now Peter thought they might ramp up the series by having me serve as editor.

All I had to do was convince a dozen or so people to write original stories for very little money.

I can't recall why I thought this was a good ideas, but once I'd said yes I found the situation curiously liberating. Because there was so little money involved, and so little likelihood that the book would get much attention, I felt free to invite whomever I wanted. Several were writers whose short fiction I knew and admired, and I even induced Science Fiction Grandmaster Robert Silverberg to let me reprint an old story of his, in which an alien spaceship lands in Central Park. But I also invited stories from people I knew who'd never written a short story, and the results were remarkable.

Erin Mitchell, who sees to my marketing and publicity, has read more crime fiction than almost anybody, but "Old Hands" was her first attempt at actually writing anything herself—and it wound up nominated for an Anthony award. Elaine Kagan, a dear friend ever since our book tours crossed paths in Pittsburgh 20+ years ago, had published four or five well-received novels and some magazine non-fiction over the years; the story I persuaded her to write was a honey. She showed it to her daughter, Eve, who responded with an unsolicited story of her own—and when I saw it I knew it was too good to turn down.

My filmmaker friends Brian Koppelman and David Levien somehow found time to write stories. My old college roommate Peter Hochstein, who'd written novels when he wasn't turning out advertising copy, wrote his first short story for me, and found the process so energizing that he's since written several more. And so on.

The best part of "and so on" came when I recalled that my daughter Jill had shown a lot of promise as a writer back in her college days. I'd read one or two stories of hers back then, and could see she had the requisite talent for a career as a writer. But it takes more than talent, you have to want it, and she decided what she wanted was to go to law school. She did, and to good effect, and has spent the past quarter-century distinguishing herself in the world of corporate real estate law, which is probably more interesting than it sounds, but just barely.

So I surprised her with an out-of-the-blue invitation to write a story, and she surprised me by agreeing. Her story struck me as quite brilliant, but I was her father, so what did I know? I sent it to Janet Hutchings, editor of *Ellery Queen's Mystery Magazine*, and Janet bought it for their Department of First Stories.

"Now I *could* include it in *Dark City Lights* as a reprint," I said, "but—"

"But it would be better if I wrote another story. How soon do you need it?"

She delivered it in plenty of time.

Now *Dark City Lights,* given the limited distribution and promotion available to Three Rooms Press, was not going to set the world on fire. The critics who reviewed it were generous, and in addition to Erin's Anthony nomination, Parnell Hall's "The Dead Client" won a Shamus award, but the book's overall sales were unremarkable, and my own earnings, as best I can calculate, worked out to something like 42¢ an hour.

Still, I have to call the whole thing a positive experience. And it evidently rendered me receptive to an anthology idea, should one happen to arise.

And, sometime in the late spring of 2015, one did.

Who knows where ideas come from? I don't, and what difference does it make? It's enough of a wonder that they turn up at all.

This one, as best I recall, was simply *there.* I was sitting at my computer one afternoon, and it would be nice to say I was thinking about an Edward Hopper painting, or about the satisfaction of having edited *Dark City Lights,* and I suppose either could be possible. But all I know is that my mind filled with the notion of an anthology consisting of stories drawn from Hopper's paintings.

A handsome and well-produced book, I realized, is what it would have to be. With each story illustrated by a high-quality reproduction of the painting that had inspired it. And with a full complement of A-list writers who would not only produce superb stories but whose name value would be capable of raising the book's profile enough to make it worth a publisher's substantial investment.

I was excited enough by the idea to get right to work on it, and within a couple of hours I'd drawn up a dream list of writers and drafted a letter of invitation. Somewhere along the line a title came to mind: *In Sunlight or in Shadow.*

I sent out invitations, and just about everybody said yes. Joyce Carol Oates, Lee Child, Jeffery Deaver, Joe Lansdale, Craig Ferguson, Megan Abbott, Stephen King, Michael Connelly. And more—some from *Dark City Lights* (Warren Moore, Jonathan Santlofer) and otherS whose work I knew and admired (Nicholas Christopher, Robert Olen Butler, Kristine Kathryn

Rusch, Justin Scott). I sought out and sat down with Gail Levin, Hopper's distinguished biographer, hoping she might furnish an introduction; she said she'd rather try a short story, and delivered a fine one.

One Jill D. Block wrote "The Story of Caroline," her third published story. And I looked at Hopper's painting of a woman sitting at a table in a cafeteria, and wrote "Autumn at the Automat."

So filling the table of contents was relatively easy, because Hopper's work triggered a remarkable response in almost every writer who heard about the idea. Finding a publisher was a little more difficult, because the industry's not all that enthusiastic about anthologies these days. But my agent believed in the project as much as I did, and he found the perfect home for it in Pegasus Books, and we were off and running.

In Sunlight or in Shadow: Stories Inspired by the Paintings of Edward Hopper was published in early December, just about a year and a half after I got the idea for it. The book got a great deal of advance publicity, and the reviewers gave it their full attention. It wound up on most lists of the season's top gift books, and some readers reported difficulty in getting their orders filled. You'd have thought it was a Cabbage Patch Doll, or some other toy on the top of every kid's Christmas list.

I was just talking to my agent earlier today, and he said he couldn't recall any book of mine that got as much play in the media. I'd made the same observation myself.

Early on, before the book made landfall at Pegasus, it looked as though I might have trouble covering my costs. In order to make sure the project got off the ground, I'd committed to paying the writers for their stories, and I'd have to pay permission fees for the art, and hire someone to handle that part of the business.

I wasn't sure where the money for all of that was going to come from. My agent nailed down a couple of foreign sales, and along with the Pegasus advance I could see that I wouldn't actually lose money, but would I match the 42¢ an hour I'd netted from *Dark City Lights?*

It looks as though I will. The book's scheduled for publication in Italy, Germany, Korea, China, Russia, Czech Republic, Bulgaria and Taiwan, with further sales pending elsewhere. It won't make me rich, anthologies never make anybody rich, but it's made me pleased and proud, and that's good enough.

And it also moved me to come up with a sequel.

I couldn't think of another artist who could equal Edward Hopper in evoking such a powerful response in writers and readers alike. But if a single painter couldn't do so, suppose each writer picked a different painter?

Thus *Alive in Shape and Color*—stories inspired by the paintings of Norman Rockwell and Salvador Dali and Hokusai and Balthus and Rene Magritte and Pablo Picasso and Vincent Van Gogh and . . . well, the list goes on.

Pegasus leapt at it; they'll be publishing the book in December of 2017, a year after *In Sunlight or in Shadow*. And the writers were quick to hop on board, with just about everyone from the first book eager to re-up for the second. A dozen of them have delivered their stories, and trust me: they're outstanding.

Isn't it remarkable what a writer will do to keep from having to write anything himself?

PART THREE: HANGING IT UP

When I first set my sights on writing as a profession, one clear vision energized and sustained me: wouldn't it be wonderful if I could come up with ideas and spin words into stories? And then they would grow into books with my name on them—and I would get paid for my efforts. Wouldn't it be wonderful?

Good morning, boys and girls.

Good morning, sir.

In some of our recent meetings we addressed the question of how to be a member of the writing profession without actually having to write anything. There were, as I recall, two ways we found. Can any of you remember what they were? Yes, Arnold?

One was the anthology game, sir. You dream up a premise for a collection of stories, find other writers to turn out the actual stories, write a few words of introduction, and sit back while the money rolls in.

Rolls may not be the word we're looking for here, Arnold. It's more of a trickle. But that's the essence of it, and I've done it a dozen times over the years, most recently with *In Sunlight or in Shadow: Stories Inspired by the Paintings of Edward Hopper.*

Hasn't that just been published in Taiwan, sir?

It has, Rachel. in a very attractive edition from Faces.

You must be very proud, sir.

I am, and thank you. Do you happen to recall the other way we discussed to be a writer without writing anything?

You get other people to write whole books and put your name on them. They're co-writers or ghost writers, whatever you want to call them, and they write books with your series characters in them, or sequels to books of yours, or books from ideas you thought up. They do all the work and you pay them as little as you can get away with.

It sounds like a grim business, doesn't it? And it's one I've managed to avoid thus far, but can one ever know for certain what the future may hold?

No, sir. That's what makes it the future. As opposed, say, to the present or the past.

Mine was a rhetorical question, Arnold, but it's still nice of you to provide an answer. But let's move on, shall we? Today it's my pleasure to report on a third way to be a writer without writing anything, and it may be the simplest one of all.

You stop writing.

*   *   *

Writers don't retire.

Or at least that's what the world prefers to believe. It's curious, because in just about any other line of work the presumption exists that, sooner or later, enough is enough. Whatever we spend our lives doing, there's a point where we're entitled to stop.

More often than not, we don't even have a choice in the matter. In the corporate world, there's almost always a mandatory retirement age. In academia, there's a similar mark on the calendar, after which one becomes a professor emeritus, with all the dignity (and free time) attendant to the designation.

But for writers (and to an extent all in the arts) the calendar exists only to call one's attention to deadlines and delivery dates. "Of making many books there is no end," wrote the author of *Ecclesiastes*, and every writers since has has to decide whether the statement is a blessing or a curse.

A few years ago, Philip Roth announced that he did not intend to write any more novels. The declaration seemed reasonable enough. The man was closing in on his eightieth year, and he'd been writing abundantly and to great acclaim since college. He's received every imaginable award aside from the elusive Nobel Prize, which the Swedes had apparently decided he was never going to get. Awards aside, he'd produced a towering body of work, and he felt he was done.

What I found most remarkable was not Roth's decision, clearly a private matter, but the public response to it. It was astonishing how many individuals had an opinion to offer, one they felt compelled to share with the world.

One contingent was overwhelmed with empathetic sadness. "Alas, poor Philip Roth! How tragic for him! How awful that he wasn't going to be able to write more books!" Their hearts went out to him, secure in the presumption that Roth himself would surely wish it otherwise, that he'd be far happier and feel ever more fulfilled if he could keep on putting in long hours and writing more books until his dying day.

I found this lot misguided, but too earnest to be held in contempt. The others—and there were quite a few of them, and they were fiercely vocal—were furious with Roth. How dare he stop writing! Where did he get off, withholding his unwritten thoughts and unrealized books from the world? What nerve! Get back to work, Philip!

Like most comments, I suspect these reactions tell us rather more about their authors than they do about Mr. Roth. But they underscore a home truth: writers don't get to retire. Their vocation is a calling to which they are forever compelled to respond.

HOW WE'VE CHANGED

I wrote this for the December 1994 issue of American Heritage,
*in response to the question: "What do you think is the most
important, or interesting, or overlooked way in which America
has changed since 1954, and why? And what does this change
say about us as a people?"*

From my own self-centered perspective, the most astonishing change in
America over the past forty years is that I have somehow been transformed
from a boy of sixteen to a man of fifty-six. I find this astonishing, and I don't
know how to account for it.

When I look at the Bigger Picture, two remarkable changes suggest
themselves to me, and I have the sense that they are somehow related. First,
the regionalism that was such a defining aspect of this country has been
eroded beyond measure. When you drove across America in 1954, bouncing along on bad roads, risking ptomaine in dubious diners, holing up nights
in roadside cabins and tourist courts, you were rewarded with a constant
change of scene that amounted to more than a change of landscape. There
were no chain restaurants, no franchised muffler-repair shops, and even the
brands of beer and gasoline were apt to change when you crossed a couple
of state lines,

Nowadays you take the Eisenhower administration's most enduring
legacy, the interstate highway system, and eat at Burger Kings and sleep in

Days Inns, and when the scenery palls, you duck into a mall, walk past thirty franchised shops, and catch a movie at the fourplex theater. Even the local accents have lost their edge, weathered away by forty more years of national television. We have become more nearly a single nation than we used to be.

And at the same time, the complexion of the nation is infinitely more varied than it was forty years ago. America was people by persons of Northern European stock. Most had been here for many generations. Immigration had slowed to a trickle, and the more recent arrivals were also European—Irish and Italians and Greeks and Armenians, and refugees from what we were still calling war-torn Europe. There were fewer blacks, and they were far less visible, found mostly in the largest Northern cities and the rural south. There were a few Mexicans in the Southwest, a handful of French Canadians in New England.

And now? Nearly a third of the population of my own city, New York, is foreign-born, arriving in the same numbers they were a hundred years ago. And the new immigrants stream in from every continent but Antarctica. You see it most vividly on both coasts, but it's just as true in the heartland, where it's more apt to surprise you—the Gujarati family operating a motel in rural Mississippi, the cluster of Vietnamese restaurants in Denver, the Hmong craftsmen in Minnesota and Wisconsin.

All changed, changed utterly. Or, in another light, not changed at all. America has spent the past forty years evolving, becoming more completely what it has indeed been from its beginnings. It has taken one more step (or a series of steps, or a glide) in that ceaseless process called Self-Realization.

Even as you and I . . .

Oh my. That was what, twenty-five years ago? We seem to have gone on changing, and in ways that resonate oddly with my 1994 observations . . .

HUNTING BUFFALO

Okay, let's start off with a big one, a major triumph. February 27, 1989. We spent the previous night in a Best Western in Durant, Oklahoma. Now, after a quick breakfast, we're packed and on our way. This is southeast Oklahoma, just a few miles north of the Red River and the Texas border, and we head northeast on U.S. 69 and U.S. 75 for thirty-two miles to Atoka, then cut east on State 3 for another thirty miles. At Antlers we pick up U.S. 271, and we're going northeast again. It's a pretty drive on 271, but it figured to be; the road has a dotted line next to it on the map, Rand McNally's indication of scenic beauty. We pass through Finley and Snow and Clayton, and then something makes me abandon 271 and head due north on Route 2.

"I think this'll be more scenic," I say. "We get to cross Sardis Lake this way, and we'll be going through Yanush."

"Sounds good," Lynne says.

"Of course we'll be missing Tuskahoma and Albion, but we'll be hooking back into 271 in about twenty miles anyway, at Talihina. The road less traveled and all that."

"You're the pathfinder," she says.

We proceed about half a dozen miles on 2, across the lake and through the town of Yanush. A little ways outside Yanush Lynne spots a sign on a small frame-wood building, and we go back and look at it. BUFFALO VALLEY HEAD START PROGRAM, it says. Something like that.

"Some kind of administrative district," I tell her. "Maybe there's a stream in the area called Buffalo Creek. You throw a handful of stones over your shoulder in this part of the country, one of 'em's odds-on to splash in something called Buffalo Creek."

A couple of miles farther we head east again, on Route 1. This will run us right into Talihina and 271, but before it does, we come round a bend and come upon a batch of houses. Some of them have signs, and all the signs say BUFFALO VALLEY.

It wasn't just a school district. It's a community, no question about it. I don't know what you'd call it, a hamlet, a wide place in the road, but it is definitely a community. It even has a population, for God's sake.

That hasn't always been the case. Some of our best Buffalos have been deserts compared with this place, and few have been so abundantly supplied with photo opportunities. Buffalo Valley clearly exists, and it has people living in it, and it even has signage to tell the world what it is.

"Where's the camera?" I want to know. "Where are our Buffalo shirts?"

"Somewhere in back. I didn't think we were going to need them today."

"Neither did I. Buffalo Valley, Oklahoma! It's not on any of the maps. It wasn't in the industrial-strength atlas. We weren't even looking for it, we just wandered off on a back road, and . . . and—"

"And here it is." Her eyes are shining. She has never looked more beautiful. "It's as if we were led here," she says.

"I know."

"It's—"

"I know."

Wordless, we locate and put on our Buffalo T-shirts. Lynne grabs the camera, and we pile out of the car. I strike a pose in front of a sign. COLLINS BAR-C RANCH, it says. BUFFALO VALLEY OK.

Lynne snaps a picture. Now it's her turn, and I hurry her across the road. There's a white house set back a hundred yards or so, but out at the road's edge is one of those large signboards they have at service stations that usually proclaim special rates on brake jobs. But this sign announces BUFFALO VALLEY TAX SERVICE.

Where better to pose a retired accountant? Lynne stations herself beside it and smiles hugely, and I take her picture.

In no time at all we're back in the car, and in not much more time Buffalo Valley is a speck in the rearview mirror. For miles, all through the day, all the way into Arkansas and on to Hot Springs, we keep babbling at each other.

"It's really amazing. I mean, it's like it was a gift."

"I know. We weren't even looking for it—"

"Because who knew it was there to look for? According to the maps, there's only one Buffalo in Oklahoma, and we hit it last year."

"In Harper County, and then last month we picked up the one in McCurtain County, which isn't on any map, but I found it in the marketing atlas in the library."

"The industrial-strength atlas."

"Right. So who thought there would be a third Buffalo? Buffalo Valley! I think it's our first Buffalo Valley."

"Is it? I think you're right. What is it, our twenty-sixth Buffalo? I want to note it on the back of the Polaroids."

"Put down Latimer County. Twenty-six Buffalos. That's got to be a record."

"No question."

"I mean, we're getting good at this, don't you think? When you can just drive right into an unrecorded Buffalo without even trying—"

"You're right. Pretty soon we'll be able to find 'em in our sleep."

I can explain. I spent June 1987 at a writers' colony in Virginia, working on a novel called *Random Walk*. The book chronicled a group of people walking across America, and there was a lot of geography in it. Throughout the month, when I wasn't actually typing, I was most often studying a map.

One thing I noticed: There were a lot more Buffalos than I'd suspected.

Growing up in Buffalo, New York, I'd always known it wasn't the only one of its species. There was a Buffalo, Wyoming. I knew that, and I knew there were a couple of others, although I wasn't too clear on where they were. Now, looking with purpose in the index of my Rand McNally Road Atlas,

I found there were Buffalos as well in Iowa, Kansas, Kentucky, Minnesota, Missouri, North Dakota, Ohio, Oklahoma, South Carolina, South Dakota, Texas, West Virginia, and Wisconsin. There were three Buffalo counties, in Nebraska, South Dakota, and Wisconsin, and three towns with Buffalo as part of their title—Buffalo Grove, Illinois; Buffalo Center, Iowa; and Buffalo Lake, Minnesota.

Eighteen towns named Buffalo!

It soon developed, though, that I had merely scratched the surface. Several scenes in *Random Walk* are set in Texas, and I was estimating how long it would take my serial-killer character to drive from Wichita Falls to Abilene, and what route he ought to take, when I noticed the town of Buffalo Springs a little ways southeast of Wichita Falls. I was still light-headed from this discovery when I spotted Buffalo Gap just fourteen miles south of Abilene.

The index, then, was not the last word on Buffalos. They were apt to hide in plain sight, right smack in the middle of a map. I went through the atlas page by page, state by state. I stared long and hard at every map, like an astronomer scanning the skies in a search for new stars.

Later that summer I was booked to work two writers' conferences, one in Yellow Springs, Ohio, the other in Muncie, Indiana. The two were separated by a scant hundred miles, but they were scheduled three weeks apart. Lynne and I rose to the occasion, taking three weeks to drive from Yellow Springs to Muncie, proceeding first to Buffalo, New York, then cutting across Ontario to Detroit, then rambling up through Michigan's Upper Peninsula and down through Wisconsin and, oh, here and there.

After the Muncie conference we took another week getting back to Florida. For a while we had been thinking about leaving Florida, where we had been living for two years after many years as New Yorkers. We didn't want to stay in Florida, but neither did we know where we wanted to live next.

"Maybe we don't have to live anyplace," I said. "We could just live on the road. We've been living out of this car for the past month. It hasn't been so bad, has it?"

"Where would we go?"

"I don't know, but there's a pretty big country out there, and we've got friends scattered all over it. We could just go anywhere." We fell silent for a few moments. "You know," I said, "there are twenty-five Buffalos."

"That many?"

"At last count. There may be more. Scattered all over the country."

"Like our friends."

"Twenty-five or more. I think we should go to some of them."

Lynne thought for a moment, then shook her head. "I think we should go to all of them," she said.

Buffalo, Alabama, is on the map. It's in east-central Alabama, three miles north of Lafayette and not far from the Georgia border.

It was our third day out of Florida when we hit Buffalo, Alabama. It was to be our first Buffalo—we weren't counting Buffalo, New York; we wouldn't count it until we bagged it in the course of our travels—so the anticipation was enormous. We had spent the previous night in Eufaula, a charming antebellum town, and we drove up to Buffalo, skirting Phenix City and passing through Opelika. North of Lafayette we kept watching for highway-department markers. Every town in Alabama has a green sign at its limits, stating its name and population.

Not Buffalo. Our first Buffalo had been delisted. It was still on the map, but the highway department had taken it off the books. We would have missed it altogether but for a sign hand-painted in irregular white capitals on the gray stucco wall of an out-of-business gas station. BUFFALO ALA., it announced. It looked like subway graffiti, only not as neat.

Half a mile farther on we came to Jack Tomlinson's general store. Just beyond it stood a two-acre lot with nothing in it. A large and forceful sign proclaimed the property a private club and assured us that trespassing was strictly forbidden.

"What's that?" I wondered. "How can that be a club, and who would want to trespass there, and why would anybody else want them not to, and what the hell is the point of that sign?"

"That's to keep the Jews out," Lynne explained.

We didn't ask Jack Tomlinson about the private club— maybe it was a secret society, maybe you're not supposed to talk about these things—but we did learn something about the town. It had originally been called Buffalo Wallow, he advised us, because there was a place over yonder where you couldn't get anything to grow, and the conjecture was that this was because buffalo used to wallow there. The town itself had dwindled when the railroad stopped providing service north of Lafayette.

We put on our Buffalo shirts. We took pictures—with Jack in front of his store, and by ourselves in front of the Buffalo sign.

Our first Buffalo!

Buffalo, Mississippi, was almost as much of a surprise as Buffalo Valley, Oklahoma. It did not just fall into our laps, however, or we into it. It, too, was given to us, but we had to do a little work for it.

We were in Mobile, to visit Lynne's mother, but it turned out she had gone off on her own to visit friends in Lucedale, Mississippi. There was something on television that evening that I found irresistible, or at any rate less resistible than a visit to my mother-in-law. Lynne felt restless enough to go to Lucedale alone. I wished her Godspeed and turned on the TV and put my feet up.

She came back the next morning bursting with news. Alone in the car on the way back and starved for companionship, she'd put on the CB radio. In among the bursts of static she'd heard two truckers jawing about something or other, and one of them mentioned Buffalo, Mississippi. She cut in with a breaker asking for information on that very place, and before their signal faded altogether, one of them managed to say that he wasn't actually sure, but he thought there was a place called Buffalo near McLean or McLain or McClayne or something, she wasn't sure just what.

McLain, Mississippi, is on the road from Mobile to Hattiesburg and wasn't much out of our way, since I'd been planning to drive up to Meridian so that we could check out the Jimmie Rodgers Museum. (It's housed in an old railway building, a fitting memorial to the Singing Brakeman, and I'd have to say it's well worth a visit: pictures of Jimmie, drafts of songs, and tapes for sale you can't get elsewhere.)

A lady at a gas station in McLain directed us to Buffalo. We didn't have to go more than a few miles. There were no official signs, but we could tell when we were there. The woods were posted against trespass by the Buffalo Hunt Club, and there was also the Buffalo Baptist Church and a vast graveyard that called itself the Buffalo Cemetery, Inc.

"This one's not on any of the maps," I told Lynne after I'd taken her picture in front of the big old boneyard. "Or in any of the atlases."

"Well, I can see why," she said. "Our first Buffalo isn't a town any more, and our second Buffalo has a negative population. The only people who live here are dead."

Some people, informed of our pursuit of the wily Buffalo, just don't get it. If they're not nonplussed, neither are they plussed.

When pressed, I am apt to explain that the Buffalo hunt is a matchless vehicle for serendipity. Chasing a Buffalo, one finds something unsought but by no means unappreciated.

In June 1988, for example, we were heading east after having spent a month in Sedona, Arizona. We drove through Colorado and into Kansas, passed a night in Garden City, then headed south, detouring to have a run at Buffalo, Oklahoma—the large one, in Harper County, at the eastern end of the Oklahoma panhandle. En route to it, we stopped for a look at a private museum in the house where the Dalton Boys holed up. There's an underground tunnel from the house to the barn. Once a posse surrounded the house, and the Daltons scuttled through the tunnel, emerged in the barn, got on their horses, hooted at the lawmen, and rode off.

After logging our sixth Buffalo, we proceeded eastward across northern Oklahoma. We were going to be very near Bartlesville, so we stopped at Woolaroc, the museum and wild-animal preserve established by the founder of Phillips Petroleum. We could have spent several days looking at his collections of Western art and Plains Indian artifacts—they're that good and that well displayed—but we wanted to get to Buffalo, Kansas, before nightfall.

We had time, though, for a stop at Coffeyville, Kansas, where there was a second Dalton Boys museum. This one was housed in one of the banks that they'd tried to rob and where they met their Waterloo. Emmett Dalton, youngest of the gang, was the sole survivor of the raid. He took a load of buckshot in the back and was not expected to live, but he pulled through, got out of prison in 1907, went to Hollywood, wrote his memoirs, appeared in films, became a screenwriter, and then made his fortune in Los Angeles real estate. (I'm not making this up.)

Now if you were to set out to visit the two Dalton museums, or even Woolaroc, you'd very likely have a good time. But it's just not the same as coming upon them while looking for something else altogether. You have to take time to smell the flowers, certainly, but the whole point of your life can't be sniffing around flower beds. The time you take to smell the flowers has to be taken from something else.

My friend Don Westlake understood immediately. "It gives the illusion of direction and purpose to something that has neither," he observed. "It makes it possible to decide whether to turn left or right at an intersection, and you don't even have to flip a coin. And there's something else."

"There is?"

"Yes," he said. "The name of the town is very important. It's the fact that it's Buffalo you're going to that makes a difference. I mean, you could do the same thing with Springfields, but who would want to?"

The more Buffalos you find, the more other Buffalos you find out about.

By the time we left Florida, in February 1988, our list of huntable Buffalos ran to around forty. As I write these lines, we have managed to visit fifty-one Buffalos—and we have about two dozen to go. Not only have we found Buffalos we didn't know about, but we have kept finding out about Buffalos we didn't know about.

I feel like one of those physicists looking for smaller and smaller particles. The mere fact of our search must be creating them. Microscopic Buffalos, smaller than quarks and twice as crafty, are sprouting all over the landscape.

Every once in a while we've been able to rule one out. The atlas of a 1911 edition of the Britannica supplied Buffalo Meadows, Nevada, situated due north of Reno in Washoe County. More recent maps don't show it, and a visit to the public library in Reno cleared things up. Buffalo Meadows had existed, all right; but then the railroad went somewhere else, and in 1913 the town ceased to exist.

Of course, there might still be a community there, a couple of tumbledown houses. Maybe we ought to drive through, on the rather uncertain dirt road that wanders in that direction. If nothing else, we ought to be able to log a Ghost Buffalo. It wasn't a drive we much wanted to make this time, but I suspect we'll get there sooner or later.

Tentatively, though, we've crossed it off our list. Same goes for Buffalo Gap, Texas, the one in Travis County. We've already been to the Buffalo Gap south of Abilene. As a matter of fact, we've been there twice because we liked it so much the first time. We found a great restaurant there, Judy's

Gathering Place, run by Judy Laughter Nalda, and decided that either she or her restaurant alone would be worth a detour of several hundred miles. But that's in Taylor County. In fact, it was once the seat of Taylor County, until the railroad (does a subtle pattern begin to emerge?) passed fourteen miles north of Buffalo Gap, to the great detriment of that town and the great advantage of the new town of Abilene. The County Commission had to vote to transfer the county records and all to the new county seat, Abilene, and the commissioners dead-locked, 2 to 2, and the chairman cast the deciding vote for Abilene. When he got home, he found that somebody had murdered all his chickens.

In Buffalo, Missouri, we opened a bank account. We might have done this earlier, but it's a rare Buffalo that has a bank in it. Our eighth Buffalo had a perfectly nice bank, and a perfectly nice woman helped us open a savings account with an initial deposit of twenty dollars. When she found out about our Buffalo hunt, she got into the spirit of the thing right away and scurried around, presenting us with every promotional item the bank had handed out in the past dozen years. We drove off with two Buffalo Bank caps, a Buffalo Bank outdoor thermometer, several embossed pencils, and a Buffalo Bank plastic fly swatter.

Buffaloville, Indiana, is deep in southwest Indiana, midway between Santa Claus and Lincoln City, site of the Lincoln Boyhood National Memorial, maintained by the National Park Service. We spent a couple of hours at the memorial, then pushed on to Buffaloville. A highway marker pointed the way from three miles off, but when you got there it was hard to tell you were there. No signs, no business establishments, just a long-abandoned gas station and a dozen or so scattered houses. We took a picture in front of the gas station, not one of our choicer photo ops. Three girls, probably eleven or twelve years old, came to see what we were up to. We asked them what they could tell us about Buffaloville.

"This is it," they said.

Did they like it here?

No, it was terrible, they said. They were all from elsewhere and would have preferred to be anywhere else. There was nothing to do and no one to do it with, they reported, and the local people were terribly prejudiced. Once a black kid had come to town for some sort of school athletic event, and they'd run him straight out of town.

Lynne gave each girl a Buffalo Bank pencil, and we got in the car and headed for Santa Claus.

Why were buffalo wallowing in Alabama? And what were others of their ilk doing in South and North Carolina, in Pennsylvania and Kentucky and Maryland and West Virginia? There are seven, possibly eight, Buffalos in Pennsylvania; we've been to two of them. There are ten of the beasts in Virginia. Ten! In Virginia! I always thought of the bison as a Western animal, thundering across the plains, supporting the whole culture of the Plains Indians. There are, to be sure, Buffalo place-names scattered throughout the plains states, but why are there just as many in the East?

"If the fool will persist in his folly," Blake wrote, "he will become wise." I don't know about that, but if you persist in anything long enough, you wind up learning something. There were two strains or subspecies of the buffalo, or American bison: the plains buffalo and the wood or mountain buffalo. Thus, much of the East was full of the critters, and it didn't take the organized slaughter of the plains buffalo hunters to root them out. There seems to have been a universal human response to the beast. When a man saw one, all he wanted to do was kill it.

The Indians were no less savage. They'd doubtless have exterminated the species themselves if they'd had the technology. As it was, their hunting method in suitable terrain consisted of cornering a whole herd and stampeding them over an obliging cliff, slaughtering them to the last buffalo.

Growing up in Buffalo, New York, I was given to understand early on that the city was not named after the animal and that no bison had ever been anywhere near the area until the local zoo acquired a brace of them. The name of the city, I was given to understand, was a corruption of the French *beau fleuve*, "beautiful river." Presumably some English settlers ran into some French trappers and asked them where they were, and the French thought the question related to the Niagara River and responded accordingly.

You know something? I don't believe a word of it. I don't think a Frenchman would call the spot *beau fleuve* in the first place, and I don't think an English colonist would hear *beau fleuve* and turn it into Buffalo.

When Buffalo was first settled, there was another town a few miles distant called Black Rock, which Buffalo later grew to absorb. I think Black Rock got its name from the presence of a rock in the neighborhood, and a dark rock at that. And I likewise believe that Buffalo got named after a buffalo. Someone either saw one hanging around, not a far-fetched notion, or thought he saw one, or saw something that looked like one, or something.

There's a place in Arkansas named Toad Suck. I haven't been there, not yet, and I don't know how it got its name, but don't expect me to believe that toads didn't have something to do with it. I won't accept that it was named for an itinerant Rhinelander named Taussig or that there was a plague of tussock moths in the area. There's a toad at the bottom of this one. I'm fairly sure of it.

I should probably say something about our T-shirts. They appear in photo after photo. Going through our album, you get the impression that these two weirdos have worn the same outfit all over the country. Actually we put them on only to get our pictures taken, and we take pictures only when we come to a Buffalo. We've been to national parks and natural wonders all over the place, and the only pictures we've taken are these crummy Polaroids of each other standing in front of churches and cemeteries and grocery stores and road signs.

The shirts are made by a firm called New Buffalo Graphics, located on Elmwood Avenue in Buffalo, New York. It makes twelve or more different designs, and we own three of them. One shows a road sign with a buffalo on it and bears the legend BFLO-XING. Another, dopily surrealistic, shows a reinterpreted Camel cigarette pack, with a bison replacing the familiar humped quadruped and a couple of clarinets sticking up from the opened pack. BUFFALO, the legend reads, JAZZ & GEOGRAPHY BLEND CLARI-NETS. If you can sort of sense what they're getting at, don't drive or operate machinery. Our favorite shirt simply shows a noble bison surrounded by the best municipal motto I've ever read. BUFFALO, it says, CITY OF NO ILLU-SIONS.

Where will it all end? It's beginning to look as though it won't. We've been doing this for fifteen months, and I suspect we'll keep at it for another year before we latch on to a house or apartment somewhere and settle down. We'll be spending this summer in the northern plains and the Pacific Northwest. There aren't any Buffalos in Washington or Oregon, but there's a strong herd in Montana and the Dakotas. By September we'll be in the Southeast, trying to round up some of the Virginia Buffalos. After that, well, it's hard to say.

But there's no way we're going to bag all of the outstanding Buffalos within the next twelve months. I doubt we'll get up to Buffalo Center, Alaska, or Buffalo Narrows, Saskatchewan, and Buffalo Springs, Kenya, would seem to be out of the question. (Once, I shouldn't wonder, it was a hot prospect for selection as the capital, but then they ran the railroad through Nairobi instead . . .)

For an ostensibly endangered species, the Buffalo is a resourceful beast. New specimens keep turning up. Just the other day I learned of the existence of a second Buffalo in New York State. It's called Buffalo Corners, and it's in Wyoming County near Letchworth State Park, not a hundred miles from the City of No Illusions itself.

I don't think we're going to run out of Buffalos or of the urge to hunt them. What began as a lark is starting to look like a lifelong commitment. As long as we can get gas for the car and film for the camera, we'll never really settle down. It's no longer a matter of choice. It's an imperative. When you hunt the Buffalo, you have to let the chips fall where they may.

There you have it, the chronicle of what could arguably qualify as an obsession. When American Heritage *ran it in 1990, they illustrated it with photos of our Polaroids, and listed all of the Buffalos in our virtual trophy case.*

And here, thirty years later, is an updated list:

1. *Buffalo, New York – I arrived in The Big Bison on 6.24.1938. Lynne's first visit would have been sometime in the spring of 1983.*
2. *Buffalo, Alabama – 2.4.1988*
3. *Buffalo, Mississippi – 2.8*
4. *Buffalo, Texas – 2.12*
5. *Buffalo Gap, Texas – 2.13*
6. *Buffalo Creek, Colorado – 2.28*
7. *Buffalo, Oklahoma – 6.8 (Harper County)*
8. *Buffalo, Kansas – 6.9*
9. *Buffalo, Missouri – 6.10*
10. *Buffaloville, Indiana – 6.12*
11. *Buffalo, Ohio – 8.4*
12. *Buffalo, Indiana – 8.5*
13. *Buffalo, Illinois – 8.5*
14. *Buffalo Hart, Illinois – 8.5*
15. *Buffalo Prairie, Illinois – 8.5*
16. *Buffalo, Iowa – 8.8*

17. *Buffalo Center, Iowa – 8.10*

18. *Buffalo Grove, Illinois – 8.11*

19. *New Buffalo, Michigan – 8.12*

20. *Forks of Buffalo, Virginia – 9.30*

21. *Buffalo, Tennessee – 10.1 (Humphreys County)*

22. *Buffalo, Oklahoma – 1.7.1989 (McCurtain County)*

23. *Buffalo Hill, California – 1.?*

24. *Buffalo Springs, Texas – 2.26*

25. *Buffalo Valley, Oklahoma – 2.27*

26. *Buffalo City, Arkansas – 3.3*

27. *Buffalo Valley, Tennessee- 3.4*

28. *Buffalo, Tennessee – 3.4 (Scott County)*

29. *Buffalo Springs, Tennessee – 3.5*

30. *Buffalo, North Carolina – 3.5*

31. *Buffalo Cove, North Carolina – 3.6*

32. *Buffalo Ridge, Virginia – 3.6*

33. *New Buffalo, Pennsylvania – 3.10*

34. *Buffalo Springs, Pennsylvania – 3.11*

35. *Buffalo Crossroads, Pennsylvania – 3.15*

36. *Buffalo Corners, New York – 3.16*

37. *Buffalo Hill Village, New York – 3.16*

38. *Buffalo, Wisconsin – 5.21*

39. *Buffalo City, Wisconsin – 5.22*

40. *Buffalo, Minnesota – 5.25*

41. *Buffalo Lake, Minnesota – 5.25*

42. *Buffalo Trading Post, South Dakota – 5.26*

43. *Buffalo Ridge, South Dakota – 5.26*

44. *Buffalo Springs, North Dakota – 5.29*

45. *Buffalo, South Dakota – 5.29*

46. *Buffalo Gap, South Dakota – 6.4*

47. *Buffalo, Wyoming – 6.6*

48. *Buffalo, Montana – 6.16*

49. *Buffalo, Alberta, Canada – 7.10*
50. *Buffalo Gap, Saskatchewan, Canada – 7.10*
51. *Buffalo, North Dakota – 7.12*
52. *Buffalo, Pennsylvania – 7.17*
53. *Buffalo Mills, Pennsylvania – 8.18 (Bedford County)*
54. *Buffalo Gap, Virginia – 8.19*
55. *Buffalo Station, Virginia – 8.20*
56. *Buffalo Hill, Virginia – 10.1*
57. *Buffalo Junction, Virginia – 10.2*
58. *Buffalo Springs,Virginia – 10.2*
59. *Buffalo Forge, Virginia – 8.20.1990*
60. *Buffalo Bridge, Pennsylvania – 11.23.1991*
61. *Buffalo Run, Pennsylvania – 11.23*
62. *Buffalo Creek, Pennsylvania – 11.24*
63. *Buffalo Mills, Pennsylvania – 11.24 (Armstrong County)*
64. *North Buffalo, Pennsylvania – 11.24*
65. *Buffalo, Nebraska – 6.2.1992*
66. *Buffalo Grove, Nebraska – 6.2.1992*
67. *Buffalo, Maine – 6.23, 1993*
68. *Buffalo Run, Maryland – 3.25.1997*
69. *Buffalo, West Virginia – 3.25*
70. *Buffalo Creek, West Virginia – 3.26*
71. *Buffalo Bluff, Florida – 9.13.1999*
72. *Buffalo, South Carolina – 9.14*
73. *Buffalo Valley, Tennessee – 9.23*
74. *Buffalo, Tennessee – 9.25 (Sullivan County)*
75. *Buffalo Bend, Virginia – 9.26*
76. *Buffalo Creek, British Columbia, Canada – 7.18.2001*

So is that it? Are we done?

Ah, who can say? The Heisenberg Principle still seems to apply, and we know of seven or eight Buffalos, or rumors of

Buffalos, we've yet to track down. Some are the ruminative quadruped equivalent of low-hanging fruit; we know right where they are, and all that is required of us is the will to drive there . . .

INTRODUCING MANHATTAN: A DARK DUET

In 2004, Akashic Books published Brooklyn Noir, *an anthology of original fiction edited by Tim McLoughlin, launching a never-ending series of regional anthologies. (One waits for* Pleasantville Noir *and* Happy Valley Noir . . .)

Akashic's Johnny Temple recruited me to put Manhattan Noir *together, and published it in 2006; two years later I followed it with* Manhattan Noir 2: The Classics, *consisting of stories published over a couple of centuries. (And three very noir poems!)*

My two introductions are about the stories. They're also very much about the city.

MANHATTAN NOIR

The City.

See, that's what we call it. The rest of the world calls it the Apple, or, more formally, the Big Apple, and we don't object to the term. We just don't use it very often. We call it the City and let it go at that.

And, while the official city of New York is composed of five boroughs, the City means Manhattan. "I'm going into the City tonight," says a resident of Brooklyn or the Bronx, Queens or Staten Island. Everybody knows what he means. Nobody asks him which city, or points out that he's already *in* the city. Because he's not. He's in one of the Outer Boroughs. Manhattan is the City.

A few years ago I was in San Francisco on a book tour. In conversation with a local I said that I lived in the City. "Oh, you call it that?" he said. That's what we call San Francisco. The City."

I reported the conversation later to my friend Donald Westlake, whose house is around the corner from mine. "That's cute," he said. "Of course they're wrong, but it's cute."

The City. It's emblematic, I suppose of a Manhattan arrogance, of which there's a fair amount going around. Yet it's a curious sort of arrogance, because for the most part it's not the pride of the native. Most of us, you see, are originally from Somewhere Else.

All of New York—all five boroughs—is very much a city of immigrants. Close to half its inhabitants were born in another country—and the percentage would be higher if you could count the illegals. The flood of new arrivals has always kept the city well supplied with energy and edge.

Manhattan's rents are such that few of its neighborhoods are available these days to most immigrants (though it remains the first choice of those fortunate enough to arrive with abundant funds). But it too is a city of newcomers, not so much from other countries as from other parts of the United States, and even from the city's own suburbs and the outer boroughs as well. For a century or more, this is where those young people most supplied with brains and talent and energy and ambition have come to find their place in the world. Manhattan holds out the promise of opportunity—to succeed, certainly, and, at least as important, to be oneself.

I was born upstate, in Buffalo. In December of 1948, when I was ten and a half years old, my father and I spent a weekend here. We got off the train at Grand Central and checked in next door at the Hotel Commodore, and in the next three or four days we went everywhere—to Liberty Island (Bedloes Island then) to see the statue, to the top of the Empire State Building, to a Broadway show (*Where's Charlie?*), a live telecast (Ed Sullivan), and just about everywhere the subway and elevated railway could take us. I remember riding downtown on the 3rd Avenue El on Sunday morning, and even as my father was pointing out the Skid Row saloons on the Bowery, a man tore out of one of them, let out a blood-curdling scream, turned around, and raced back inside again.

I think I became a New Yorker that weekend. As soon as I could, I moved here.

"Why would I want to go anywhere?" my friend Dave Van Ronk used to say. "I'm already here."

Manhattan Noir.

While I might argue Manhattan's primacy (assuming I could find someone to take the other side), I wouldn't dream of holding that everything worthwhile originates here. Even as so many Manhattanites hail from somewhere else, so do many of our best ideas. And the idea for this book originated on the other side of the world's most beautiful bridge, with a splendid story collection called *Brooklyn Noir.*

It was that book's considerable success, both critical and commercial, that led Akashic's Johnny Temple to seek to extend the *Noir* franchise, and it was Tim McLoughlin's outstanding example as its editor that moved me to take the reins for the Manhattan volume.

I sat down and wrote out a wish list of writers I'd love to have for the book, then emailed invitations to participate. The short story, I should point out, is perforce a labor of love in today's literary world; there's precious little economic incentive to write one, and the one I was in a position to offer was meager indeed. Even so, almost everyone I invited was quick to accept. That gladdened my heart, and they gladdened it again by delivering on time, and delivering what I think you'll agree is material of a rare quality.

My initial request wasn't all that specific. I asked for dark stories with a Manhattan setting, and that's what I got. Readers of *Brooklyn Noir* will recall that its contents were labeled by neighborhood—Bay Ridge, Canarsie, Greenpoint, etc. That's not the case here; while some of these stories have very specific settings, others pay less attention to urban geography. Still, the book's contents do a good job of covering the island, from C. J. Sullivan's Inwood and Charles Ardai's Upper East Side to Justin Scott's Chelsea and Carol Lea Benjamin's Greenwich Village. The range in mood and literary style is at least as great; noir can be funny, it can stretch to include magic realism, it can be ample or stark, told in the past or present tense, and in the first or third person. I wouldn't presume to define noir—if we could define it, we wouldn't need to use a French word for it—but it seems to me that it's more a way of looking at the world than what one sees.

Noir doesn't necessarily embody crime and violence, thought that's what we tend to think of when we hear the word. Most but not all of these stories are crime stories, even as most but not all are the work of writers of crime fiction, but the exceptions take place in a world where crime and violence are always hanging around, if not on center stage.

Noir is very contemporary, but there's nothing necessarily new about it. In cinema, when we hear the word we think of the Warner Brothers B-movies of the Thirties and Forties, but the noir sensibility goes back much further than that. When I was sending out invitations, one of the first went to Annette and Martin Meyers, who (as Maan Meyers) write a series of period novels set in old New York. Could Maan perhaps contribute a dark story from the city's past? They accepted, and in due course the same day's mail brought Maan's "The Organ Grinder" and a present-day story from Marty.

Every anthologist should have such problems. Both stories are here, both show the dark side of the same city, and both are far too fine to miss.

Most of our contributors live in New York, though not necessarily in

Manhattan. (It's hard to afford the place, and it gets harder every year. New York is *about* real estate, and Justin Scott's "The Most Beautiful Apartment in New York" illustrates this fact brilliantly.) Jeffery Deaver lives in Virginia and John Lutz in St. Louis, yet I thought of both early on; they both set work in Manhattan, and reveal in that work a deep knowledge of the city, and, perhaps more important, a New Yorker's sensibility.

It seems to me that I've nattered on too long already, so I'll bring this to a close. You're here for the stories, and I trust you'll like them. I know I do . . .

Manhattan Noir 2: It's Been Noir Around Here For Ages

Manhattan Noir Two. How did that happen?

Almost inevitably, it seems to me. A couple of years ago, Tim McLoughlin edited and Akashic Books published *Brooklyn Noir*. The book earned a warm reception from critics and readers, and spawned a series for the publisher that is rapidly taking over the world. Early on, I had the opportunity to turn the noir spotlight on my part of the world, the island of Manhattan. Because I had the good fortune to recruit some wonderful writers who sat down and wrote some wonderful stories, *Manhattan Noir* drew strong reviews and sold (and continues to sell) a gratifying number of copies.

Meanwhile, Akashic expanded the franchise with *Brooklyn Noir Two,* consisting of previously published stories. (I could hardly be unaware of the book, as Tim McLoughlin was gracious enough to reprint a story of mine, "By the Dawn's Early Light.") And this sequel, too, was very well received.

While I was editing *Manhattan Noir,* it struck me that Manhattan was a natural setting for noir material, not least because it had served that function ever since Peter Minuit's celebrated $24 land grab. I thought of all the writers who'd found a home in Manhattan, and of the dark stories they'd set here, and one day I emailed Johnny Temple at Akashic to propose the very book you now hold in your hand. Johnny, it turned out, had already noted in his calendar "Q block re *Manhattan Noir* sequel." Great minds work alike, as you've no doubt been advised, and so do mine and Johnny's.

You would think compiling a reprint anthology would be a far simpler matter than putting together a book of original stories. I certainly thought so, or I might not have rushed to embrace the project. Curiously, it was the other way around.

For the first *Manhattan Noir,* all I had to do was persuade some of the best writers in the country to produce new dark stories set in Manhattan, and to do so for a fee that fell somewhere between honorarium and pittance. They turned in magnificent work, and I turned in the fruits of their labors, and that was pretty much it. Nice work if you can get it.

But this time around I had to find the stories, and that's not as easy as it sounds. I knew that I wanted to include O. Henry and Damon Runyon—but which O. Henry story? Which story of Runyon's? I did not want to resort to the anthologist's ploy of picking stories from other people's anthologies—this, of course, is one reason everybody knows "The Gift of the Magi" and "Little Miss Marker," while so many equally delightful stories remain unknown to the general reader. So what I had to do was read all of O. Henry's New York stories, and all of Damon Runyon's stories, and that was effortful and time-consuming but, I must admit, a very pleasurable way to get through the days. And then I had to narrow the field, until I'd selected a single story from each author.

I also had to filter everything for a Manhattan setting. For example, I knew I wanted to include a story by Jerome Weidman, author of novels like *I Can Get It For You Wholesale* and plays like *Fiorello*. And I even knew which one I wanted, a haunting story narrated by a young boy who has to find a way to inform his parents of the sudden death of a beloved cousin. I read that story forty or more years ago, and it stayed in my mind, and when I managed to track it down I discovered one aspect of it which had *not* stayed in my mind; to wit, the damn thing was set in Brooklyn.

No problem. Weidman wrote a good many stories, and I have now read them all, and I'm pleased to include herewith "My Aunt From 12th Street." And when Tim McLoughlin is ready to gather up yarns for *Brooklyn Noir Three*, have I got a story for him . . .

I've always had a problem with introductions to collections and anthologies. If the material's good, what does it need with an anthologist's prefatory remarks? And if it's not good, who needs it?

Still, people who read anthologies seem to expect some concrete evidence of the anthologist's involvement in his material, even as those who publish them want to see proof that the anthologist has expended sufficient effort to get words on paper. I won't say much about the stories, they don't require it, but I will say a word or two about the short story as a literary form, and its virtual disappearance in our time.

It should surprise no one with a feeling for noir that it all comes down to money.

Consider this: In 1902, William Sydney Porter, whom you and the rest of the world know as O. Henry, moved to New York after having served a prison sentence in Ohio. (He'd been convicted of embezzling $1050 from a bank in Austin, Texas.) Within a year he had contracted to write a weekly short story for a newspaper, the *New York World*. For each story he was to receive $100.

This was at a time when a dollar a day was considered a satisfactory wage for a workingman, and when you could support a family quite acceptably on

$20 a week. O. Henry published his first short story collection in 1904, and his tenth in 1910. He never wrote a novel. He never had to.

Consider Damon Runyon. Today's readers know him chiefly for *Guys and Dolls*, the brilliant musical based on his stories, but Runyon himself wrote short stories almost exclusively. "My measure of success is money," he wrote. "I have no interest in artistic triumphs that are financial losers. I would like to have an artistic success that also made money, of course, but if I had to make a choice between the two, I would take the dough."

Already a great success as a Broadway columnist, Runyon began publishing fiction in magazines in 1929, with the bulk of his work appearing in the Thirties. Magazines like *Cosmopolitan* and *Collier's* and *The Saturday Evening Post* paid him upwards of a dollar a word for his work.

Damon Runyon never wrote a novel. He never had to, either.

Throughout the 1930s and '40s, a majority of American writers made their living turning out short fiction for magazines. The upper crust wrote for the slicks, the lower echelon for the pulps, and in either tier it was possible to make a decent living.

Then the world changed, and the publishing world with it. After the Second World War, inexpensive reprint fiction in the form of mass-market paperbacks killed off the pulp magazines almost overnight. Television finished the job and essentially took the slick magazines out of the fiction business. Few magazines published much in the way of short fiction, and those that did were able to pay only small sums for it.

And writers stopped producing short fiction.

Not entirely, to be sure. Samuel Johnson wasn't far off when he said that no one but a blockhead writes but for money, but the fact remains that virtually all writers are driven by more than the hope of financial reward. E. E. Cummings explained in an introduction that a poet is a person who makes things, and so is a writer of fiction. One may indeed make it in the hope of being well compensated for its manufacture, but one nevertheless makes it too for the sheer satisfaction of the task itself. Witness the many very fine stories being written today, rarely for more than an honorarium or a pittance, and often for magazines that pay the author in contributor's copies.

Still, money makes the mare run, or keeps her stalled in her traces. A surprising proportion of today's leading commercial writers have written no short fiction whatsoever, and few of them have written enough to be particularly good at it. They're not to be blamed, nor can one hold the publishing industry to account. If readers cared more about short fiction, more short fiction would be written.

And is the same thing even now happening to the novel? Are video games and hi-def cable and the World Wide Web doing to it what paperback novels and broadcast TV (Three networks! Small screens! Black and white pictures!) did to the short story?

But we don't really want to get into that, do we?

Before I could select a story for this volume, it had to meet two requirements. It had to be noir, and it had to be set in Manhattan.

The boundaries of noir, as we'll see, are hard to delineate. Those of Manhattan, on the other hand, are not. It's an island, and the waters that surround it make it pretty clear where it ends.

But two of my choices are rather less obvious in their Manhattan settings.

Evan Hunter knew Manhattan intimately, and set a large portion of his work here. His Ed McBain Eighty-seventh Precinct novels are very clearly set in Manhattan, although for fictional purposes he tilts the borough ninety degrees and calls it *Isola*. (That's Italian for *island,* in case you were wondering.)

Evan wrote a great deal of short fiction, all of it good and much of it superb. Many of the early stories were set in unspecified locales, and while he may well have had Manhattan in mind, there's no textual evidence to show it. The Matt Cordell stories, with their Bowery bum private-eye hero, have specific Manhattan settings, but I opted instead for "The Last Spin," because

I simply couldn't resist it; it's been a favorite story of mine ever since I read it fifty years ago.

But you have to read closely to determine that it takes place in Manhattan. The two characters, champions of warring teen-age gangs, never get out of a featureless room. Still, the one called Dave makes it clear where they are. "My people come down from the Bronx," he says. When you come down from the Bronx, you land in Manhattan. Case closed.

If there's a line in "The Last Spin" that places the story firmly in Manhattan (and, I would guess, somewhere in the northern reaches thereof, East Harlem or Washington Heights, say) that's not a claim I can make for Edgar Allan Poe's entry. Now you would think Poe would have set something in Manhattan, given that he spent so much time in residence here. He lived on West 3rd Street for a time, and there was a great outcry a few years ago when New York University, clearly determined to turn all of Greenwich Village into dormitory space, set out to knock down the Poe House and build something in its place. And he lived on West 84th Street, which the city fathers have subsequently named after him. (But don't give that street name to a cabby. These days it's hard enough to pick one who can find 84th Street.)

I read my way through all of Poe's stories, or at least enough of each to determine where it took place, and while the man set stories in Charleston and Paris and in no end of murky landscapes, he doesn't seem to have set anything in Manhattan. He spent quite a few years here, and while they may not have been terribly happy years, well, how many of those did the man have, anyway?

And how could I leave this Manhattanite out of this volume?

So I stretched a point and selected "The Raven." He was living in Manhattan when he wrote it, and it takes place in the residence of the narrator, who is clearly a fictive equivalent of the author himself. How much of a stretch is it to presume that the book-lined chamber that serves as its setting (with its purple curtains and many a quaint and curious volume of forgotten lore) is situated like so many other book-lined chambers on Manhattan's Upper West Side? On, say, West 84th Street?

Works for me.

But wait, you say. (Yes, you. I can hear you.) Wait a minute. "The Raven." Uh, isn't it, well, a poem?

So?

Yes, "The Raven" is a poem—and a magnificent one at that. Nor is Poe the only poet to be found herein. It's my great pleasure to present to you the work of two other poets, Horace Gregory and Geoffrey Bartholomew. Both are, to my mind, superb practitioners of their craft. Both are represented here by works set very specifically in Manhattan. And the works of both, like "The Raven," are indisputably noir.

I became acquainted with Horace Gregory's work almost as long ago as I read "The Last Spin," and it too made an enduring impression. Specifically, I was taken with a group of Gregory's early poems, originally published under the title *Chelsea Rooming House,* and consisting of poetic monologues by the various inhabitants of that building. There is a lingering darkness in the work that made my only problem that of deciding which of the poems to include, and the reader who samples these may well be moved to go on and read the rest of them.

Much more recently, Geoffrey Bartholomew published *The McSorley Poems.* McSorley's is an historic saloon in the East Village—*We were here before you were born,* proclaims the sign over its door, and the sign itself has been making that claim since, well, before you were born—and Geoffrey has been tending its bar for a quarter of a century. He's a longtime friend of mine, and when he offered me a pre-publication look at *The McSorley Poems,* I found myself reminded of *Chelsea Rooming House.* The work of either of these poets, dark and rich and ironic and dripping in noir, would sweeten this book; together, they complement one another; with "The Raven" for company they make an even more vivid statement.

Yes, they're poems, all of them, and fine poems in the bargain. And who is to say that the notion of noir ought to confine us to prose? The term (which really only means *black* in French) first came into wide usage as a label for certain films of the 1930s and '40s. When it moved into prose fiction, it seemed early on to be inextricably associated with big cities, as if the term *urban noir* were redundant. The novels of Daniel Woodrell have since been categorized quite properly as *country noir,* and Akashic's great noir franchise, ranging as far afield as Havana and Dublin, makes it abundantly clear that noir knows no geographic limitations.

Nor does time serve as a boundary. If the term came about in the middle third of the past century, that doesn't mean that the noir sensibility had not been in evidence before then. Consider Stephen Crane; his first novel, *Maggie, A Girl of the Streets,* could hardly better epitomize the noir sensibility, and our selection, "A Poker Game," shows a dark soul indeed confounded by a rare example of innocent grace. Consider "Mrs. Manstey's View," the first published story of Edith Wharton, which appeared in *Scribner's Magazine* in 1891.

Noir seems to me to transcend form. Film and theater can fit comfortably in the shade of its dark canopy, and so surely can poetry. Some operas make the cut—Verdi's *Rigoletto,* it's worth noting, had its plot lifted line for line in Damon Runyon's oft-anthologized "Sense of Humor." And who could look at Goya's black paintings and not perceive them as visual representations of noir? And what is Billie Holliday's recording of "Gloomy Sunday" if it isn't noir? Or the Beatles' Eleanor Rigby, who died in the church and was buried along with her name? I'd include them, and I'd pull in Beethoven's late quartets while I was at it.

Rather than exercise false modesty (which is the only sort of which I'm capable) I've included a story of my own, "In For a Penny." It was commissioned by the BBC, to be read aloud, and their request was quite specifically for a noir story. Such commissions rarely bring out the best in a writer, but in this case the resultant story was one with which I was well pleased, and I'm happy to offer it here.

Really, how could I resist? How could I pass up the opportunity to share a volume with Stephen Crane and O. Henry and Edgar Allan Poe and Damon Runyon and Irwin Shaw and Edith Wharton and, well, all of these literary superstars?

My mother would be so proud...

LISTOWEL, A SPECIAL PLACE

One very useful contribution of the language of texts and tweets is IIRC. "If I recall correctly," it means—or If I remember correctly, the initials being the same. The longer one lives, the more useful the phrase becomes—and the less likely that one does recall or remember correctly.

So. IIRC, the piece that follows was written for a magazine called The Walker, *a publication aimed at recreational pedestrians. I don't remember when they asked for it, or when I wrote it. I don't know how long the magazine lasted, or if they stayed around long enough to publish my article. Did they pay me anything? I don't think they did, but who's to say?*

I tried to Google my way to some information about either my article or the magazine. Perhaps your Googling might produce results. But, really, why would you bother?

"If your travels bring you someplace special, if your trip is particularly enjoyable, never go there again. Because your memory will have enhanced it, and a return visit will inevitably be a disappointment."

I don't remember the source of this piece of advice, but it has always made sense to me. And, because it has ever been my nature to strike out for the new and unknown, I've had little difficulty following instructions. My wife and I have traveled widely, and have almost always enjoyed ourselves, and have only rarely gone any place a second time. London and Paris have been exceptions; my work has often taken me there, and both are too familiar to disappoint. But there's one other spot to which I've returned innumerable times over the past 40 years, and I've rarely been disappointed.

The only problem is I can never go there again.

Do you believe in past lives? I do or don't, depending on when you ask me, but I've never been able to find another explanation for my affinity for Ireland. One of my earliest childhood memories is of responding to Irish music on the radio, and it was soon joined by an interest in Irish history, and a collecting enthusiasm for Irish coins and tokens. I have no Irish ancestors, and grew up without any close acquaintances of Irish descent.

In 1964 I made my first visit abroad, and it was to Ireland. I got off the plane feeling as though I'd somehow returned home. My then-wife and I rented a car and drove around the country, winding up in Dublin.

Driving as an adventure—there were always sheep and goats and donkeys in the road, though not many cars. And Dublin was still a 19th Century city, with horse-drawn lorries and a pall of peat smoke in the air.

We returned almost annually, and on our third or fourth visit discovered the town of Listowel, in County Kerry. Listowel is the Literary Capital of Ireland; a market town of 3000, it has been the birthplace of a remarkable number of writers, and since the early 1970s has hosted an annual Writers' Week festival, five days of plays and book launches and poetry readings and workshops and singsongs and nonstop good fellowship. I kept going back, and made many friends there, and even toyed with the idea of moving there.

Then my first marriage broke up and my life went through changes, and I lost touch with Listowel, and with Ireland, for something like 20 years. I returned in 1995, and again it felt like coming home. It had changed some, of course, and too many old friends had died, but I loved it all the same. My wife felt the same way, and we came back every year, and one year I arrived early, holed up in the hotel, and spent six weeks writing a book before my wife flew over to join me for Writers' Week. (The book was set in Burma. Make what you will of that.)

I became an official of Writers' Week, led a workshop one year, launched a book another. I made new friends, and renewed my ties with old friends.

And, after last year's festival, my wife and I realized something. While we'll probably go back again—old habits die hard, after all—I don't think our visits from now on will be frequent ones. Because the Ireland I found in 1964, and kept returning to, has gone.

Ireland's economy has flourished over the past decade or two. The European Common Market benefited the country enormously, and business has flourished. It's become a rather expensive place to visit, but that's the least of it. Tiny villages, largely unchanged for a couple of centuries, are now ringed with suburban developments; thatched-roof cottages are being pulled down and replaced by McMansions; farmland, those blindingly green fields chopped up into crazy-quilt patterns by hand-made unmortared stone fences, is simply disappearing. The roads are wider, and unblocked by sheep or goats or donkeys; instead, far too many cars create unprecedented traffic problems.

Well, the Irish certainly have a right to prosper, and to embrace the 21st century, with all that's good and bad in it. I wouldn't have them sacrifice their own comfort in order to maintain a living museum for tourists. But listen in the pubs and you'll note that the locals themselves are well aware that, whatever's been gained, something irreplaceable has been lost. "We've become prosperous," a woman told me, "and we've lost our soul."

So I think our visit last year will be our last, at least for a while. It was our first time back since the death of our good friend John B. Keane, a founder of Writers' Week, an internationally successful playwright and novelist, and the keeper of Listowel's foremost pub. We felt the loss keenly, and it made us more acutely aware of all the other losses.

Ah, but if I could just go back there thirty years ago . . .

THE MAGIC OF MINNEAPOLIS

Bouchercon, the foremost annual convention of aficionados of mystery fiction, must draw inspiration from the hermit crab. Every year it's in a different city, and each year it seems to be larger and more ambitious—and put together by a whole new group of enthusiasts, who are charged with reinventing the wheel in order to make it all work.

One constant is the Bouchercon program, a book with a schedule of events, an array of ads and illustrations, and, alas, a section with photographs and capsule biographies of all the participating authors. Why alas? Because one winds up being called upon to sign one's entry again and again and again, from ad infinitum all the way to ad nauseam.

In 1996, when Bouchercon was in St. Paul, I was asked to write something for the program about the 1987 conference, held on the other side of the Mississippi River. I'd been the Guest of Honor that year.

I was happy to oblige. Of course that meant I had to sign all those programs twice—once on my capsule biography, and once on the first page of the essay.

There are certain experiences that change your life forever. After them, you're not the same person anymore. You don't see things the same way. It is, in the immortal words of William Butler Yeats, "all changed, changed utterly."

There are experiences like that. And there are other experiences altogether, like Bouchercon in 1987.

It may be hard for some of you to believe this, but I haven't always been a fixture in the mystery conference circuit, a bad penny that—heads or tails—always turns up. There was a time when I actually had a life. I dropped in briefly at a couple of Bouchercons—in New York in 1983, in Chicago a year or two later.

Then in 1987 I was invited to be the Guest of Honor.

Well, I'll tell you: Flattery will get you almost anywhere with me. I was flattered and delighted and pleased as punch. I was also unsure I belonged at Bouchercon in any capacity, let alone that of honored guest, given that I had just written a novel outside the field of crime fiction and had no idea whether I would spent my remaining years writing mysteries, writing other things, or metamorphosed into a kangaroo, hopping furiously across the Australian outback. That last seemed unlikely, but what do we ever know for sure?

Still, a free flight? A free room? I came, and felt honored. I was interviewed, I signed books, I hung out. Had a hell of a time.

Then came Saturday night, the banquet. Steve Stilwell, appearing as harried as every Bouchercon organizer always seems to be by Saturday night, caught up with me a few minutes before we were all to sit down to dinner. He told me what the program was to be, which struck me as considerate but unessential. Wouldn't I discover what the program was just by sitting through it?

". . . And then after the awards," he said, "you'll give your speech."

"Huh?" I said.

"Your talk. And then . . ."

"Wait a minute," I said. "What talk?"

"The talk I told you about. The talk the Guest of Honor gives at every Bouchercon banquet."

Well, go know. This was my first Bouchercon banquet.

I don't remember exactly who said what from that point on, because both of us were too busy with our respective panic attacks. Steve had to confront the prospect of a banquet with nothing but dead air issuing from the mouth of the principal speaker, while I had to make a speech in front of a few hundred people despite having Nothing To Say.

(Remember, this was nine years ago. I have come a long way since then, and have long since learned that having Nothing To Say is no handicap to a speaker, and indeed can be something of an advantage. I rarely have anything to say, and I give talks all the time. A few weeks ago I was walking in the country and saw five cows dozing under a tree. I went over and gave them a little talk about series characters in crime fiction. It turned out that four of them had heard me before.)

Well, the problem turned out to be no problem at all. Somehow, sitting on the dais, I recalled that I had never heard anyone remark, upon leaving a banquet, that the only thing wrong with the whole affair was that the speeches were too short. So I said whatever the hell I said, letting brevity be the soul of my wit, and that was that.

Except for the magician.

Now this will give you an idea of the shape I was in—I can't remember at this point whether the magician came on at the end of the program or whether he preceded the awards and my talk. I think it must have been the latter, because it seems to me that, if he had done his routine at the end, everybody would have walked out on him. Only a captive audience could explain the continuing presence of bottoms in chairs.

He was terrible.

He was so terrible he made you appreciate mimes.

He did close-up magic in a room full of several hundred people. His patter was tedious. None of his tricks worked. And the saddest thing of all is that, even if he'd been good, even if he'd been Houdini, nobody cared. Nobody wanted to see that poor son of a bitch do anything but disappear.

And that was the one thing he wouldn't do. Maybe he tried, maybe it was one more trick he couldn't quite pull off. All I know is that he was out there forever.

And then he was gone, at last. But not without adding a phrase to the language, one that will endure, I suspect, as long as there's a Bouchercon.

"It was bad," I heard someone say a couple of years ago at Malice Domestic, "but not as bad as the magician in Minneapolis."

I can't attend this year, but I want to lay to rest the rumors that my absence is a consequence of my fears that the magician will be back. I'm pretty sure he won't. But I have a high school reunion in Buffalo, and I just don't want to miss it. Bouchercon, after all, comes every year. High school reunions, thank God and all His angels, do not. I'm sure I'd enjoy Bouchercon in St. Paul, as I've enjoyed it everywhere, having formed the habit of regular attendance back in 1987. I'm not entirely sure I'll enjoy my high school reunion, and to tell you the truth I don't know what to expect.

But I'm sure of one thing. It won't be as bad as the magician in Minneapolis.

I don't get to every Bouchercon these days, but I show up more often than not. An increasing and profound distaste for air travel helps me make my choice to attend or not. If I can get there by train, sign me up. If a flight is required, well, then my presence is not. This year we met in Dallas, and when I booked the conference I expected to take a train—well, a couple of trains—from New York. But fall of 2019 found me as writer-in-residence at Newberry College in South Carolina, and it would take me many trains and many days to get there, so I flew.

That wasn't much fun. The weekend got off on the wrong foot (or the wrong wing, if you prefer) and my enjoyment of the conference was hampered by the distaste I felt for the flight back. But the programs were interesting, and the barbecue joint where my friend Lee Goldberg and I had lunch lived up to its billing, and I got to renew acquaintance with some old friends and meet some online colleagues for the first time.

So it may not have been perfect, but you know what? It was a whole lot better than that magician in Minneapolis.

THE MEAN STREETS OF GOTHAM

Gotham Central was a run of comic books featuring the cops of Gotham City without Batman. In 2008 the first five installments were collected for hardcover publication, with Ed Brubaker, Greg Rucka, and Michael Lark sharing the byline. I was invited to furnish an introduction . . .

We always knew they meant New York.

Oh, sure, they called it Gotham City. That's where the Bat Signal hung in the night sky like the moon, and where the Batmobile never had to circle the block looking for a parking space. Gotham was home to the Joker and the Riddler and the Penguin, and in its streets and upon its rooftops Batman and Robin the Boy Wonder waged their endless noble battle against the forces of evil.

That was Gotham City, all right, and that was a perfectly fine thing to call it in the alternate universe of comic book fiction. But we're not dim. We knew well and good what town we were talking about, whatever name they fastened on it, and whatever they called its streets and newspapers and citizens.

They were talking about New York.

I mean, why else call it Gotham?

The original Gotham, it may interest you to know, was in England, a village in Nottinghamshire. The name meant "goat town" in Anglo-Saxon, which would seem to suggest that some of the inhabitants kept goats, and didn't care who knew it. Back in the thirteenth century, the Gothamites earned a reputation as "wise fools" by feigning insanity in order to avoid paying taxes to King John. (There was evidently something about King John that put people's backs up; it was he, you'll recall, who in 1215 inspired the peers of the realm to force upon him the Magna Carta, that Great Charter that stands as the foundation of all our freedoms, granting the citizenry such rights as trial by jury. But I digress . . .)

King John had long since gone to his reward when the Dutch bought the island of Manhattan and founded a town they called Nieuw Amsterdam. And it was almost two centuries after that, in 1807, when Washington Irving published a series of essays entitled *Salmagundi, or the Whims and Opinions of Launcelot Langstaff and Others,* wherein he referred to the city as Gotham. Irving's use of the name implied that Gothamites were self-important and foolish, but the name shrugged off its connotations and endured.

(And wasn't Washington Irving the lad for naming things? Salmagundi, which he seems to have cobbled up out of a handful of leftover Scrabble letters, became the name of an artists' club; founded in 1871, it endures to this day, and its brownstone clubhouse boasts the only remaining stoop on 5th Avenue. Meanwhile, Irving followed *Salmagundi* with *A History of New York,* which he wrote under the pen name of Diedrich Knickerbocker, ostensibly an embittered old codger of Dutch extraction. There's another name that's hung on, and you'll find it attached to any number of present-day New York institutions, including a group of tallish fellows who pass the time throwing a round ball through a hoop. But there I go, digressing again . . .)

In 1844, Edgar Allan Poe wrote a series of satirical reports on daily life in New York, which he called *Doings of Gotham.* (He lived at various New York locations—in Greenwich Village, on West 84th Street, and in a cottage in the Bronx that survives to this day as a Edgar Allan Poe museum.) The author of "The Raven" doesn't seem to have found New York's streets all that mean, but did trouble to call them "with rare exception, insufferably dirty." He went on to lament the $50,000 spent annually for street cleaning, and proposed a novel alternative: "Contractors might pay roundly for the privilege of cleaning the streets, receiving the sweepings for their perquisite, and find themselves great gainers by the arrangement. In any large city, a company of market gardeners would be induced to accept a contract of this character."

Believe it or not, Poe's notion never did reach the right ears, and to this day the city actually spends money to clean the streets. In some years the tab runs even higher than $50,000.

William Sydney Porter, whom you'd know as O. Henry, lived in New York from 1902 until his death in 1910. Many of his stories, especially those in *The Four Million,* were set in New York, but when he called the place Gotham he was just using a sobriquet that had long since been incorporated into the local language. He had other names he invented for the city, most notable "Baghdad-on-the-Subway." Now there's a phrase that must have resonated very differently a century ago than it does today.

Forget the name. Suppose they called the city something else, or nothing at all. Could it be any place but New York?

In 1940, when Bob Kane started drawing *Batman,* the urban landscape alone could have told us what town he had in mind. The high-rises and sky-scrapers defined New York in an era where not all that many cities boasted a building much taller than the local water tower.

Things are a little different now, and you don't have to look all that far to find a one-horse town with a genuine skyline. But it's not just the height of the buildings that makes New York the right setting for Batman, and the perfect home for these Gotham cops—dressed, I don't doubt, in GCPD Blue—who fight the good fight in these pages.

It's not the actual meanness of the streets, either. New York, its image notwithstanding, has a lower crime rate than most of the rest of the country, and one that continues to drop. Gentrification has upgraded Harlem and made the Lower East Side unrecognizable, and you pretty much have to leave Manhattan and do some real searching to find a genuinely bad neighborhood these days.

So it's not the crime rate, and it's not the tall buildings. What is it? The answer's somewhere in the following gag:

> *Tourist to New Yorker: Can you tell me how to get to the Empire State Building, or should I just go %@&!!! myself?*

The New York energy goes beyond anything you'll find anywhere else. It's too much for some people and it grinds them down, but it lifts up and animates the rest of us.

It gives us the New York edge, which is attitude and something more. Reggie Jackson, who had some of his best years at that ballpark in the Bronx, smiled when someone asked him how he felt about the city. "If you give a New Yorker the first line," he said, "he's got the whole page."

Hey, get a grip, will you? Can you imagine the Joker, trying to make his bones by putting one over on the cops in Albuquerque? Or the Riddler, trying out conundrums on Fargo's Finest? Can you picture Catwoman in Cleveland, or the Penguin in Peoria, or Two-Face in the Twin Cities? Or our villain du jour, the chilling Freeze, in, say, Fresno?

I didn't think so.

It's Gotham City, baby. Get used to it.

NO SLINGS, NO ARROWS

In the mid 1980s I was invited to contribute to James Charlton's
Bred Any Good Rooks Lately?, a collection of short pieces of
word play terminating in a Spooneristic pun. Many of the
offerings were old tales retold, the originator's identity lost in
the mists of time, but I'd actually devised one of these things
myself, and was quick to seize the chance to make it immortal.

To make assurance doubly sure, here it is again:

David Garrick, the eighteenth-century English actor who made his reputation as Richard III, won even greater renown as Hamlet. Shortly before his
first performance in that role, Garrick fell and sustained a fractured tibia.
While some gossips hinted that the cast was merely a device to permit his
continuing the limp that had served him so well as Richard, theatergoers by
and large accepted the performance, limp and all.

Garrick went on to play Hamlet on many other occasions, and of course
did not limp in the part once his leg had healed. Other lesser actors, however, borrowed not only his interpretation of the role but the limp that had
gone with it. Although there is nothing in the play to suggest that the melancholy Dane ought to limp, several generations of English actors hobbled in
the part, and, while the theatrical world today has forgotten this curious bit
of business, it survives in that perennial opening night wish: "Break a leg!"

It endures, too, in that show biz bromide: *"You can't make a Hamlet*
without breaking legs."

A PEN NAME? REALLY?
AFTER ALL THESE YEARS???

*When Jill Emerson came out of retirement in 2011, I wrote
a batch of blog posts to give her a helping hand. This one for
Mystery Readers Journal, while indisputably a bent nail, may be
of at least passing interest . . .*

The first book I wrote was about a young woman who'd come straight from
her college graduation to Greenwich Village, in search of her sexual identity.
My agent sent it to Crest, where it was bought and published. I had called
it *Shadows*; they called it *Strange Are the Ways of Love,* and they called me
Lesley Evans.

The second book I wrote, though the first published, was written for
Harry Shorten at Midwood. I called it *Carla* and I called myself Sheldon
Lord, and Harry didn't feel a need to change either of those names.

I wrote those books in 1958, and it's no secret (and was never much
of one) that I wrote a great many over the next two decades, many of them
under one pen name or another. I was never Lesley Evans again, but I went
on being Sheldon Lord. And Andrew Shaw and Ben Christopher and John
Warren Wells. I wrote one book (*Such Men Are Dangerous*) with a first-person protagonist named Paul Kavanagh, and put his name on the cover; then
I wrote two more books, told in the third person and peopled with other
characters, and used Paul Kavanagh's name on them, too. I wrote another

book (*No Score*) with a first-person protagonist named Chip Harrison, and put *his* name down as author. (There were three more books by Chip, but they were also *about* Chip.)

And then there was Jill Emerson.

Jill was a little different. After I'd parted company with an agent, I sat down and wrote a sensitive novel of the lesbian experience. I put the name Jill Emerson on it, and I put Jill's name on the letter I wrote to the editor at Midwood. This was really dumb, as I'd published maybe a dozen books with Midwood and the door would have been open for me. Instead I elected to fling my manuscript over the transom, and I got a contract by return mail. (Call me insane, but you can't say I'm without talent.)

The mail came addressed to Jill Emerson, whose name I'd already added to my office mailbox so that I could receive *The Ladder*, the publication of the Daughters of Bilitis. Which was a national lesbian organization, to which Jill belonged. (Call me insane, but you can't say I'm not resourceful.)

I called the book *Shadows and Twilight*. Midwood called it *Warm and Willing*. That seemed reasonable to me. I mean, they only changed two of my three words.

Jill's second and last novel for Midwood was *Enough of Sorrow*. Throughout, no one there had a clue that Jill was anyone other than the young gay woman she purported to be.

By the end of the '60s I was done writing pseudonymous erotica. I'd long since stopped writing for Midwood and Nightstand and Beacon. Then Berkley started up a line designed to elevate the genre, and my agent peddled me to them. He told them the author's real name was Lawrence Josephson—a name he made up on the spot for no discernible reason—but that LJ would be using a pen name. When he asked me what name I wanted to use, I figured it sounded like a job for Jill Emerson.

Jill wrote three books for Berkley, *Thirty*, *Threesome*, and *A Madwoman's*

Diary. (They came out with other titles, but forget it; they're eBooks now, with my original titles restored.) They were stylistically experimental; *A Madwoman's Diary*, as you might expect, was in diary form, as was *Thirty. Threesome* was even more of a tour-de-force, with the three characters writing alternate chapters of a *Naked Came the Stranger*-type novel.

Next I wrote an epistolary novel that would have been Jill's sixth book, and her fourth for Berkley. But everybody who read it thought it deserved better, and my agent sent it to Bernard Geis, where it was published as *Ronald Rabbit is a Dirty Old Man,* by Lawrence Block.

Jill wrote two more books, a Berkley hardcover called *The Trouble With Eden* and an Arbor House literary mainstream novel called *A Week as Andrea Benstock.* There are some good stories about both books, but I won't tell them here. (You can find them, and far more detail on all the others, in *Afterthoughts*, a piecemeal memoir of my writing life. It's composed of the afterwords I wrote for my Open Road eBooks, and will be out soon as a 99¢ eBook. The bargain price is there because we hope it'll induce you to buy some of the other books. Hey, call me insane, but you can't say I'm not enterprising.)

A Week as Andrea Benstock came out in 1975, not long after the fourth Chip Harrison and the third Paul Kavanagh. And that was that. I was done being Jill, and I was done with pen names altogether. When the Harrison and Kavanagh books were reissued by new publishers, they came out with my own name on them.

No more pen names.

Yeah. Right.

*   *   *

Cut to, oh, sometime last year. I'd written a couple of short stories about a hot and homicidal young lady, and now I watched as they coalesced into a book. (This had happened before; a short story about a wistful hitman named Keller grew into four books about the fellow.)

The book was an utter joy to write, and I couldn't remember when I'd had more fun. But it was very different from Matthew Scudder's line of country, and I decided the ideal publisher would be Charles Ardai at Hard Case Crime. He loved the book and wanted it as his first-ever hardcover original.

And I knew how I wanted the byline to read:

GETTING OFF
A Novel of Sex and Violence
By Lawrence Block writing as Jill Emerson

For a couple of reasons.

One's the experience I had with *Small Town*. That was my post-9/11 book, the big jam-packed multiple-viewpoint New York novel I'd been wanting to write for years. It was well-received by readers and reviewers, and sold reasonably well, but it also brought an unsettling amount of negative email. Some of it was downright hostile, and what it came down to was that the book's sexual side was more than some readers were prepared to handle. The ones who came to the book from an affection for my lighthearted burglar and his faux-Manx cat were just plain not ready for Susan Pomerance and her Brazilian landscaping.

Fair enough. I knew what to do with those emails, being the happy owner of a keyboard with a DELETE button, but that doesn't mean I wanted to go through all that again. I decided to make it very clear what sort of book I had this time around, so that it only got into the hands of readers who'd welcome its excesses.

Reason enough for a pen name. An *open* pen name, because I do want people to be able to find the damn book, but a pen name nonetheless.

As I said, reason enough. But not the only reason.

See, it just felt right.

Being Jill again. I'd accessed something within myself when I heaved *Shadows & Twilight* onto Midwood's slush pile. And I felt its creative empowerment while I wrote *Getting Off.* Part of it originally was based on its clandestine aspect, and this time around I'd be out there, my name twinned with Jill's on the cover, even as all Jill's early work now bears the same dual byline.

Hey, call me insane, but you can't say I'm not having a good time.

A RARE AND RADIANT MOTHER

In 1998, Jill Morgan requested a piece for Mothers and Sons, *a collection in which sons would write about their mothers and mothers about their sons. (Well, mostly.) New American Library published the book in hardcover in 2000 and reprinted it a year later in paperback. I was especially taken with the contributions of two friends of mine, Peter Straub and Stuart Kaminsky; less so with my own:*

It was in 1959, and it seems to me it would have been in early June, a couple of weeks before my twenty-first birthday. I was back in Buffalo after what would turn out to have been my last year at college, and in a week or two I would go to New York, where I intended to support myself writing fiction until it was time to go back to school.

It was dinner time, and we were at the table in our house on Starin Avenue. My mother and father and sister and I were joined this evening by my Aunt Mim and Uncle Hi, and my cousins Peter and Jeffrey. I don't remember anything about the dinner, but I'm sure it was a good one, because that was the only kind my mother ever put on the table. And I don't remember anything about the conversation, until at some point Leo Norton came into it.

One of the men, my father or my uncle, mentioned Leo Norton, and the other allowed as to how he believed the man was dead. A reasonably intense discussion ensued, and it became evident that, while there was a certain division of opinion on the subject, no one at the table could say with anything approaching certainty whether Leo Norton was in fact alive or dead.

For my own part, I'd never heard of the man before. I don't know who he was or how his name came up, but I think it's safe to say he didn't play a central role in the life of any of the eight of us, or somebody would have known whether or not the man had a pulse.

The discussion proceeded apace, until my cousin Jeffrey stood up and left the table. He consulted the phone book, picked up the hall phone, and dialed a number. The table went silent as we waited to see what the hell Jeffrey was up to. "Hello," he said. "Is Leo there?" There was a pause, and he beamed. "Just checking," he said, and hung up.

Leo, Jeffrey assured us, was alive and well. We acknowledged Jeffrey for his resourcefulness in solving the puzzle, and we speculated on the reaction the phone call must have produced in the Norton household, and then the conversation turned to another topic, and that was that.

A year and a half later, in December of 1960, my father died suddenly and unexpectedly the day before his fifty-second birthday. An aortic aneurysm ruptured during the night, and an hour or two later he was dead.

I was in New York when this happened. I had indeed moved there shortly after the Leo Norton dinner, and had moved back to Buffalo six weeks later. I wrote paperback novels and pulp short stories, bought a half interest in a downtown jazz club, and began dating a woman. In March of 1960 we got married and moved to New York. I sold my half of the business back to my partner and went on writing fiction, and in the middle of the night the phone rang and Moe Cheplove, doctor and family friend, told me my father was dead.

It was a shocking death. My father was one of the first in his social set to die, and there'd been no warning; he was apparently fine one day and gone the next. My mother was devastated, and so was my sister, and so was I.

I could dredge up memories of the several days in Buffalo following his death, and indeed I've been unable to avoid them, but I'll spare you. There's just the one incident that's relevant here, and it happened at the funeral parlor, as I sat next to my mother while one person after another came over to express regrets. There were a great many people there whom I knew, and many I did not, and I wasn't expecting anything when a man I'd never seen before walked up to my mother.

"Lenore," he said, "I'm very sorry. I'm Leo Norton . . ."

Well, I lost it.

Perhaps you saw that classic episode of the Mary Tyler Moore show, the one centered on the funeral of Chuckles the Clown. (He was dressed up as a peanut, and an elephant tried to shell him.) Nobody could resist making jokes about his death, and Mary thought they were in very bad taste. Then, at the funeral itself, with everybody appropriately solemn, Mary can't keep from laughing.

Jesus, I know just how she felt. I'd been bawling like a baby for a couple of days, and shell-shocked to numbness the rest of the time, and here was this doofus I'd never seen before, and the only other time I'd heard his goddamn name was when eight of us sat around the dining room table arguing about whether he was alive or dead. "Is Leo there? . . . Just checking!"

I could not stop laughing. I knew I shouldn't be laughing—I was at my father's funeral, for God's sake, and you don't laugh at your father's funeral—but there was nothing I could do about it, and the inappropriateness of my laughter just made the whole thing that much funnier.

And here's what my mother did: She put an arm around me, and she *soothed* me! "It's all right, Larry," she said. "Go ahead and cry. It's all right."

She knew I wasn't crying. She knew I was laughing, and she knew *why* I was laughing, but she was the only person in the room who did. Because she played her part so superbly, everybody else believed just what she wanted them to believe—that her son, overcome with grief, was sobbing uncontrollably.

I got it together, as one does, and the day went on. And that night we were talking, and we laughed about our Leo Norton moment. "God, that was funny," she said. "Your father would have loved it." Her face clouded. "And I can never tell him," she said, and we wept.

It must have been fifteen years later when I got an envelope in the mail addressed in my mother's handwriting. I opened it up and took out a newspaper clipping, with a two- or three-paragraph obituary for Leo Norton.

The name didn't register at first, and I turned the piece of paper over to see if there was something relevant on the reverse. There wasn't. Then I read it again and the penny dropped.

I called Buffalo. "I got that clipping," I told her, "and it took me a minute, but then all I could do was laugh."

"I had the same reaction when I read it in the paper," she said. "It's a fine thing. The poor man drops dead and we laugh."

That story may be familiar. I've told it before, fictionalized, in a short story I called "Leo Youngdahl, R.I.P." I changed Leo's last name, and some other names as well—Jeffrey to Jeremy. I moved the family from Buffalo and changed our background from Jewish to Pennsylvania Dutch. I made the narrator a woman, and had her recount the story to the man she was living with. I chose some of these changes, I suspect, in order to distance myself from the story, to make it less about me, less about us.

Because, you see, it is not my nature to write about my own self, my own life, my own family. All honest fiction, to be sure, is autobiographical, in the sense that every character is a projection of oneself, every incident a projection of one's own experience. In that sense, who I am and what I've done and where I come from informs everything I've written.

But my characters rarely bear much resemblance to me, and the stories I tell hardly ever derive from experience. I almost never base a character on someone I know. There is, I believe, an unconscious process of synthesis that operates, so that characters are comprised of bits and pieces of people I've known or glimpsed or heard about, but that's about as far as I go. I've observed elsewhere that fiction writers fall into two basic categories, those who report what they've seen and those who recount what they've imagined. I'm not a reporter, I'm an imaginer.

I'm thus not terribly eager to sit down and tell you about my mother, and my natural reluctance is greatly augmented by my sense that my mother is probably equally reluctant to be written about. I have reason to believe this. On two occasions, Buffalo expatriates of my generation have written revealingly about their parents, and in both instances my mother found the whole business upsetting. David Milch, the television writer, included in a memoir one chapter about his late father, a prominent and respected heart surgeon. My mother thought it was deplorable that David portrayed his father as a pill-popping compulsive gambler. What David wrote seemed to me to be enormously affectionate and loving, but all my mother could see was that he had told truths about the man that should have been kept private.

Similarly, Elizabeth Swados, the writer and composer, wrote at length about her Buffalo family, about her schizophrenic brother, about her problematic relationship with her father. My mother found the whole business unfortunate and questioned why she'd had to go public with that sort of thing.

I have no family secrets to reveal in these pages. I'm not here to show you my mother's dark side; if she has one, I haven't seen it myself. I have, and have always had, a warm and loving relationship with the woman. I visit her in Buffalo once or twice a year, talk to her on the phone several times a week. And, when I finally sat down to write this piece after months of stalling, I wrote three sentences and had to go lie down.

I'd just as soon go lie down now. But I'll keep at it, and I'll tell you a thing or two about my mother. Some facts, some memories, some impressions. Make of them what you will.

*   *   *

She was born September 21, 1912, in Buffalo, New York, to native-born parents who were themselves the children of immigrants. She grew up in a two-family house on Hertel Avenue. Her father had bought the house, occupying the lower flat with his wife and children, installing his mother and his two unmarried sisters upstairs.

We lived less than a mile from that big white house, and I spent much of my childhood there. My father's parents died young, and what family he had was geographically and emotionally remote, so our extended family was in fact my mother's family. My grandmother was a legendary cook—everybody says this, but for a change it's true—and I think we must have gathered around her dining room table every couple of weeks. I know all holidays and family occasions were celebrated there.

My grandmother was widowed in 1952 and died in 1963. After her death, my great aunts, Sal and Nettie, moved downstairs and rented out the upper flat. Nettie died in 1983, Sal in 1990. We put the house on the market, and somebody bought it.

My mother's name was Lenore Harriet Nathan. She had two younger brothers, Hi and Jerry. She went to PS 22, just a block from her house, and Bennett High School, just a few blocks away on Main Street. She was salutatorian of her high school class, and should have been valedictorian on the basis of her grade-point average. There was, I gather, some question as to just why she was screwed out of the higher office. One school of thought held that it was because she was Jewish, the other that it was because she was female. (A little of both would be my guess, but who cares?)

On a recent promotional tour to Florida, I met a woman who told me she'd known my mother as a girl. She and her older sister would come over to my mother's house, and the three of them would cut through the back yard as a shortcut to PS 22. "Your mother was always so nice to me," the woman remembered. "She was my sister's age, and I was eight years younger, but she didn't treat me like a baby."

"I remember her," my mother said. "She was a pest."

My mother won a scholarship and went to Cornell University. In due course, both of her brothers followed her to Cornell. I suspect they were there on scholarships as well. The Nathans were a bright family.

These were competitive scholarships, awarded through examination and sponsored by Cornell University and the New York State Board of Regents. I don't know if she would have qualified for a scholarship based on need. My grandfather, who dropped out of high school to support his widowed mother, had a company called Buffalo Batt & Felt, with a factory in Depew, New York. I don't know what they did there, but gather it had something to do with by-products of the cotton industry. (One summer my grandfather delivered a load of cottonseed waste to our house, where my mother spread it on the gardens for fertilizer. It lay there stinking for months.)

In high school, my mother had shown more than a little talent at the piano and as a visual artist. Her piano teacher encouraged her to think about a concert career, while her art instructor hoped she would draw and paint professionally.

Did she ever seriously entertain such hopes? I don't know, but my sense is that she did not. She was, I gather, vastly popular at Cornell. Family lore has it that she once had three dates of a Saturday night, and somehow contrived to keep them all. (If I wrote sitcoms I probably would have found a use for that one.) She was nearsighted, and evidently vain enough to go without her glasses on all social occasions; while she attended all Cornell's home games, she never actually saw a football game until, married, she put her glasses on. According to my father, who exaggerated wildly for the sake of a story, she was surprised to discover that there were men down there on the field.

She was an English major. I don't know how seriously she approached her studies, but her grades were always good. (She signed up for second-year Spanish because it fit her schedule, without having taken first-year Spanish. She got a B. The rest of her grades were generally A's, and she made Phi Beta Kappa.)

In 1974 I fell in with a small crowd of people who went to jazz clubs six nights a week. (They stayed home on Saturdays; Saturdays were for amateurs.) They were older than I, and one had been at Cornell at the same time as my mother. When I told him her maiden name his eyes widened. He knew right away what sorority she was in (Sigma Delta Tau) and had the wistful look in his eyes of someone who'd gone to school with Grace Kelly. "Please remember me to your mother," he said later that evening.

When I did, she allowed that his name was familiar, but she didn't remember who he was.

Arthur Jerome Block, a New Yorker, won the same scholarship and attended the same college. He was four years older than my mother, and got to Cornell a couple of years earlier than she did. After three years as an undergraduate in the arts college, he transferred to the law school.

His mother had died while he was an infant, and he'd been raised by his father and by a couple of aunts. His father was a plumber who made some money in real estate, and my father was forever moving and changing schools. During his first year in law school, his father, 42, died suddenly of pneumonia.

I think being abruptly orphaned must have predisposed my father to early marriage. He felt entirely alone, and he wanted a wife and a family. And he met my mother and they fell in love, and they did something that was both dramatic and unusual.

They ran off and got married in secret.

This was in 1932, when college students did not get married. Indeed, most colleges had a rule against it. If two students did get married, it was generally for an obvious reason. She was pregnant, and he was Doing the Right Thing.

That wasn't the case with my parents. Their plan, you must understand, was to keep the marriage a secret from virtually everyone. (My father's roommate, Jimmy Gitlitz, was in on it, and served as best man. I suppose my mother must have had an attendant as well.) They went off to Cortland and got married by a Baptist minister. (Their first choice, a justice of the peace in Trumansburg, turned them down.) Then they drove to Albany for a weekend honeymoon, intending to return to Ithaca, where my mother would continue to live in the dormitory. They'd be married, but nobody would know.

Why, for God's sake? Not to thwart parental opposition; my father had met my mother's parents, and they liked him, even as he was drawn to the warmth and solidity of their family circle. Not to legitimize an impending birth; she wasn't pregnant, and wouldn't become pregnant for four more years. (She had a miscarriage two years or so before I was born in 1938.) Did they marry so that they could sleep together lawfully? Or was it simply that my father wanted to be married, wanted the security of it?

I know it was his idea, and he must have been persuasive. His was not the first marriage proposal my mother received. There were, I gather, several young men who wanted to marry her. She found it easy to turn them down, so you'd think she wouldn't have found it difficult to put my father off for a couple of years.

I guess they were crazy in love. I think that must have been it.

Anyway, the plan went kerblooey. Student marriage was a genuinely rare occurrence at the time, and the local paper in Cortland ran an item about two Cornell students having gotten married there. Jimmy Gitlitz drove all over Ithaca in his Model T Ford, heroically buying up all the copies of the Cortland paper before anyone could read it. But the item was somehow deemed newsworthy beyond Trumansburg, and another paper—Albany?

Maybe—picked up the story, and that was more papers than Jimmy could buy.

Word got out. The bridal couple went directly from Albany to Buffalo and had a religious ceremony with the bride's family present. "And you'll celebrate this as your wedding anniversary," my grandmother said.

No, said my father. They'd celebrate the first date, February 26th. "Would you want your daughter to have lived in sin for four whole days?" he demanded. "And believe me, did she sin!"

They lived briefly in New York, where my mother spent a semester at Barnard. My father had finished law school and was admitted to the bar, and had a promising future in New York, through a connection with the successful law firm that had represented his late father. But they wound up in Buffalo instead. I think my mother missed her family, and I think my *father* missed her family. He had a stepmother whom he detested, and . . . well, this is her story, not his, but I think he may have been more eager than she to relocate to Buffalo.

So they found an apartment in Buffalo, and he found a job, and she spent the next twenty-eight years as a wife and mother.

It was a very different world. There were, to be sure, women who entered the professions, women who made careers for themselves in the arts. But I don't think my mother even saw this as an option. It was not what women in her circle did, and she was very much a member of her own social circle.

Nowadays, as my wife would say, the worm is on the other foot. Nowadays a woman who does not work, who allows her husband to support her while she devotes her time to küchen und kinder, feels guilty about it, or thinks she ought feel guilty about it. She's presumably wasting her talents, her education, her whole life.

It was different then. When the wife of a man of the business or professional classes took employment, she was not only reflecting unfavorably upon her husband's ability to provide for her. In addition, she was depriving her children of a full-time mother while taking a job away from a woman who genuinely needed one.

My father always supported us, and we never missed any meals, but we were a far cry from well off and could certainly have used a second household income. It was never a consideration. Did any of my friends' mothers work? I can't think of a single one that did.

This is not to say that my mother's life was one of idleness. She did have household help while my sister and I were growing up, but she kept an immaculate, well-ordered home and prepared an excellent dinner every night. She did volunteer work and belonged to high-minded organizations, frequently serving as secretary. ("Sometimes," she told me, "I'd like to write the minutes the way they ought to be written. 'Mrs. Fingerhut suggested that the window be closed. Mrs. Wisbaum responded that it was warm in the room, and that if Mrs. Fingerhut didn't dress like a tramp she wouldn't feel the draft.'")

She played cards regularly—bridge in the evening with my father and other couples, bridge and canasta and mah jongg on regularly scheduled afternoons with her friends. Often enough there would be a game at our house, and I'd be playing on the floor in the next room while a table of nicely-dressed ladies moved cards or tiles around and dished their absent friends. Looking back, I'm struck by what an opportunity it provided for a future writer, and how I let its knock go unanswered. They prattled on, destroying reputations on a regular basis, and I never paid any attention.

And she played the piano. There was a Gulbrandsen upright in our front room for years, and I took lessons and practiced on it, to no purpose and with no discernible effect. Sometimes she played, by herself and for herself. Chopin, more often than not, but sometimes Czerny, and sometimes show tunes. She could play anything by ear, and could transpose from one key to another with relative ease.

When I was in high school, she took up painting again. There was a class given once a week at the Jewish Center, and once a week she attended it, and while she was there she painted. Her work was representational at first, and became increasingly abstract; for several years, until she gave it up a decade or so ago, she painted hard-edge acrylics reminiscent of the work of Al Held.

Once, when I was eighteen or so and home from college for a few days, my parents and sister and I were going out for dinner. Betsy was in the car, and my folks thought that I was there as well, and that they were alone in the house. But I'd forgotten something, and had come back to get it from my room.

Betsy had a parakeet at the time, and you were supposed to cover its cage when you left. and I overheard the following conversation between my parents:

My Mother: Are you ready? We're running late.
My Father: Okay, let's go. Oh, wait a minute. We have to cover the parakeet's cage.
My Mother: Oh, the hell with the little bastard.

I couldn't believe it. While I wouldn't have phrased it so inelegantly, I had until that moment regarded my mother as a woman who wouldn't have said shit if she had a mouthful. And here she was, talking like you or me.

"Oh, the hell with the little bastard." With those astonishing and unforgettable words, my mother unwittingly allowed me to realize that she was a real person.

I think their marriage was a good one. If they fought or argued, I never knew it. It seemed to me that their interests diverged over the years, but not in such a way as to imperil the marital bond. I've no idea if either or both of them sought fulfillment elsewhere, and I have to say I'm perfectly content not knowing. It is manifestly none of my business . . . and, if I did know, it would be none of yours.

My father was an unhappy man. I suspect today he'd be diagnosed as having a bi-polar personality. He was certainly a depressive, with occasional periods of elation. His moods were never uncontrolled, never required hospitalization, never led him to seek treatment.

In the last half-dozen years of his life he would wake up very early—four or five in the morning—and would get up and have breakfast and start the day. After dinner he would get in bed with the television set on and be unable to stay awake past eight or nine o'clock. On the weekends, when he and my mother had a social engagement, I think he stayed awake without difficulty, but during the week he drifted into this pattern of early to bed, early to rise.

She would be up until midnight or one in the morning. I lived at home from August of 1959 until I got married the following March. I was writing paperback novels at this point, and worked out a curious schedule; I would have a cup of coffee with my mother around midnight. She would go to bed, and I'd go to my room and work all night, finishing in time to have another cup of coffee with my father around five or six. Then I'd go to bed.

I think my father probably regarded himself as a failure. He wanted to be rich, and became impatient with work that didn't reward him quickly enough. Consequently he changed careers prematurely. If he'd stayed with any of several things he tried, he probably would have been rewarded in the long run. But it was not in his nature.

On the way to the hospital, he said this to my mother: "I hope you get a better guy next time." Then he was admitted, and joked with his nurses. And died.

*　　　*　　　*

I was a good student, and, while I was never a candidate for valedictorian, I was always on the honor roll. The only academic difficulty I got into was in the first semester of my third year in high school. I was taking intermediate algebra, and during the first two of three marking periods, I did the homework and took the tests and got grades in the 90s.

Then, abruptly and for no particular reason, I stopped doing the daily homework assignments. Don't ask me why. I guess they struck me as boring and stupid. I stopped doing them, and nobody said anything, and life went on.

At the end of the semester, we all took the regents exam. The following week, Miss Kelly announced that only one person in the class had earned a perfect score on the final. "And that same person didn't hand in any of his homework assignments during the past six weeks," she said. "So on his report card I've given him 100 for the final examination, and 65 for the last marking period."

Everybody thought it was pretty funny. Then I went home, and my mother asked me what grades I'd received.

"Well," I said, "I got the seven in English."

"The seven? What does that mean?"

"Ninety-seven," I said. "And, let's see, I got the two in Spanish."

"The two?"

"Ninety-two. And I got the five in algebra."

"What does that mean, ninety-five?"

"No, sixty-five," I said, sarcasm dropping like acid.

"And how about Latin? What did you get in Latin?"

It was a good stratagem, but only for a day or so, until I brought the card home and showed it to her. Her sense of irony and poetic justice was at least as good as Miss Kelly's. I got a dollar for aceing the final, and grounded for a month for the 65.

*   *   *

It was in my junior year at high school that I decided to become a writer. In English class, I wrote a composition on career plans, discussing the various career choices I'd entertained since early childhood. (At four I'd announced that I wanted to be a garbageman, abandoning that dream when my mother told me they all got chapped hands.) I concluded with the observation that, uncertain as my future was, one thing was clear: I could never be a writer.

My teacher, Miss Jepson, wrote in the margin: "I'm not so sure about that!" And I decided on the spot that I would be a writer, and never had a moment of second thoughts on the subject. I'd never previously considered being a writer, and from that day on I never considered anything else.

I'd already had some success. In eighth grade, I had to write an essay on the subject of Americanism, for a contest jointly sponsored by the American Legion and the *Buffalo Evening News*. A year before then we had to write essays on the plight of the Buffalo waterfront, and for some reason I couldn't understand what the hell the teacher was getting at, and never turned in the assignment. I suppose my mother wanted to make sure this didn't happen again, and this time around she gave me a little coaching. I wrote the essay, but in retrospect I can see that she put ideas and phrases in my path.

Well, I won a trip to Washington. Not a bad payoff for 250 words.

When I announced that I wanted to be a writer, I got nothing but encouragement from both my parents. They read the poems and sketches I turned out and found something to praise in them. In my senior year I applied to two colleges—to Cornell, of course, which was essentially the family school, and to Antioch, which my parents suggested. They'd heard about it through a friend, and thought it might be a nurturing environment for me.

Both colleges expressed a willingness to admit me. I took the same exam my parents had taken years earlier, and won the same scholarship. It would have substantially reduced the cost of sending me to Cornell, and was of no use at an out-of-state school.

We were not in great shape financially—I'm sure I would have been eligible for financial aid at Antioch, had my father not been unwilling to fill out the requisite forms. As it was, I could have saved a good deal of money by going to Cornell, and I'd have received in Ithaca an education every bit as good and rather more prestigious than what was on offer in Yellow Springs, Ohio. I wanted to go to Antioch, but I can't say I had my heart set on it, and at any rate I wouldn't have dreamed of making a fuss. But there was never a suggestion that I take the money and go to Cornell. They completely supported my going to Antioch.

They were just as supportive when I dropped out two years later. I had sold a story and found a summer job at a literary agency, and I decided the job was too good to give up to return to school.

In February of 1958, I had my first story published. It was called "You Can't Lose" and it appeared in *Manhunt*, a crime fiction magazine. I'd written it in 1956, in the fall, and had sold it the following summer. By the time it appeared in print, I had dropped out of college and was living in New York, working for a literary agent. I was nineteen years old, and thought of myself as mature beyond my years. I was misinformed.

My parents in Buffalo had been awaiting the story's appearance in print, and were quick to buy copies and tell their friends, some of whom dutifully bought copies of their own. (It may have been *Manhunt*'s peak month in western New York.) The story, such as it was (and it wasn't much), is narrated by a thoroughly unscrupulous young man, living by his wits, and getting started in a life of crime. For at least one of my mother's friends, it embodied nothing so much as a loss of innocence—specifically, that of the young fellow who'd written it.

"Oh, Lenore," she said with a sigh. "How do they grow up so quickly? Where do they learn it all? You tell them to dress warm, you hope they'll wear their rubbers . . ."

"Now more than ever," my mother said.

*   *   *

My sister, Betsy, was five years younger than I. Just as I took after my mother's side of the family, so did she take after our father's. "She has my features," he said, "but on her they look good." (He was being unnecessarily modest, and was in fact a handsome man.)

As a child I could never detect this sort of resemblance, and now I wonder how I could have missed it. Betsy definitely looked like my dad, and there is a picture of his mother that could be a picture of Betsy in a period costume. The resemblance is uncanny.

She also inherited his emotional makeup, and on her it didn't look good at all.

My father was certainly depressive, and probably bi-polar. What amounted to moodiness in him manifested far more severely in his daughter. She began acting out around the onset of puberty, and was hospitalized after a psychotic break a couple of years later. The eventual diagnosis was manic-depressive psychosis, and it had her in and out of state mental hospitals for the rest of her life.

She was tall and beautiful, bright and funny, and she had a terrible life. She was married twice, had a child with each husband, and wound up in Roswell, New Mexico, where lithium finally seemed to be keeping her emotionally stable. She died there in 1978, a few months after her thirty-fifth birthday, a few days after my fortieth. Her lithium levels created problems, and a doctor prescribed something to help, and instead it killed her.

My mother never knew what the hell to do about Betsy. There are, I am sure, worse things than being the parent of a mentally-ill child, but I'd be hard put to tell you what they are. Nowadays I suppose there are support groups for this, as there are for everything, and I suspect they help. God knows my folks could have used one.

Instead, they blamed themselves. Forty years ago, few people were apt to suggest that madness might be cellular or biochemical in origin. If a kid didn't turn out right, the logical assumption seemed to be that it was the parents' fault. For years my mother was haunted by the thought that there was something she might have done wrong, or something she might have failed to do, that had led to Betsy's difficulties.

I think she got over this. What lasted longer, I suspect, was the nagging sense that there ought to be something she could do to help.

What she didn't like to do was talk about it. She talked with my father, and later with her second husband, and she talked a great deal with me, but she avoided discussing the subject with her friends. Part of this stemmed from a natural inclination to keep family matters private. She was concerned, too, at least early on, that Betsy might recover and resume her rightful place in society, only to be handicapped by widespread knowledge of her past.

There was something else, though, and it took me a while to understand it. What she wanted to avoid was having the same futile and tedious conversation over and over with well-meaning friends. I'm sure they thought she was avoiding the subject, and consequently politeness and consideration led them to avoid bringing it up. And that was fine with her.

I used to think she was being hypocritical, or playing ostrich with her head in the sand. I've long since ceased to see it that way, perhaps because I've found out how annoying it is to wind up having the same conversation over and over, even on a subject that is not painful but merely tedious.

Well, I take after her. But on her it looks good.

My sister's first marriage ended abruptly. Her husband was a Hawaiian, a lifer in the Marine Corps. He was also an alcoholic, and she told me he abused her physically, but I never knew whether to believe her. When Betsy reported something, you couldn't be sure if it was true. She never lied, but she sometimes remembered things that hadn't happened.

His name was Everett Collins Poohina, and he was called Po. At the end he was based at Camp Pendleton, in southern California. My sister bore his son, David, and was hospitalized again at Patten State, near San Bernardino. While she was there, Po went AWOL, wandered around drinking for a couple of days, then picked up a hand grenade and took it out onto the range. He pulled the pin and didn't stop counting at ten.

My mother and I flew out there and saw the baby, who was being cared for by friends of Betsy and Po. Po's father was planning to come over from Hawaii, and had expressed the intention of taking his grandson back to the islands with him.

After we left the couple's house in Oceanside, my mother kept stressing the baby's physical appearance. He looked Hawaiian, he said. He looked like his father. He didn't look like us at all.

I was confused. That sort of racial observation was uncharacteristic of her. But then I realized what she was doing. She knew that the baby was going to wind up in Hawaii, that he would be separated from his mother and indeed from all of us, and that it was probably better for him that way. And so she was preparing herself for lifelong separation from her grandson by stressing his otherness as a way of distancing herself from him. He was one of them, not one of us.

My mother was forty-eight when she was widowed, and left with nothing aside from the cash on hand, the house on Starin Avenue and the proceeds of a small insurance policy. My father had bought the house in 1943 for $8500, and she sold it in 1961 for just about twice that. (I suppose it would bring $200,000 now, something like that.)

She moved to an apartment a few blocks away and got a job at a library, where she quickly made herself indispensable, taking evening courses in library science toward a masters or some sort of certification. After an appropriate interval she began accepting dates, and began keeping company with a man named Bill Bregger. They dated for a year or two, and had come to an understanding. Then he went into the hospital for a routine prostate operation. A successful pharmacist, he knew all the doctors and hospital personnel, and was assured of the best care.

And one thing after another went wrong post-op, and he stayed in the hospital for weeks until finally his kidneys failed and he died.

She was in a curious position, a sort of unofficial widow. His daughters knew and liked her—she's still close to them—and she was in some respects the chief mourner.

I was living in Buffalo at the time. My wife and daughter and I had moved back from New York several months after my father's death, probably out of guilt from not having been there at the time. We were there for two years, and then I accepted a job editing a numismatic magazine in Racine, Wisconsin. I took it, it seems to me, as a graceful way of getting out of Buffalo.

Shortly after we settled in Racine, my mother mentioned that Frankie Rosenberg, who'd been in poor health for some time, had died. The Rosenbergs lived directly across the street from us, and Joe and Frankie had painted in the same weekly class as my mother. He was an otorhinolaryngologist, and had taken out my tonsils when I was five years old.

I never held it against him. And, when I got off the phone with my mother, a curious thought flashed through my mind. Now she and Joe can get married, I thought. It was, really, a ridiculous thought, and I let it go and forgot about it.

And a year or so later, they did.

Her second marriage was just about perfect. With Joe she found a true companion, and the delight they took in each other's company was remarkable to see. They traveled widely, collected art together, painted together, and obsessed together over the decor of their home. (She was back on Starin again, directly across the street from the house I grew up in.)

Joe had lost a kidney early on to diphtheria, and had survived bladder cancer, but he was the furthest thing from an invalid. He was wonderfully energetic and enthusiastic. They had eleven great years together, and then, driving to work one morning, he had a heart attack and died.

She sold the house, bought a condo in a good building downtown. She had quit work at the library to marry Joe, and wished in hindsight that she'd stayed on another six months to qualify for Social Security. She didn't go back to the library, or look for anything elsewhere. She was 64, and young for her age, but I was not surprised when the years passed without any more men coming into her life. That chapter had ended on a high note, but it had ended.

Some months after Joe's death, before she sold the house, I came to visit for a few days. I overheard her talking to a friend on the phone, and she was saying that it was good to have a man in the house. "I'll tell you," I heard her say, "it's a pleasure to find the toilet seat up!"

Nice line, but here's what I really liked about it: Years before their marriage, Joe had had a bladderectomy. He wore a prosthesis, a bag that he emptied at appropriate intervals, and he didn't have to raise the toilet seat to do it. So he never left the seat up.

She'd been widowed about a year and a half when Betsy died. Coincidentally, she was visiting New York when the call came, so we were able to fly out to New Mexico together for the funeral. Betsy, who'd had a Reformed Jewish upbringing, had become Christian somewhere along the way—attending her total-immersion baptism into one denomination or other had been a peak experience for Joe and Lenore—and belonged to the Salvation Army toward the end. I wondered how my mother would handle the service, with the hymns and the eulogy, but she was fine with it.

Afterward, back at our motel, she said, "Well, now at least I don't have to worry about where she is and what she'd doing."

Huh? Where she was was in the ground, and what she was doing was lying there. We no longer had to worry that something bad might happen, because the worst possible thing *had* happened. Where was the relief in that?

I didn't get it. Now, just over twenty years later, I'm beginning to. It's easier to endure the worst, I guess, than to sit around waiting for it.

After the funeral, she had a drink. I kept her company, but I didn't have one with her. I'd stopped doing that about fifteen months earlier.

When I was three or four months sober, I'd flown to Buffalo for the weekend. I'd decided to tell my mother that I'd stopped drinking, and I knew what her response would be. "Don't you think you're overreacting?" she would say. "Why do you have to take everything to extremes? Why can't you just drink sensibly?"

It was not a conversation I was eager to have. But I blurted it out, told her I'd realized I had a drinking problem and that, a day at a time, I was staying away from the stuff.

"I think that's wonderful," she said. "I think you've made a very wise decision, and I'm happy for you."

Go know.

In July, 1988, Lynne and I attended an international conference of crime writers in Gijón, an industrial port in northern Spain. I got a phone call from my cousin David, who had tracked me down, God knows how. My mother had been in an auto accident. She was in critical condition, and it was impossible to say whether she would survive.

Early the following morning we flew to Madrid and continued on to New York and Buffalo, not knowing whether we were rushing to a bedside or a funeral. When we arrived she was alive but her outlook was uncertain, and it stayed that way for a long time. She was in intensive care for a full month, and comatose throughout. She had sustained broken ankles and a cracked pelvis and had gone into respiratory failure.

When she finally recovered consciousness and got out of the ICU, there was a period of a couple of weeks during which she was not herself. That's an overused expression, but in this instance it was literally true. The personality inhabiting her was not her own. She was nasty to her nurses, mean-spirited, and, well, not herself. Lynne and I were put in mind of Stephen King's *Pet Sematary*, in which the dead return to life, but incompletely, their souls misshapen, their psyches with pieces missing. She was alive, but who he hell *was* she?

Maybe this sort of thing happens frequently after such massive insults to the body and soul. I wouldn't know. It was clear, though, that the internal decision she had made to return to life was not one she endorsed wholeheartedly. She was back, but she wasn't entirely sure it was where she wanted to be.

I remember that I brought her a book of Gary Larson's *Far Side* cartoons while she was in the hospital, and it turned out to be an unfortunate choice. She kept finding cartoons she didn't get, and it bothered her profoundly that their humor eluded her. "Why is this funny?" she kept demanding. "What's funny about it?"

I knew what was bothering her. She was afraid that some mental impairment might have resulted from the accident, and that was something she had always dreaded far more than death. "If I ever get like that," she'd said, of someone suffering from Alzheimer's, "I hope I can count on you to kill me."

I don't think she really relaxed until I brought her a book of Double-Crostics, and she knocked one off in half an hour. If she could still do that, the brain damage couldn't be too severe.

Lynne and I stayed in her apartment while she was in the ICU, and for the first few weeks after she came to. Then we went on with our lives, and, a few weeks later, she was discharged from the hospital and went on with her own.

I made one executive decision before we left. I found the packs of cigarettes she had on hand and tossed them.

She'd been a heavy smoker ever since college, and had never attempted to quit, or even considered it. Smoking may have been a contributing factor to her post-traumatic respiratory failure; it certainly slowed her recovery.

I figured she would probably start smoking again after she got out of the hospital, and I felt she had the right, but I also figured if it meant that much to her she could damn well go out and buy a pack. So I rounded up the cigarettes and got rid of them.

She never did resume smoking. I eventually mentioned what I'd done, and she said she'd almost certainly have started again if there had been cigarettes around the house. But there weren't, so she didn't.

The September before her accident, she'd thrown herself a 75th birthday party at the country club. Dozens of her friends attended, and all the family. She was the belle of the ball, young for her years, and very much on top of her game.

The auto accident constituted an abrupt transition from middle to old age. She'd become a traveler after my father's death, traveled extensively with her second husband, traveled again in her second widowhood. She went to India, to China. When my daughters Amy and Jill each graduated from college, she took them in turn to Europe.

She'd have taken Alison, too, but the accident intervened. There have been no more trips to Europe, or even to New York. But she has remained very active, going to plays and concerts, playing cards with her friends, dining out at restaurants several nights a week. She watches a good deal of television, and is especially fond of *East Enders*, the British soap, and HBO's *Oz* and *The Sopranos*. ("I was watching *Oz* the other night," my daughter Jill told me, "and trying to come to terms with the fact that Nana never misses an episode. I mean, is that a show for your grandmother to watch?")

Three years ago I bought her a computer for Christmas. Arthritic fingers don't exactly dance on a keyboard, and the requisite memorization is easier for the young than the old, but she got the hang of it and surfed the Net like a kid.

She still reads, though less than she used to. I send her my books in manuscript now, so she won't have to wait for the printed book, and because the typeface is larger and easier to cope with. She still knocks off Thomas Middleton's Double-Crostics in twenty minutes. Mentally, she really hasn't lost a step.

But her feet never entirely recovered from the accident, and arthritis complicated by late-onset diabetes has her in pain pretty much all the time.

Well, she's eighty-six years old.

I had this piece mostly written when Lynne and I flew up to Buffalo to spend Passover with her. Our visits, once or twice a year, are like time-lapse photography. Every time we see her it's a little harder for her to get around, and she has more hours where the pain and discomfort immobilizes her. It's always a joy to see her, and I always come home deeply saddened.

We ate in several different restaurants, and each time she brought half her entree home in a doggie bag. Her sense of smell had faded in recent months, she told me, and perhaps as a consequence her appetite was considerably diminished. She still enjoyed her food, but she didn't eat as much of it.

In our family, that's not a good sign. Hearty appetites are a birthright, and emotional blows don't interfere. My mother certainly endured some crippling losses in the course of her life, but nothing ever stopped her from eating a good dinner.

In Gijón, after I'd made arrangements for our flight the following morning, Lynne and I went out with another couple as planned, and fell to like loggers. My mother, I assured Lynne, would understand.

I don't know what it means, this ebbing of the appetite.

One afternoon I had her windshield wipers replaced. The car's the one she bought to replace the one in which she had the accident, and it must be ten years old by now. The mileage is low, though, and the car seems to be in good shape.

"This will be my last car," she said. "It'll outlast me."

I had printed out what I'd thus far written, and brought it along, thinking I might let her have a look at it. Once, when she asked what I was working on, I was on the verge of telling her about this piece. But I didn't.

Maybe, now that it's done, I'll print out a copy for her. Maybe I'll wait until the book comes out.

We'll see.

I spent weeks trying to figure out how to approach this essay, or article, or whatever the hell it is. I'm by no means thrilled with the result. What does it say, really, about her, or about me, or about anything?

What do I know about writing this sort of thing?

She is, to my mind, a remarkable woman, but I don't know that you could prove it from what I've written. She's hidden somewhere under all these damned words, but where?

I haven't even known what to call her. "My mother." "She."

When I talk about her—to Lynne, to my daughters, to anyone who knows her—I call her Lenore. (My father used to quote Poe: "A rare and radiant maiden whom the angels call Lenore.) When she's in the room I call her Mom.

There is a metaphysical school of thought that holds that you choose your own parents. The soul, buzzing around in hyperspace, picks out the vessel in which to be reincarnated.

I'd say I chose well.

❧❦❧

I did in fact show her the piece, and she found it underwhelming. "I'm more interesting than that," she said.

No argument there.

Did she ever see it in printed form? I don't believe so. In the summer of 2001 her foot problems worsened, and she had to have a couple of toes amputated. She tried mightily to refuse the surgery, preferring death to disfigurement, but the doctors finally persuaded her.

I flew to Buffalo and saw her at Millard Fillmore Hospital, just across the street from her apartment. The doctor wanted to do further surgery, saying she'd die without it, and arguing that her mental state was such that she was incompetent to veto the procedure. I had her checked by a psychiatrist who was a family friend, sure she'd get a clean bill of mental health, but that's not what happened. She'd evidently had a bunch of mini-strokes over the preceding year, and in retrospect I could see the symptoms I'd managed to overlook.

She'd always been very clear that her direst fear was of outliving her mind. Death before dementia was her unequivocal choice, and she also preferred death to further amputation.

I made arragements for her to be transferred to a hospice and flew back to New York, and a day after I got there, two planes flew into the twin towers of the World Trade Center. Lynne and I watched from our twelfth-floor window as the towers fell.

Sixteen days later, and six days after her 89th birthday, my mother died. Here's the notice that ran in the New York Times *and the* Buffalo News:

ROSENBERG - Lenore Nathan Block. Of Buffalo NY, died peacefully September 27, 2001, in her ninetieth year. She is deeply mourned by her son, the writer Lawrence Block of New York City; her stepsons, Richard Rosenberg of Laguna Beach and Arthur Rosenberg of Albuquerque; her daughters-in-law, Lynne Block, Karen Rosenberg, and Loretta Mackay; her grandchildren, Amy Reichel, Jill Block, Alison Pouliot, Gretchen Faber, Diane Sweeney, Kenneth Rosenberg, David Poohina, and Jennifer Reyes; her great-grandchildren, Sara and Marisa Reichel, Joseph Harrison, and Laura Rosenberg; and her brother and sister-in-law, Hi and Mim Nathan. She was predeceased by her two husbands, Arthur Jerome Block and Joseph Rosenberg; her daughter, Betsy Molina; and her brother, Jerry Nathan. A Phi Beta Kappa graduate of Cornell University, an accomplished painter, a woman of infinite warmth and wit, she's gone where the Saturday Review still publishes a Literary Cryptogram every week, and where there's an endless supply of unworked Double-Crostics; where Rubinstein and Horowitz and Art Tatum take turns at the piano, and where her favorite cities of New York and Paris and London are just around the corner. She was a great and gallant lady, and her absence leaves an enormous permanent gap in the skyline.

RAYMOND CHANDLER AND THE BRASHER DOUBLOON

Sometime in 1960, a friend's enthusiasm for coin collecting
proved contagious, and I began sorting through pocket change
and noting dates and mint marks. Before I knew it I was
subscribing to a weekly numismatic newspaper and buying
coins from dealers and at auctions. I'd collected stamps as
a boy, and now I was collecting coins with at least as much
passion, and a little more money to commit to the pursuit.

I'd been doing this for three years or so when my writing
career hit a bad patch. A falling-out with my agent led to my
losing access to the publishers who had long sustained me.
Fortunately, I had nothing else to fall back on—no college
degree, no vocational experience. So I had to keep at it, and I
developed some additional markets for my work.

And while I was at it I wrote a couple of articles for
numismatic publications. "Raymond Chandler and the Brasher
Doubloon" was the most interesting of them, and it opened
a door for me in Racine, Wisconsin. That's where I sent it, to
a fellow named Kenneth E. Bressett who was editing a new
magazine called the Whitman Numismatic Journal. He snapped
it up, and before long he found an excuse to visit Buffalo, where
I was living. Our meeting led to a job offer, and by July of 1964
I'd sold our house at 48 Ebling Avenue, in the Township of
Tonawanda, and relocated with wife and two daughters to 4051

*Marquette Drive, in Racine, where I worked on the magazine
and related enterprises for a little over a year and a half.*

*It was the only job I ever had after college, and I surprised
myself by discovering an unexpected ability to survive and even
flourish in a corporate atmosphere. Toward the end of my stay,
I learned that my boss planned to move me out of the backwater
of the Coin Supplies Division and into general marketing, which
told me that I had found for myself, astonishingly, A Job With A
Future.*

*This was enormously heartening. But, even as I realized all
this, I realized too that it was not a future I wanted. I was, alas,
doomed to be a writer, and had in fact sustained myself during
that year and a half by writing and publishing a couple of
novels and several shorter works. I had in fact just finished the
first Evan Tanner novel,* The Thief Who Couldn't Sleep, *when
I made my decision to give up my job and return to the East
Coast.*

*It was good to return to my real life. But I've never regretted
a single day that I spent in Racine, and I'm pleased to present
the piece that started it all.*

One of the stock components of the contemporary mystery novel is the disappearance of some item of great value or importance. This missing article
serves as the focal point for the mystery, with various agents attempting to
recover it and various complications arising in due course. If the article itself
is interesting, the book is made more interesting for its readers.

The nature of this sort of item is infinitely variable. It may be a unique
objet d'art, as in Dashiell Hammett's *The Maltese Falcon*. It may be a vital
document, as in any of a plethora of espionage novels. In the recent movie
Charade, a batch of rare stamps filled this role.

Occasionally a coin or a collection of coins is used in this fashion as the core of a mystery novel. Perhaps the most noteworthy instance of numismatics in detective fiction occurs in Raymond Chandler's *The High Window*, where the plot spins around the mysterious loss of an uncirculated specimen of the Brasher Doubloon. The book is of particular interest to a numismatist not only because a coin is involved but because several interesting facets of numismatics, including a clever counterfeiting method, are treated in some depth.

Raymond Chandler himself was one of the fathers of the tough or hard-boiled detective story. Born in 1888, he did not begin writing professionally until his mid-forties. His total production from that time until his death in 1959 was relatively small—seven novels, five Hollywood screenplays and a handful of short stories and articles. The quality of his output is considerably more impressive than the quantity. The sound plotting and swift pace of Chandler's books won him a large public following; his depth of thought and brilliance of style earned him acclaim from more loftily intellectual readers and critics as well.

The High Window was published in 1942, although Chandler had the book in the planning stage at least three years earlier. In a letter to his publisher in April of 1942 he discussed possible titles for the script and commented on the doubloon itself, revealing as he did so the depth of his research:

> "The title, *Brasher* or *Brashear Doubloon*, was the origin of the story, but that's not important. I never thought of your idea that booksellers might pronounce Brasher as brassiere. I can see the point now.
>
> "Brasher, more commonly Brashear, is an actual name. There was an Ephraim Brashear or Brasher, and he actually did make this coin for the State of New York in 1787. It is not the most valuable American coin, but except possibly the 1822 five-dollar gold piece it is the only one existing in sufficient numbers, and being of sufficient value, to be of any use for my purpose. There

were a couple of small towns named Brashear and also a Brasher Falls . . .

"All I can think of along this line at the moment is *The Lost Doubloon, The Lost Doubloon Mystery, The Stolen Coin Mystery, The Rare Coin Mystery*. All rather pedestrian. I'd like something with a bit more oomph."

A few days later Chandler suggested *The High Window* as the title, and this was used when the book came out. When the book was made into a movie five years later, the film carried Chandler's original title, *Brasher Doubloon*.

In the book itself, Chandler's detective, Philip Marlowe, is hired to recover "a rare gold coin called a Brasher Doubloon." The owner of the coin is the widow of a collector who described the piece as the prize of her husband's collection and estimates its worth as over ten thousand dollars. A clause in his will forbids her to dispose of his collection during her own lifetime. She explains that her husband "seemed to feel that I ought to have taken more interest in his little pieces of metal while he was alive."

Marlowe's client discovered the doubloon was missing after a coin dealer called to inquire if it was for sale. In due course Marlowe goes to the dealer's office to question him. While it is unlikely that Chandler's interest in numismatics went any deeper than the research for this book itself, the following description indicates that he was not entirely unfamiliar with the vagaries of professional numismatists:

"I turned the knob and went into a small narrow room with two windows, a shabby little typewriter desk, closed, a number of wall cases of tarnished coins in tilted slots with yellowed typewritten labels under them, two brown filing cases at the back against the wall, no curtains at the windows, and a dust gray floor carpet so threadbare that you wouldn't notice the rips in it unless you tripped over one . . . The inner office was just as small

but had a lot more stuff in it. A green safe almost blocked off the
front half. Beyond this a heavy old mahogany table against the
entrance door held some dark books, some flabby old magazines,
and a lot of dust."

In conversation with the coin dealer, Marlowe determines that someone
has attempted to sell the coin to the dealer, who immediately became suspi-
cious and called Marlowe's client. Marlowe offers to buy back the coin for
the owner for one thousand dollars, and the dealer is interested in acting as
the go-between in the recovery of the coin. In the course of the conversation,
the dealer supplies the following background information on the Brasher
Doubloon:

"An interesting coin . . . In some ways the most interesting
and valuable of all early American coins . . . It is a gold coin,
roughly equivalent to a twenty-dollar gold piece, and about the
size of a half dollar. Almost exactly. It was made for the State
of New York in the year 1787. It was not minted. There were no
mints until 1793, when the first mint was opened in Philadelphia.
The Brasher Doubloon was coined probably by the pressure
molding process and its maker was a private goldsmith named
Ephraim Brasher, or Brashear . . . .

"The two halves of the mold were engraved in steel, in
intaglio, of course. These halves were then mounted in lead. Gold
blanks were pressed between them in a coin press. Then the
edges were trimmed for weight and smoothed. The coin was not
milled. There were no milling machines in 1787. . . . And, since
the surface hardening of steel without distortion could not be
accomplished at that time, the dies wore and had to be remade
from time to time . . . in fact, it would be safe to say that no two
of the coins would be identical, judged by modern methods of
microscopic examination."

Concerning the quantity of Brasher Doubloons in existence, the dealer estimates the number at "a few hundred, a thousand, perhaps more," an estimate which is clearly out of line. Of these, he adds, very few are uncirculated specimens, and places the value of such a piece at upwards of ten thousand dollars.

With the amount of research obviously devoted to the numismatic background of *The High Window*, it would seem unlikely that Chandler could have been so far out of line on the quantity of Brasher pieces in existence as he was by accident. It's probably more likely that he deliberately bent the truth for the sake of the plot. This becomes more apparent when we consider that the other piece which he considered was the 1822 half-eagle, of which only three specimens are known. For plot purposes, Chandler required a coin with an extremely high value but with sufficient specimens in existence so that counterfeiting on a small scale would be feasible. With today's dramatically high coin prices, it would be easier to come up with such a coin; twenty years ago, coin prices were considerably lower, and a little distortion of the truth for the book's sake seems unavoidable.

Later in the book, Marlowe receives the coin in question anonymously, through the mail. At this point we are given the following description of the coin:

> "The side facing me showed a spread eagle with a shield
> for a breast and the initials E. B. punched into the left wing.
> Around these was a circle of beading, between the beading and
> the smooth unmilled edge of the coin, the legend E PLURIBUS
> UNUM. At the bottom was the date 1787 . . . . The other side
> showed a sun rising or setting behind a sharp peak of mountain,
> then a double circle of what looked like oak leaves, then more
> Latin, NOVA EBORACA COLUMBIA EXCELSIOR. At the bottom
> of this side, in smaller capitals, the name BRASHER."

For safekeeping Marlowe pawns the coin with a pawnbroker who is unaware of the value of the piece and simply loans him fifteen dollars on the basis of the coin's gold value. He mails the pawn ticket to himself and continues with his investigation.

Later in the book we learn that this particular specimen of the Brasher Doubloon is a particularly unusual one. Marlowe's client explains that "the coin maker's initials, E.B., are on the left wing of the eagle. Usually, I am told, they are on the right wing."

One wonders whether or not this was simple invention on Chandler's part. As it happens, there is a unique specimen of the Brasher Doubloon in which the initials are punched not on the wing but on the breast of the eagle. Chandler no doubt moved the variation from breast to opposite wing to make the difference less obvious, and labeled the piece a rare variety rather than a unique one for reasons in line with those hypothesized above.

At the close of the book, in the course of the solution of several murders, Marlowe discovers that the Brasher Doubloon was stolen not specifically for resale but in order to make counterfeit copies of the piece. Because Chandler is a great believer in detail, we have the following elaborate description of the counterfeiting process:

> "The method they thought of was about what a dental technician uses to make a gold inlay. . . . That is, to reproduce a model exactly, in gold, by making a matrix in a hard white fine cement called albastone, then making a replica of the model in that matrix in molding wax, complete in the finest detail, then investing the wax, as they call it, in another kind of cement called crystobolite, which has the property of withstanding great heat without distortion. A small opening is left from the wax to outside by attaching a steel pin which is withdrawn when the cement sets. Then the crystobolite casting is cooked over a flame until the wax boils out through this small opening, leaving a hollow mold of the original model. This is clamped against a crucible on a centrifuge and molten gold is shot into it by

centrifugal force from the crucible. Then the crystobolite, still hot, is held under cold water and it disintegrates, leaving the gold core with a gold pin attached, representing the small opening. That is trimmed off, the casting is cleaned in acid and polished, and you have, in this case, a brand-new Brasher Doubloon, made of solid gold and exactly the same as the original."

This whole process sounds only slightly more complicated than performing brain surgery with boxing gloves on, and I find it hard to believe that anyone about to plunk down ten grand for a Brasher Doubloon would not give the coin enough of a look-see to determine that it was a cast copy, let alone demand a pedigree for the coin. But this is a petty objection. Chandler was writing a mystery novel, not preparing a paper for presentation at the A.N.S., and the casting method is certainly of numismatic interest, however unlikely it may be to deluge the market with perfect Brusher Doubloons.

After Marlowe breaks things open, one of the counterfeiters is picked up in another city with a dozen fakes in his suitcase. Appallingly enough, the counterfeiter goes free! As Marlowe explains, "He had bought the gold legally and counterfeiting an obsolete New York State coin didn't come under the federal counterfeiting laws."

A most unsuccessful conclusion from a coin collector's standpoint! What happened to the phonies? I suppose we have to take it on faith that some agent of Providence saw they were melted down. A dozen "perfect" counterfeit Brasher Doubloons floating around the country is frightening to contemplate.

A fine book, *The High Window*, as absorbing now as when it was written. One shouldn't need a special excuse to read it, but the numismatic tie-in should make it doubly interesting for a coin collector.

TRAVEL BY NUMBER

This piece on the Travelers Century Club ran in the New York Times *travel section May of 2003. (It had a different and more newspapery title: "In This Club, Countries Are Collected.")*

The local guide in Odessa explained it all to us. Although our itinerary called for our tour bus to proceed from Odessa to Tiraspol, en route to Kishinev, it would be simpler and quicker to skirt that portion of Moldova east of the Dniester and cross directly from Ukraine into Moldova proper. We'd be spared a border crossing that way. "And it is all gangsters there," she said. "Very dangerous. Nothing to see. Boring."

The twelve of us sat around and talked it over. One of our group pointed out that he'd never known a place to be both dangerous and boring.

"When my folks and I went to Albania," a woman recalled, "they were shooting over our heads all the time. I can't believe it's going to be any worse in—what's the name of the place?"

"Transdniester," I said. "Or Transnistria, or the breakaway People's Republic of Moldavia."

When the Soviet Union fell apart, the portion of the Moldavian SSR east of the Dniester River didn't want to be part of the new nation of Moldova. Their ties were with Russia, while the western portion of Moldova leaned toward Romania. They fought a war of independence in 1992, and five hundred people died in it. Since then five thousand Russian troops have been stationed in Transdniester, maintaining an uneasy peace and guaranteeing the region's autonomy.

"Is it on the list?" someone wanted to know.

It wasn't.

"But it might get there eventually," someone else pointed out. "And did you say they have their own stamps? And their own currency?"

"Hell, they're a country," said the woman who'd been under fire in Albania. "Where's the guide? Tell her to forget about her damn shortcut. We want to go to Tiraspol."

I'm not sure when I first heard of the Travelers Century Club, but my first encounter with one of its members came in 1996, on a day trip from Reykjavik to Greenland. The highlight for one of our party was the opportunity to get his passport stamped and add Greenland to his list of visited countries. It was his 129th, and he was eager to send a postcard to a friend and fellow club member. "She's got 154 countries," he said, "but she just hops around the Caribbean, scooping up all the islands. She never goes to the hard countries."

You have to understand that my wife, Lynne, and I are compulsive when it comes to travel. (And most things; we feel that, if you're not compulsive about something, you just don't care about it very much.) I've written elsewhere of our Buffalo hunt, and we were slack-jawed with admiration when we heard about a man whose mission was to set foot in every county in America. How could we not want to join an organization that required prospective members to have visited 100 or more countries, and whose members aimed at a perfect score of 314?

We were ready to play.

*   *   *

The odyssey that led to Tiraspol was a Wilderness Travel trip that started out in Minsk. We were to tour four countries—Belarus, Ukraine, Moldova, and Romania. It would be an unlikely choice for anyone's first trip abroad, and indeed the twelve of us were seasoned travelers, club members or wannabes. One of our party, his passport as thick as a novel, logged country #273 by the time we reached Bucharest.

At dinner that first night, one fellow told us about a friend of his who wanted to go to Diego Garcia. This chunk of rock in the Indian Ocean got some attention when planes refueled there en route to Afghanistan, but in 1999 not many people had heard of it.

It was on the club's list, but you couldn't go to it. The whole island was a British naval base and access was restricted to authorized personnel. So this lunatic and his equally intrepid friend got in their boat and sailed as close to Diego Garcia as they dared.

Then they scuttled the ship, and put out an SOS. And were in due course rescued, and towed ashore to Diego Garcia, where they made a quick repair to their vessel, thanked their unwitting hosts, and sailed away in triumph.

Everyone in our party had the same reaction, one of unqualified admiration. Resourceful, said the man with the 273 countries. Brilliant, said the quiet man from Florida. Committed, a woman said—that they were, not that they ought to be.

I glanced at Lynne. She was beaming. These were our kind of people.

The club's rules are permissive and inclusive. Any contact with the surface of a listed country—even a refueling stop—counts as a visit. And political sovereignty is not the only criterion for listing a country. If historical or geographical aspects render a place discrete, it may wind up on the list. Accordingly, Hawaii and Alaska count as separate countries.

The list waxes and wanes. Czechoslovakia was one country; the Czech

Republic and Slovakia are two. Germany was two countries; with reunification, it became one.

The distinctions are arbitrary, and this drives some people crazy. Why does Trinidad and Tobago count as one country, while the Dutch and French sides of St. Martin are two? Why are some of the states of Malaysia counted separately while others are not?

I find such arguments tiresome, and about as purposeful as going to a ballgame and insisting that the infield fly rule is illogical. It's a game, you dimwit, and games have rules. If you don't want to play by them, then pick up your passport and go home.

And what are the rewards of this unquestionably loopy way to see the world?

When we drive around this country, hunting Buffalo, serendipity rewards us periodically with out of the way attractions the guidebooks don't even know about. Similarly, our pursuit of new countries gets us where we wouldn't otherwise go.

A couple of summers ago we seized the chance to add a country by making a quick trip to St. Pierre & Miquelon, a pair of French islands off the coast of Newfoundland. We went because they were on the list, and we found a charming French village that might as easily have been on the coast of Brittany or Normandy, entirely different from (and quietly hostile toward) Quebec. It's like going to France without crossing an ocean, and it was our commitment to traveling by the numbers that got us there.

Transdniester, I should report, was well worth the extra border crossing. The guide and the bus driver, at first resigned to the whole thing, perked up when they remembered they could buy really cheap brandy in Tiraspol. (I don't want to think about their return trip to Odessa.) We hit the Post

Office, where I converted two dollars into People's Republic of Moldavia currency, bought a slew of stamps, and still had a half-inch thick stack of PRM 100,000-rouble notes.

Membership in the Travelers Century Club is open to anyone who's been to 100 countries, and you can join as a member-in-training at 75. (You don't have to show proof. They take your word for it.) I'd explain how to contact the club and obtain the list of qualifying countries, but in this age of search engines and ready access to information, I think I'll let you work that out on your own. If you can't find the club's website, how do you expect to find Diego Garcia?

And how are Lynne and I doing? Well, we were trainee members on the Belarus-Ukraine-Moldova-Romania trip, but we've been busy since then, and qualified for full membership during a January voyage to Antarctica. Right now our count stands at 104 countries.

Or 105, if you count Transdniester.

And of course we did indeed count Transdniester—and so does the Travelers Century Club. A few years after I wrote this piece, the TCC newsletter announced that the Club now recognized the breakaway region of Transnistria. You can imagine our excitement at having officially added another country to our total simply by opening an envelope.

I'm not sure when the club recognized the country, albeit under a name different from the one we'd learned. I know I'd come to think of it as Transnistria when I wrote the following in my Linn's Stamp News *column in 2010, subsequently collected* in Generally Speaking:

"On a group trip through Belarus, Ukraine, Moldova and Romania, we and some fellow Travelers Century Clubbers persuaded the tour leader to cross into Transnistria, the

breakaway Moldovan province whose separate status has been
guaranteed by a couple of thousand Russian troops. They had
their own stamps, and at their post office I changed a single US
dollar into Transnistrian rubles, bought some stamps, and still
had a few million left in Transnistrian 100,000-ruble notes. A
powerful currency, the Transnistrian ruble."

I'm not sure of our country count, either. We were keeping
track carefully until we got past 160, and I'm pretty sure we've
yet to reach 170, but that's as precise as I can come. There's a
point—we reached it with Buffalos, and with countries as well—
when we tend to lose interest in the numbers.

Incidentally, when I'd heard the Diego Garcia anecdote
at that dinner in Minsk I'd thought might be apocryphal. I
certainly wanted it to be true, but how could it be? Later I was
to meet Bill Gigante, a Navy guy who turned up at an event I
spoke at in Singapore. I included the TCC in my remarks, and
told the Diego Garcia anecdote to illustrate how far some of the
club's members were prepared to go.

Bill, it turned out, had been stationed at Diego Garcia, and
was able to report that what I'd talked about had actually
happened, and more than once. "Every now and then somebody
scuttles a ship or fakes engine trouble," he said. "All in order
to set foot on that island. It's nuts, but I have to say it's also
inspiring."

THE WHOLE WORLD IS LISTENING

Some months after I had become a devoted follower of the
Overheard in New York *website, one of their principals got in
touch with me. They were about to publish a book of selections
from web posts, and wondered if I'd be interested in providing
an introduction. As recompense, they'd promote my latest book
on their site.*

    Well, okay . . .

*A car, stuck in traffic behind a garbage truck, starts blowing its
horn loudly and insistently. A nicely dressed lady shouts: "Shut
the fuck up, you moron! Haven't you ever seen a garbage truck
before? Fucking moron tourists."*

—W. 4th & Perry

A month or so ago as I write these lines, I read the garbage-truck vignette on
the *Overheard in New York* website. I had by then been a fan for a couple of
months, having grown into the habit of checking the site a couple of times a
day, and having burrowed my way through the complete archives, as happy
as a mole in a grub-infested lawn.

    When I read about the well-dressed lady, I had a frisson, and how often
does that happen? Frissons, let me tell you, are thin on the ground these days.

They're still to be found, though, and I had one, all right. I knew beyond a doubt, reasonable or otherwise, just who that well-dressed lady had to be.

And she was a mere room away. "Lynne," I called, "I think you're in the media."

She read it for herself, and admitted she was the WDL in question. "This moron was honking and honking," she said.

"Don't explain."

"I guess there were people at those outdoor tables. I guess somebody heard me."

"So it would appear. You look puzzled."

"At least they said well-dressed," she said. "I'm just trying to remember what I was wearing."

I don't remember how I first found my way to *Overheard in New York*. I think somebody must have sent me a link, possibly my eldest granddaughter, who's as devoted to the site as I am. (A month or two ago I found a contribution sent in by Sara R of Flushing. "You're a published author," I IM'd her. "It runs in the family," she replied.)

One thing that strikes me about OINY is how utterly New York it is. If you had, say, *Overheard in Los Angeles*, it'd be the closest thing to a blank page. Because Angelenos, and indeed virtually all Americans outside of New York, spend all their time in their cars. The only time you overhear them is when they're in restaurants, talking too loud on their cell phones.

We New Yorkers are out on the street, and down in the subway, living our lives in public, and delightfully unconcerned about being overheard. And we say interesting things. Some of them are stupid, and some of them are nuts, as this compendium clearly demonstrates, but a remarkable percentage of them are somehow illuminating, and graced with that unmistakable New York edge.

I've been writing books and stories set in New York for half a century, and a couple of years ago I wrote one called *Small Town,* a big multiple-view-point novel in which I attempted to cram in as much of the city as I could. I don't know that it worked, though I was pleased with it at the time. But it strikes me that the book you're holding in your hand is the true Great New York Novel, written, albeit unintentionally, by its citizens and visitors.

And here's the best part—there'll be a sequel every day.

WRITING MY NAME

The Village Voice ran this piece under the title "Signature Collection" in April of 2004. I never saw it until I found it online while I was compiling this collection. See, I was out of town when it appeared—writing my name, over and over and over . . .

Last summer I spent six weeks at the Ragdale writers' colony. I worked all day every day and came home with a novel, *The Burglar on the Prowl*. I gave it to my agent, and he gave it to my editor and the book was designed and the cover prepared, and on March 16, just two weeks ago as I write this, the book went on sale nationwide.

That's when my real job began. Writing the book, that was the easy part. Now it was time for the heavy lifting. It was time for me to start signing my name.

Lawrence Block, Lawrence Block, Lawrence Block. Over and over, on book after book. On the title page, in the space the designer was thoughtful enough to provide for that purpose. Again and again and again.

Actually, the book signing began before the book went on sale. In February I drove out to the HarperCollins warehouse in Scranton, where I signed around a thousand copies of *Prowl* for booksellers who'd ordered them. There's enough demand for this sort of thing to prompt HarperCollins to assign a special ISBN to the 10-copy signed cartons.

On March 16, I flew out to San Diego. I spent the next five days in Southern California, where I did events at five libraries and six bookstores and more drop-in stock signings than I could possibly remember.

After my final event Saturday evening, I flew home on the red-eye. On Sunday afternoon I was at Partners & Crime on Greenwich Avenue, to do my usual dog-and-pony show. I spent Monday and Tuesday dropping in at New York stores—Murder Ink, Black Orchid, Mysterious Bookshop, and a batch of chains. Otto Penzler had around 300 books waiting for me at Mysterious, all carefully flapped so they opened readily to the appropriate page for signing. Black Orchid and Murder Ink also had their books flapped. They've done this before, you see, and so have I.

Wednesday morning I rented an SUV big enough to house six families of Hmong refugees. I filled it up with T-shirts and out-of-print books and hit the road, heading for the Hunterdon County Library outside of Flemington, New Jersey. Seventy people showed up to hear me, and, not incidentally, to buy books and get them signed. I enjoyed myself, and it's a good thing, because that's what I'm going to be doing from now until the eighth of May—reading and talking at libraries and bookstores, driving around in my one-man Bookmobile, and, yes, writing my name.

How the hell did this happen? Not to me, that's my problem, but to the business in general? When did signed books become such a hot ticket?

Unless you count Saint Paul, book tours are a recent phenomenon. The first authors who toured were those whose books seemed likely to get them on local television—celebrities who'd written (or "written") books, authors of topical nonfiction, and cookbook authors who could go on afternoon TV and whip up something on the spot.

With time, the author tour ceased to be media-driven and became bookstore-centered. In recent years live local TV has disappeared throughout much of the country, and it's hard to book anybody anywhere, especially someone as gormless as your average novelist. If *Live at Five*'s not interested, though, a local bookstore might be. People could meet the author, ask questions, and buy his book—and, well, get it signed as a memento of the occasion.

A dozen or so years ago, somebody worked out what to do with the author's spare time. Instead of sitting around the hotel all day waiting for an evening event, he could improve each shining hour by hopping from store to store signing stock. Early on, store personnel were hard put to know what to make of the notion, but they got the hang of it, even as the writers learned to overcome their natural reserve and set about forcing their signature on stores whether they wanted it or not.

And the stores caught on big-time when they noticed that signed books tended to sell. A signed book quickly became a *sine qua non* for collectors. The best comparison I can think of is to the dust jacket. Until 50 years ago, the book's paper wrapper was there to draw attention in a store, and to protect the book until someone actually sat down and read it. At that time it was commonly discarded—which is why so few books with intact dust jackets survive from those early days.

Collectors collectively decided that a book with a dust jacket was more desirable, and hence worth more, than an unjacketed one. Indeed, only a jacketed copy was regarded as truly complete. Books from the '20s and '30s are still collectible without jackets, but a rare book of that vintage may be worth 10 or 20 times as much if it has a jacket. More recent books, unless of great rarity, are essentially worthless without a jacket.

Over the past decade, collectors have come to regard an unsigned book as similarly incomplete. "I have it," you'll hear someone say, "but it's not signed." If the author is still alive, the sentence ends a little differently. "But it's not signed *yet*," the collector will say.

Can you see where this is going? You have to sign the new books in order to get them sold, and you have to sign the old ones to make your readers happy.

*   *   *

Book collectors are a quirky lot, but that's true of all hobbyists. Still, how many collectors can there be? And how much impact can they have?

Lots.

One mystery specialty store owner told me a book or two ago that her order of my new one depended on whether or not she could get signed copies. If not, she'd take 10 or 20. If they were signed, her initial buy would be 200.

Because 200 hardcore collectors would buy them? No, but because the collecting tail wags the dog here. Folks buying the book to add to their library, or give as a gift, have been schooled by collectors to want a signed copy. And, since so many signed copies do exist, a sort of mutation of Gresham's Law operates; the signed books drive the unsigned out of circulation, and into Remainder Hell.

The whole signed-books issue got accelerated with the 1992 publication of John Dunning's *Booked to Die*, which noted that books simply signed by the author had more collector value than those inscribed to a specific reader. Almost immediately, I noticed an upsurge of buyers who murmured "Signature only, please." It's much quicker just signing one's name, and not having to write "To Cathy, I'll never forget that heavenly night in Sioux Falls." And was that Cathy with a C or Kathy with a K, and does it end in Y or I?

"Thank you, John Dunning," many of us said under our breath when another signature-only appeared. But there was a downside. If more folks were content with a simple signature, they were also intent on getting their *entire collection* signed.

Because I have been doing this a long time, I have a backlist that extends halfway down the street and around the corner. During a tour in 1998, when a couple of Dallas suitcase dealers brought in cartons of old stuff, I instituted a policy I've clung to ever since: I'll sign up to three of the books you bring from home for every copy of the new hardcover you buy at the signing. Most people figure this is fair, and the others—like the dame in Charlottesville the other day who frowned and said, "If I do that, how am I gonna make any profit on the deal?"—the others, all things considered, can go to hell.

In 1999, a fellow in Madison set a record that stands to this day. He brought in 53 items, cheerfully bought 18 copies of *The Burglar in the Rye*, and got everything signed. He was happy, I was happy—and the store owner was over the moon.

Item: James Ellroy signed the entire first printing of *My Dark Places*, some 65,000 books in all. He wrote two words, James and Ellroy, 65,000 times each. That's 130,000 words, which is more than he took to write the whole damn book.

Why, I sometimes wonder, does anybody want a book signed? I have a whole wall of books by friends, and it never occurs to me to ask them to sign them.

My wife, who has an abiding passion for hagiography—we have a surprising number of editions of *Lives of the Saints*, not one of them signed—has her own theory. As she explains it, a book signed by its author is a second-degree relic, not as precious as a finger bone, but on a par with a pair of cast-off sandals.

I like the explanation, but how long before the bastards start wanting the damned books signed in blood?

And what bittersweet irony that the miracle of alphabetical order makes this the last piece in the book! I'm done putting it together. Now all I have to do is sign my name.

Repeatedly . . .

My Newsletter: I get out an email newsletter at unpredictable intervals, but rarely more often than every other week. I'll be happy to add you to the distribution list. A blank email to lawbloc@gmail.com with "newsletter" in the subject line will get you on the list, and a click of the "Unsubscribe" link will get you off it, should you ultimately decide you're happier without it.

Lawrence Block has been writing award-winning mystery and suspense fiction for half a century. His newest book, a sequel to his greatly successful Hopper anthology *In Sunlight or in Shadow*, is *Alive in Shape and Color*, a 17-story anthology with each story illustrated by a great painting; authors include Lee Child, Joyce Carol Oates, Michael Connelly, Joe Lansdale, Jeffery Deaver and David Morrell. His most recent novel, pitched by his Hollywood agent as "James M. Cain on Viagra," is *The Girl with the Deep Blue Eyes*. Other recent works of fiction include *The Burglar Who Counted The Spoons*, featuring Bernie Rhodenbarr; *Keller's Fedora*, featuring philatelist and assassin Keller; and *A Drop Of The Hard Stuff*, featuring Matthew Scudder, brilliantly embodied by Liam Neeson in the 2014 film, *A Walk Among The Tombstones*. Several of his other books have also been filmed, although not terribly well. He's well known for his books for writers, including the classic *Telling Lies For Fun & Profit* and *Write For Your Life*, and has recently published a collection of his writings about the mystery genre and its practitioners, *The Crime Of Our Lives*. In addition to prose works, he has written episodic television (*Tilt!*) and the Wong Kar-wai film, *My Blueberry Nights*. He is a modest and humble fellow, although you would never guess as much from this biographical note.

Email: lawbloc@gmail.com
Twitter: @LawrenceBlock
Facebook: lawrence.block
Website: lawrenceblock.com

CPSIA information can be obtained
at www.ICGtesting.com
Printed in the USA
LVHW111518140220
646994LV00001B/133